University of London Historical Studies

XXVII

UNIVERSITY OF LONDON HISTORICAL STUDIES

I. HUGH TINKER. *The Foundations of Local Self-Government in India, Pakistan and Burma.* 1954

II. AVROM SALTMAN. *Theobald, Archbishop of Canterbury.* 1956

III. R. F. LESLIE. *Polish Politics and the Revolution of November 1830.* 1956

IV. W. N. MEDLICOTT. *Bismarck, Gladstone, and the Concert of Europe.* 1956

V. JOHN LYNCH. *Spanish Colonial Administration 1782–1810: The Intendant System in the Viceroyalty of the Rio de la Plata.* 1958

VI. F. H. W. SHEPPARD. *Local Government in St. Marylebone, 1688–1835.* 1958

VII. R. L. GREAVES. *Persia and the Defence of India, 1884–1892.* 1959

VIII. M. J. SYDENHAM. *The Girondins.* 1961

IX. MARGARET HOWELL. *Regalian Right in Medieval England.* 1962

X. N. M. SUTHERLAND. *The French Secretaries of State in the Age of Catherine de Medici.* 1962

XI. GWYN A. WILLIAMS. *Medieval London: from Commune to Capital.* 1963

XII. CHARLES DUGGAN. *Twelfth-century Decretal Collections and their Importance in English History.* 1963

XIII. R. F. LESLIE. *Reform and Insurrection in Russian Poland 1856–1865.* 1963

XIV. J. A. S. GRENVILLE. *Lord Salisbury and Foreign Policy.* 1964

XV. P. W. J. RILEY. *The English Ministers and Scotland 1707–1727.* 1964

XVI. J. F. BOSHER. *The Single Duty Project: A Study of the Movement for a French Customs Union in the Eighteenth Century.* 1964

XVII. JOAN MCDONALD. *Rousseau and the French Revolution 1762–1791.* 1965

XVIII. IAN H. NISH. *The Anglo-Japanese Alliance: The Diplomacy of Two Island Empires, 1894–1907.* 1966

XIX. WILLIAM URRY. *Canterbury under the Angevin Kings.* 1967

XX. PHYLLIS M. HEMBRY. *The Bishops of Bath and Wells 1540–1640: Social and Economic Problems.* 1967

XXI. N. M. FARRISS. *Crown and Clergy in Colonial Mexico 1759–1821: The Crisis of Ecclesiastical Privilege.* 1968

XXII. DEMETRIOS I. POLEMIS. *The Doukai: A Contribution to Byzantine Prosopography.* 1968

XXIII. JUKKA NEVAKIVI. *Britain, France, and the Arab Middle East 1914–20.* 1969

XXIV. G. G. HARRIS. *The Trinity House of Deptford 1514–1660.* 1969

XXV. J. T. CLIFFE. *The Yorkshire Gentry from the Reformation to the Civil War.* 1969

XXVI. JAMES L. STURGIS. *John Bright and the Empire.* 1969

XXVII. DAVID SYRETT. *Shipping and the American War 1775–83: A Study of British Transport Organization.* 1970

SHIPPING AND THE
AMERICAN WAR 1775-83

This volume is published with the help of
a grant from the late Miss Isobel Thornley's
Bequest to the University of London

Shipping and the American War 1775–83

A Study of British Transport Organization

by
DAVID SYRETT

UNIVERSITY OF LONDON
THE ATHLONE PRESS
1970

Published by
THE ATHLONE PRESS
UNIVERSITY OF LONDON
at 2 Gower Street London WC1

Distributed by Tiptree Book Services Ltd
Tiptree, Essex

Australia and New Zealand
Melbourne University Press

U.S.A.
Oxford University Press Inc
New York

0 485 13127 7

Printed in Great Britain by
WILLIAM CLOWES AND SONS LTD
London and Beccles

PREFACE

THE AMERICAN WAR was in many respects a unique experience for the British people and their rulers. It was, first of all, the only clear defeat suffered by the British in the series of wars with France that began with the Revolution of 1688 and ended with the Battle of Waterloo. It was, moreover, a war in which Britain had to maintain thousands of soldiers overseas while at the same time it faced a coalition of major maritime powers which were not fighting on the continent of Europe. Britain's strategic problems were further complicated by unprecedented administrative and logistical problems arising from the necessity of supporting a great army and a large naval force in the Western Hemisphere. The scope and difficulty of Britain's situation during the American War can perhaps best be understood if one keeps in mind that no nation in modern history faced comparable problems until the advent of the Second World War.

Britain's logistical problems during the American War comprise a neglected field of study. To a certain extent these problems are a part of the administrative, economic, military, and political history of the war, but they also constitute a subject which needs to be examined as a separate entity.[1] In the past, part of the difficulty has arisen from the attitude of most historians towards military history as a field worthy of serious consideration. Despite the fact that military conflict is one of man's most pervading occupations, academic historians have tended to view war as an aberration. To most academic historians, wars are abnormal events which occur from time to

---

[1] Edward E. Curtis's *The Organization of the British Army in the American Revolution* (New Haven, 1926) is the only study of British army administration during the American War, and there have been several unpublished Ph.D. theses on naval administration. See, for example, Roland Greene Usher, Jr, *The Civil Administration of the British Navy during the American Revolution* (unpublished University of Michigan Ph.D. thesis, 1942) and M. J. Williams, *The Naval Administration of the Fourth Earl of Sandwich, 1771–82* (unpublished Oxford Ph.D. thesis, 1962).

time generating unusual pressures which twist and distort bureaucracies, disturb or destroy trade patterns, and interfere with the normal course of diplomacy and the struggle for political power. A small band of military historians has displayed a different, but equally distorted, view of war; they were inclined to ignore every aspect of human activity during a war except the conduct of military operations. As a result, the bulk of military history consists of accounts of battles, marches, and sieges unrelated to any other field of human endeavour. The writings of Sir John Fortescue are typical of this genre. A devoted practitioner of operational military history, Fortescue's history of the British army is a masterpiece of style with great scope and force of narrative. But Fortescue's deep commitment to military operations limited his vision in such a way that he compressed all the appalling administrative and logistical problems which confronted the British during the American War into 'Germaine with his blindness to facts'.[1] In this connexion, it should, however, be stated that a younger generation of historians who for the most part have entered the profession since the Second World War have begun the task of bringing the history of warfare back into the mainstream of historical scholarship. In recent years Piers Mackesy, Eric Robson, William B. Willcox, and others have studied with great skill and in considerable depth Britain's strategic conduct of the American War. Despite such work, the fact remains that there has been comparatively little written about the administrative machinery which supported the British military effort.

The present study constitutes an attempt to illuminate the workings of the Navy Board's transport service which was a small, but essential, component of the British war machine. During the American War this service was responsible for the transport by sea of most of the men and supplies necessary for the conduct of the war. Because of the necessity of waging war in the Western Hemisphere, the transport service was of great strategic and logistical importance to the British war effort. The saga of the transport service is not, however, simply a tale of military operations and logistics, but rather the story of the

---

[1] J. S. Fortescue, *A History of the British Army* (London, 1902), iii, 397.

interaction of strategy, logistics, administration, and economics. Throughout the war the operations of the transport service were conditioned and modified by the often contradictory forces of the ministry's strategic desires, military necessity, economic reality, and administrative possibility. Because it fell to the Commissioners of the Navy to adjust those conflicting forces into a coherent plan of action for the transport service, this study is written, not from the point of view of Whitehall or the military commanders in the field, but rather from that of the Navy Office at Crutched Friars in the City of London.

This study would never have been possible without the cooperation and assistance given to the author by numerous people and institutions. The importance of naval administration during the American War was first pointed out to me by Professor Richard B. Morris of Columbia University. I am deeply indebted for the assistance given by Mr A. W. H. Pearsall of the National Maritime Museum, Greenwich; Mr Roger J. Mortimer and Mrs Janet Jones of the History Department Library of University College, London; Dr Clarke Slater of the Harvard Medical School; Professor Richard W. Emery of Queens College, City University of New York; Mr Piers Mackesy of Pembroke College, Oxford; Professor Chilton Williamson of Barnard College, Columbia University; and the staffs of the Public Record Office, British Museum, William L. Clements Library of the University of Michigan, Institute of Historical Research of the University of London, National Register of Archives, the Library of the Commonwealth Relations Office, University of London Library, and the New-York Historical Society. I am especially grateful to the Earl of Gainsborough for permitting me to examine the Barham Papers at Exton Park, to Mr Victor Montagu for the opportunity to consult the Sandwich Papers at Mapperton, and to the West India Committee for allowing me to use its minutes. I also wish to thank the Institute of Historical Research of the University of London and the late Miss Isobel Thornley's Bequest to the University of London for their generous financial support.

Professor I. R. Christie of the History Department of University College, London, has given me invaluable assistance at every stage of this project. His constant support and encouragement and his unfailingly helpful criticisms add up to a debt which I will never be able to repay.

I am wholly responsible for any sins of omission or commission in this study.

New York   D. S.
September 1969

CONTENTS

Abbreviations   xii

i. The Higher Chain of Command   1

ii. The Navy Board   17

iii. The Lower Chain of Command   37

iv. Short-term Procurement of Tonnage   61

v. Long-term Procurement of Tonnage   77

vi. The Measurement, Inspection and Fitting-out of Ships entering the Transport Service   106

vii. The Growth of the Provision Problem, 1775–79   121

viii. The Navy Board's Victuallers   139

ix. The Navy Board's Transports   181

x. Shipping and the American War: a Conclusion   243

Appendices   249

    A. Number and Tonnage of Transports and Victuallers in the Transport Service during the American War, 249

    B. Freight Rates, 251

Bibliography   253

Index   261

ABBREVIATIONS

Add. MSS.	Additional Manuscripts, British Museum
CRL	Commonwealth Relations Office Library
G	Sir John W. Fortescue, ed., *The Correspondence of George the Third from 1760 to December 1782* (London, 1927–28)
HMC	Historical Manuscripts Commission
NMM	National Maritime Museum
NRS	Navy Records Society
NYHSC	New-York Historical Society Collections
PRO	Public Record Office
SP	Shelburne Papers in the William L. Clements Library, University of Michigan

CHAPTER I

The Higher Chain of Command

IN RECENT YEARS students of the governmental process have revealed an increasing fondness for such terms as the 'art of administration' and the 'science of government', while so-called efficiency experts have shown a corresponding delight in tables of organization which purport to demonstrate the way in which decisions are made and implemented within a given organization. The quest for system and order that is inherent in most attempts to explain the machinery of modern government represents—depending on one's point of view—a degree of sophistication or a kind of naïveté that was altogether foreign to British officials during the eighteenth century, when public administration on occasion may have been an art but was never a science.[1] To the modern observer the system, if it can be dignified by such a word, often appears to be one of the most irrational features of the Age of Reason. But it was also a system that had worked, for until the outbreak of the American War it had helped Britain to become—or at the very least it had not prevented Britain from becoming—one of the great powers of the world.

The British administrative system was placed under a heavy strain during the American War. Anyone who has examined the records of the period is immediately and forcibly struck by the inordinate delays that attended the implementation of military decisions reached by the Cabinet. A case in point is provided by the Navy Board, which was the department that

---

[1] For a general description of the operation of the executive branch of the British government during the American War, see Piers Mackesy, *The War for America, 1775–1783* (London, 1964), 12–24; Richard Pares, *King George III and the Politicians* (Oxford, 1953), 143–81.

provided, fitted out, and administered the transports, storeships, and army victuallers required to put into execution many of the Cabinet's military programmes. As an administrative rather than a policy-making agency, the Navy Board could not act until the Cabinet had acted, and it sometimes took weeks, and even months, before a decision reached by the Cabinet could be translated into action by the Navy Board. The cause of such delays can be found in the ways in which military policy once decided on by the Cabinet was transformed into a command and transmitted through the bureaucratic highways and byways of the British government to the Navy Board and other administrative agencies.

The working Cabinet in the period of the American War consisted of the First Lord of the Treasury, the three secretaries of state, the Lord Chancellor, the Lord President, the Lord Privy Seal, the First Lord of the Admiralty, and after 1778, the Commander-in-Chief of the army. Cabinet meetings were usually attended by between six and eight members and were generally presided over by the secretary of state whose business was before the meeting. Military policy such as the formulation of instructions for admirals and generals was made by an individual minister who then presented his proposals to the Cabinet for a decision. Although ministers were not bound by law to lay the business of their departments before the Cabinet, they generally did so; for the collective decision by the Cabinet strengthened their hands in dealing with the King and relieved them of individual responsibility for an act which miscarried. Decisions by the Cabinet were usually unanimous, and the ministers welcomed the protection afforded by a cabinet minute in the violent world of British politics during the American War. 'Every expedition', wrote Lord Sandwich, 'in regard to its destination, object, force and number of ships, is planned by the Cabinet, and is the result of the collective wisdom of all his Majesty's confidential ministers. The First Lord of the Admiralty is only the executive servant of these measures.'[1]

After the Cabinet had resolved a question, its decision was

---

[1] NRS, *Sandwich Papers*, ii, 255, 259; iii, 14.

submitted to the King so that his pleasure might be known. The King upon receiving the advice of his ministers had the right to reject it and to refuse to allow their policy to be implemented. When the King rejected the advice of the Cabinet, a number of constitutional possibilities were open. The King could dismiss the ministers and attempt to obtain others; the ministers could resign and thereby compel the King to seek new ministers; the whole matter could be dropped; or the Cabinet could prevail upon the King to accept its advice. During the American War, when the Cabinet would not drop a measure rejected by the King, a curious situation arose. The King, although constitutionally able to dismiss the ministry, found that he was politically unable to do so because there was no other group in Parliament which could form a workable government that would hold views on the American question which were acceptable to him. At the same time the individual members of the ministry could or would not resign. Lord North, for example, in the course of the American War attempted many times to leave the government. The King, however, would not allow him to resign, for he felt that North was the only person who could form a government which would pursue the war until the Americans were forced to submit. Therefore, when the King rejected the advice of the North ministry, a test of strength followed between the King and Cabinet, and the King usually lost.

When the Cabinet's advice was rejected by the King, the ministers had to devote much time and energy to convince and cajole George III into approving the proposal in question. For example, on 16 January 1779 the Cabinet proposed to dispatch the Edinburgh Regiment to Jamaica. Although the King vetoed the proposal to send a regiment to Jamaica, six days later the Liverpool Regiment was ordered to embark for that island. Another example of the King first rejecting and then accepting the advice of his Cabinet occurred when he refused to approve the Cabinet's decision of 3 January 1781 to cede Minorca to Russia in return for a 'Great and Essential Service Actually performed'. By 19 January, however, fear of Russia entering the war against Britain had weakened the King's resolve. That afternoon he met with the entire Cabinet for three and a half hours and finally agreed to the proposal.[1] During the American War the Cabinet could override a veto by the King on a matter of policy if its members thought it important enough to spend the time and effort needed to convince him; but from the administrative point of view, the King represented a part of the chain of command that could and did retard execution of the Cabinet's war plans.

Six days intervened between the date of the Cabinet's decision to embark a regiment for Jamaica and 22 January, when the orders were issued to put the movement into effect. If, however, the King did not delay matters by first rejecting and then approving a Cabinet proposal, the interval between a Cabinet decision on policy and the issuing of orders to implement that policy could be shortened considerably. On 3 March 1781, for instance, the Cabinet resolved to send 200 troops to West Africa. Within three days this resolve had passed from the Cabinet, won the approval of the King, and the Admiralty had issued the orders for the provision of transports for these troops.[2]

When a recommendation of the Cabinet had been approved by the King, one of the secretaries of state became responsible for its execution; issuing orders in the form of a command from the King to the various administrative departments concerned. Sir Charles Middleton, the Comptroller of the Navy, explained the relationship between the Cabinet and the secretaries of state in the following fashion:

Cabinet
To consider and determine what expeditions are to take place, and at what periods; what troops are likely to be sent abroad, *when, where,* how, and the number. What service are to have preference.

Secretary of State
To issue timely orders, to the Treasury, Admiralty, Ordnance, and Commander-in-Chief of the Army on these heads, so that every

---

[1] Mackesy, op. cit., 382–4; Isabel de Madariaga, *Britain, Russia, and the Armed Neutrality of 1780* (London, 1962), 283–5; NRS, *Sandwich Papers*, iv, 23–6; G, no. 3230; NMM, SAN/T/6, Jan. 16, 1779; HMC, *Various Collections*, vi, 155; PRO, ADM/1/4138, f. 14.

[2] G, no. 3274; NMM, ADM/N/250, March 6, 1781.

necessary preparation can be made, and no delay nor disappointment happen when the services take place.[1]

The secretaries of state put the Cabinet's plans into execution and kept the government administrative machinery functioning, for they alone had the power to coordinate the actions of the various departments of the executive branch of the British government. If they failed to control, coordinate, and issue the correct commands to the various departments of the government, the whole administrative machinery became disjointed and broke down. As Middleton noted, 'If the public officers, on whose orders every preparation and movement depends, are not diligent, regular and punctual, it is of little consequence what your admirals and generals are.'[2]

During the American War there were three secretaries of state. By law they could sign any act of state, but in practice they divided up the world among themselves. The Secretary of State for the Northern Department dealt with the affairs of northern Europe; the Secretary of State for the Southern Department handled matters which related to southern Europe, Ireland, Africa, and India; and a third secretary, or American secretary, conducted North American and West Indian affairs. The secretaries of state did not always adhere to this geographical division of responsibilities.[3] During the Seven Years War the elder Pitt had set a strong precedent for secretaries of state acting out of their own departments when he ran the entire war from the Southern Department. On the whole, however, the secretaries of state stayed within their own bailiwicks during the American War.

Although the law stipulated that before letters from a secretary of state's office could be official acts of state they had to be signed by a secretary of state, a large number of orders, commands, and communications were in fact written and signed by an under secretary.[4] If a matter came up on which action had to be taken at once and the secretary of state was not in his office to sign the order himself or to order an under secretary to

---

[1] Quoted in Mackesy, op. cit., 12.
[2] NRS, *Barham Papers*, ii, 66.
[3] E.g., PRO, ADM/1/4141, pp. 51, 56–7.
[4] E.g., PRO, ADM/1/4133, f. 87; ADM/1/4145, f. 33.

issue a command in his name, the under secretary usually wrote and signed the order on his own initiative. It seems to have depended upon the circumstances whether or not this was followed up with an official confirmatory letter from the secretary of state; but often such a formality was ignored.[1] The fact that the under secretaries of state did not have the legal power to issue orders could have led to grave delays in the dispatch of important business had not the Admiralty accepted a letter from an under secretary of state as having almost as much validity as an order from a secretary of state.[2]

All commands and communications from the secretaries of state concerning transportation of troops and supplies were first sent to the Admiralty which in turn transmitted them to the Navy Board.[3] The Lords Commissioners of the Admiralty usually met three or four times a week to conduct the affairs of the navy. At these meetings either the First Secretary, Philip Stephens, or the Second Secretary, George Jackson, laid papers and communications before them for their decision. The proceedings of these meetings were recorded in minutes, and the decisions were written up either as letters or orders by the secretaries or their clerks. These orders and letters were then signed by the members of the Board and transmitted by the secretaries. The secretaries formed the only official channel of communication between the Lords of the Admiralty and the rest of the world. Not only did they transmit all communications from the Lords of the Admiralty, but all incoming letters and orders were addressed to them. This method of business when coupled with the short periods of attendance of the Commissioners at the Admiralty Board could cause delays in the conduct of naval affairs, for the secretaries alone, in many cases, had not the power to act.[4]

---

[1] E.g., PRO, ADM/1/4131, f. 76; ADM/1/4133, ff. 99–100; ADM/1/4146, f. 52.

[2] For an account of the role of the under secretaries of state, see Franklin B. Wickwire, *British Subministers and Colonial America, 1763–1783* (Princeton, N.J., 1966).

[3] PRO, ADM/1/4130–50; NMM, ADM/N/244–50.

[4] For a fuller description of this system, see M. J. Williams, *The Naval Administration of the Fourth Earl of Sandwich: 1771–82* (unpublished Oxford Ph.D. thesis, 1962), 16–17; Franklin B. Wickwire, 'Admiralty Secretaries and the British Civil Service', *Huntington Library Quarterly* (May, 1965), xxiii, 235–54.

Sir Charles Middleton speculated on how Lord Sandwich, the First Lord of the Admiralty, could conduct the business of the navy in the short time which the First Lord spent in attendance at the Admiralty.[1] Middleton also continually complained of 'the sluggish manner in which business goes through the Admiralty'.[2] On 23 October 1780 Middleton wrote to Sandwich: 'It is needless to remind your Lordship of the many remonstrances I have been under necessity of making from time to time of the notorious remissness in official correspondence'. And on 24 July 1781 he went into the subject in more detail, when he wrote:

My going to Mr Stephens, which under circumstances of punctuality and timely communication might prove of the first consequence, answers no other purpose than giving me much trouble and throwing me behindhand in my business. The dunning him perpetually on the same subject is so foreign to my practice and disposition that I cannot continue it. Unless therefore your Lordship, who is the first mover, will condescend to read the Navy Board correspondence yourself and continue what I say in consequence of it in your memorandum book till the business is executed, we shall never be free from disappointment. Mr Stephens cannot act of himself, and therefore cannot remove difficulties without references which take up much time and necessarily occasion disappointment.[3]

When the Lords were not in attendance, it appeared to Middleton that all incoming correspondence to the Admiralty piled up on the desks of the secretaries and remained there until the Lords appeared to conduct business. Middleton was overstating the case, for the secretaries did have limited powers of action expressly authorized by the Board of Admiralty. But in most instances involving any matter of importance a decision of the Board was required.

It often required many days for a paper to wend its way from the office of a secretary of state through the Admiralty to the Navy Board. For the Admiralty to transmit an order within twenty-four hours of receipt was rather exceptional.[4] Delays of three or four days were commonplace, while sometimes a fort-

[1] NRS, *Barham Papers*, ii, 3.   [2] NRS, *Sandwich Papers*, iii, 181.
[3] NRS, *Sandwich Papers*, iv, 371, 385.
[4] E.g., PRO, ADM/1/4138, f. 14; NMM, ADM/N/248, Jan. 23, 1779.

night might elapse. Responsibility for delays did not always rest entirely with the Admiralty for it often took a day or more for an order to travel from a secretary of state's office to the Admiralty.[1]

The transmission of orders could be expedited to some extent by the use of unofficial means of communication.[2] Sir Charles Middleton was occasionally consulted directly by the secretaries of state, and he carried on an unofficial correspondence about naval affairs with Lords Shelburne and Sandwich.[3] On 17 January 1781, however, after a mix-up concerning a convoy of victuallers, he wrote to Sandwich: 'If your Lordship wishes to have official reports from this [Navy] Board, the question must come officially from the Admiralty, as there is no other regular way of conducting business in a public office; and . . . I cannot be inclined to give my consent that duty shall be carried on by private messages.'[4]

Middleton was not the only Comptroller of the Navy who would not do business outside official channels. Lord Barrington, Secretary at War, on 28 October 1775 applied privately to Maurice Suckling, the then Comptroller, for information about the transports on which the 15th and 37th Regiments were to embark. He did not receive the desired information until sometime later when he applied for it officially. There was a marked reluctance in naval circles to do any business except through the proper channels, and as one authority has noted, 'Almost every act of importance in the naval service required a warrant or order properly authorized by legal authority'.[5]

The Navy Board not only received all communications from the secretaries of state concerning transports by way of the

---

[1] E.g., PRO, ADM/1/4134, f. 72; ADM/1/4137, ff. 37, 57, 70; ADM/1/4138, ff. 104, 145; ADM/1/4139, f. 43; ADM/1/4142, ff. 14, 69–70; ADM/1/4143, f. 66; ADM/1/4144, ff. 34, 121, 129; ADM/1/4145, f. 145; ADM/1/4148, f. 4. The secretaries at the Admiralty sometimes wrote on the top right hand corner of the in-letters the dates when they were received and on the back of the bottom right hand corner they wrote the action taken and the date when it was taken.

[2] E.g., NRS, *Sandwich Papers*, i, 95.

[3] G, no. 3224; NRS, *Barham Papers*, ii, 19–22, 66–7, 71–2.

[4] NRS, *Sandwich Papers*, iv, 373.

[5] PRO, ADM/1/4328, Nov. 13, 1775; Williams, op. cit., 40–1.

Admiralty, it also received all communications from every other branch of the government, except the Treasury, by the same route. Lieutenant Colonel Robert Donkin, applying directly to the Navy Board on 23 August 1782 for transport to Bermuda for clothing belonging to the Royal Garrison Battalion of Bermuda, had the chain of command explained to him by the Board as follows: 'We have received your letter of this day, and acquaint you that as the clothing viz; for the soldiers therein mentioned are ship'd by orders to us from the Rt Hon. the Lords Comm. of the Admiralty, grounded on the Secretary of State's Letter to their Lordships, your application should be made to the secretary of state.'[1] In some cases, however, the War Office, Treasury, Ordnance Board, and East India Company wrote directly to the Admiralty about transport affairs and that body forwarded the information to the Navy Board without consulting the secretaries of state. At other times these organizations wrote to one of the secretaries of state, who in turn wrote to the Admiralty which then transmitted the information on to the Navy Board.

The Treasury was the only major department of the government which dealt directly with the Navy Board on transport affairs. The Navy Board and the Victualling Board communicated with each other directly, but the Victualling Board was part of the naval establishment and considered to be inferior in rank to the Navy Board. The only channel of communication between the Navy Board which administered the transports, and the departments of the government, with the exception of the Treasury, which sent goods on the Navy Board's ships, lay through the Admiralty or through the secretaries of state and then the Admiralty. This bureaucratic isolation of the Navy Board resulted in the letters and orders concerning transports intended for that agency having to travel over some curious routes before reaching their destination.

The necessity of transmitting through the Admiralty orders concerning the Navy Board's transport service was an irrational aspect of the administrative system. The records reveal that the Admiralty, except in the winter of 1775–76, did not take an

[1] PRO, ADM/1/4149, f. 32.

active interest in the transport service.[1] The evidence indicates that in the first winter of the war, Sir Hugh Palliser, a former Comptroller of the Navy, actively supervised the Navy Board's administration of its transports.[2] After the first year of the war, however, the Admiralty appears to have been preoccupied with the fleet and for the most part left the transport service in the hands of the secretaries of state and the Navy Board except for assigning warships to escort transports.

The Ordnance Board ran its own fleet of transport vessels which for the most part carried ordnance stores and artillerymen. But the artillerymen, when on board an ordnance transport, were fed by the navy's Victualling Board. When a group of artillerymen were to embark on an ordnance transport, the Board of Ordnance wrote to a secretary of state to inform him. The secretary of state then informed the Admiralty who in turn informed the Navy Board of the coming embarkation. The Admiralty, on 11 May 1780, told the Navy Board that 156 artillerymen were going to embark on the *Brilliant*, an ordnance storeship bound for New York, and that the Navy Board was therefore 'to cause a proper quantity of provisions to be put on board the storeship for the use of said party, during the voyage'. The Navy Board's reaction to this command was to 'write to the Commissioners of Victualling accordingly'.[3] Why in such cases the Admiralty did not write directly to the Victualling Board is not known.

In general, the War Office wrote to one of the secretaries of

---

[1] A study of the orders and communications concerning transports received by the Admiralty from the secretaries of state [PRO, ADM/1/4130–50], the minutes of the Board of Admiralty [PRO, ADM/3/81–96], and the orders issued by the Admiralty to the Navy Board about transports [NMM, ADM/N/244–50] show that in most cases the Admiralty merely redrafted the order received from the secretaries of state before issuing them to the Navy Board. And letters relating to the transport service are almost totally absent from the correspondence of the Fourth Earl of Sandwich, who was the First Lord of the Admiralty. See NRS, *Sandwich Papers*, i–iv and the Sandwich MSS. at Mapperton. In his study of the administration of the British Navy, R. G. Usher, Jr has come to substantially the same conclusion as I have concerning the role of the Admiralty and its relations with the Navy Board. See Roland Greene Usher, Jr, *The Civil Administration of the British Navy During the American Revolution* (unpublished University of Michigan Ph.D. thesis, 1942), 9, 14–15, 38.

[2] NRS, *Sandwich Papers*, i, 84–98.

[3] NMM, ADM/N/249, May 11, 1780; PRO, ADM/1/4130, f. 139.

state about important matters and directly to the Admiralty about petty ones. The Admiralty, on 11 April 1782, received a direct request from the War Office for transportation to Newfoundland of four tons of camp equipage.[1] The same procedure was employed in regard to requests for transport for individual officers or small bodies of troops.[2] But when the War Office required transportation for a large number of troops or a substantial amount of stores, it wrote to a secretary of state requesting that he issue an order to the Admiralty to supply the necessary vessels.[3] The War Office, however, did not always stay within official channels, for the Secretary at War sometimes employed unofficial letters as a means to expedite an affair at the Admiralty.[4]

The East India Company communicated with both the Admiralty and the secretaries of state. The Company corresponded directly with the naval authorities over the question of making space available on board its ships to carry stores to India for the use of the King's ships there.[5] On the other hand, it wrote to the secretaries of state on matters concerning the transport of the King's troops to India on East India Company ships.[6] The company always wrote directly to the Admiralty when requesting escort for East India Company ships in the Atlantic en route to or from India.[7]

The Treasury corresponded directly with the secretaries of state, the Admiralty, and the Navy Board. The Treasury appears to have dealt directly with the Navy Board on matters relating to naval stores.[8] On occasion the Treasury consulted the Board directly about payments for the hire of vessels into the King's service under peculiar circumstances.[9] The negotiations which

[1] PRO, ADM/1/4330, April 11, 1782.

[2] E.g., PRO, ADM/1/4328, Aug. 14, 17, 22, 1775, and Feb. 26, March 6, 1776; ADM/1/4330, Jan. 12, April 4, 5, 6, 13, 1782.

[3] E.g., PRO, ADM/1/4134, f. 27; NMM, ADM/B/195, Aug. 14, 1777.

[4] E.g., PRO, ADM/1/4328, April 10, 1776, May 15, 1777.

[5] PRO, ADM/1/3912, June 16, 1781; ADM/1/3914, Jan. 31, Oct. 10, 1782, Jan. 2, 1783. See below, pp. 71–6.

[6] PRO, ADM/1/4137, f. 80; ADM/1/4146, f. 112.

[7] See PRO, ADM/1/3913, passim.

[8] E.g., PRO, T/29/46, ff. 58, 59, 67, 68, 71; T/29/49, f. 239; T/29/50, f. 229; T/29/52, f. 114.

[9] E.g., PRO, T/29/45, ff. 171, 190–1; T/29/46, ff. 50, 57, 91, 100–1, 123, 143, 153, 194; T/29/47, ff. 22, 33, 41.

resulted in the Navy Board assuming the responsibility for the transport of the army's provisions in 1779 were conducted wholly between it and the Treasury. After the transfer of responsibility had taken place, a very close working relationship quickly developed between the Treasury and the Navy Board.[1]

Ordinary business concerning the transport service moved through the hierarchy of the British government in a sluggish and inefficient manner, while the exceptional problem became so enmeshed in red tape that the administrative machinery came to a near halt. Weeks and in some cases months might be required to resolve simple problems relating to the transport service. On 1 February 1777 the Navy Board wrote to the Admiralty stating that the transport *Molly* had arrived at Londonderry from North America with a load of coal and requested that permission be given for this coal to be landed duty free at Plymouth for the use of the Royal Dockyard there. Philip Stephens forwarded the Board's request to the Treasury on 10 February 1777, and the matter was laid before the Treasury the next day. The Treasury ordered that a letter be written to 'Mr Stephens acquainting him that it appears so very extraordinary to My Lords that a ship should arrive in Ireland from North America having on board a Loading of Coals, that their Lordships desire to receive a more particular account and full explanation of this business'. Stephens sent this request to the Navy Board which reported to the Admiralty on 1 March that the *Molly* had originally been ordered to proceed from New York to Cape Breton to obtain coal for the use of the army at New York. During her return voyage to New York, however, she became separated from the convoy and was taken by the Americans from whom she later escaped. After her escape, the *Molly*'s master brought her into the nearest British port—Londonderry. The information was forwarded to the Treasury on 22 March by Stephens, but it was not until 10 April that the matter was brought before the Treasury and orders were issued to the Commissioners of Customs that the coal on board the *Molly* be permitted to land duty free at Plymouth. The Navy Board, however, was not informed of the

[1] See below, pp. 139–80.

Treasury's decision, and in a letter to the Admiralty dated 18 April it stated that the *Molly* had arrived in Plymouth from Londonderry. Once again a request was made for permission to land the coal, and this time it was granted.[1] Thus, two months and eighteen days were needed to get permission to land duty free a shipload of coal which was the property of the Crown.

The delay in receiving permission to unload the coal on board the *Molly* was not an isolated incident, for in 1778 it took some seven months before the combined efforts of the Navy Board, Admiralty, Treasury, and a Secretary of State could find a means to transport 200 butts of vinegar from Deptford to New York. John Robinson, Secretary to the Treasury, informed Lord George Germain, Secretary of State for America, on 20 January 1778 that the Treasury had managed to ship 'all the clothing and stores ordered by my Lords [in December 1777] except 200 Butts of vinegar for which no ship has yet been appointed'. The vinegar was apparently forgotten until 1 May 1778 when William Knox, one of Germain's under secretaries, wrote to the Admiralty requesting that it ask if the Navy Board could 'provide a proper Conveyance for it to sail with the Lioness storeship' to New York. The Admiralty transmitted Knox's request to the Navy Board that day, and on 9 May the Board informed the Admiralty that 'it is not in our power to provide a ship of force to carry the vinegar, that can be ready to sail with the Lioness', which had already left the Downs for Spithead.[2] By 12 May this information had reached Germain, who then had Knox write to the Treasury requesting that the vinegar be sent immediately to Cork and shipped from there to New York on board a Treasury victualler. The Treasury did not consider the matter until 19 May when it resolved:

that it is with concern that their Lordships are informed that the Vinegar is not yet gone . . . [and] . . . that their Lordships think that sending the Vinegar now round by Corke, would . . . delay it so long as might put the Army to great Distress, since their Lordships

[1] PRO, T/29/46, ff. 24, 54–5; NMM, ADM/B/194, Feb. 1, March 1, April 18, 1777.
[2] PRO, ADM/1/4135, ff. 9, 92; NMM, ADM/B/196, May 9, 1778; ADM/N/248, May 1, 1778.

apprehend the Troops may now be in want of the supply, besides it is probable the victualling ships now under dispatch at Corke, would be sailed before the vinegar could arrive there. And that their Lordships upon Consideration of the state of their shipping find it at present not possible for them to undertake the service.[1]

The day after he was rebuffed by the Treasury, Germain directed Knox to issue an order to the Admiralty commanding it to provide transport for the vinegar. The Admiralty sat on Knox's order for twenty-nine days until 18 June, when it ordered the Navy Board to load the vinegar on an unemployed transport and have her proceed to Spithead and await further orders. The vinegar was put on board the transport *Felicity* at Deptford, and on 28 June the Navy Board requested that twenty soldiers be ordered to embark on the *Felicity* to help defend her. Because the soldiers reporting to the ship were not commanded by a commissioned officer, the Navy Board on 30 June requested that a commissioned army officer be embarked on board the *Felicity*. Finally, on 17 July 1778 the vinegar left Deptford on board the *Felicity*.[2]

If the administration could spend several months arranging for the transportation to New York of 200 butts of vinegar, petitions from owners of ships requesting payment for services rendered could hardly be expected to receive speedy consideration. Vice Admiral Thomas Graves, naval commander-in-chief in North America, in 1775 impressed into the King's service at Boston the ship *Glasgow* for use as a transport. The *Glasgow* was released from the King's service late in 1776, and her owners, Glasgow merchants John and George Buchanan, petitioned the Admiralty for £775 2s 0d in payment for damages resulting from the detention of their ship by the navy at Boston. The Admiralty referred the matter to Germain's office, and on 11 November 1777 William Knox referred the petition to the Treasury. The Lords of the Treasury considered the Buchanan petition on 29 May 1778 and resolved to 'Transmit the several papers to Mr. Stephens & desire him to move the Lords of the Admiralty that they will refer the same to the Navy Board and

[1] PRO, T/29/47, f. 62.
[2] PRO, ADM/1/4135, f. 106; NMM, ADM/B/196, June 26, 30, July 17, 1778; ADM/N/248, June 18, 1778.

direct them to take into consideration the charges made by the petitioners . . . [and to] report whether they are proper & reasonable and what sum ought to be allowed thereon'. The Board took the petition under consideration and on 20 June 1778 informed the Admiralty that the Buchanans should be paid £500 for the freight of the *Glasgow* and that their claim for damages should not be allowed. Stephens transmitted the Navy Board's report on the Buchanan petition to the Treasury on 23 June. The Treasury did not consider the matter until 7 July when they resolved 'that the Articles of Charge as specified by the petitioners should not be admitted, but that they think in lieu thereof £500 may be a resonable Allowance', and that the whole matter ought to be referred back to Knox because 'It appears to them, that the ship was stopped by an officer of the Navy, on a Naval Account, and if my Lords should direct the £500 Mentioned in said report to be paid, it must be out of money [appropriated] to the Navy Services'. Knox laid all the relevant papers before Germain, who on 24 July 1778 ordered the Admiralty to direct the Navy Board to pay £500 to John and George Buchanan for the freight of the ship *Glasgow*.[1] The Buchanans were fortunate—it took only months for a decision to be made on their petition. In some cases years were consumed in resolving similar problems.

Countless other examples exist of the delays and obstacles encountered by orders concerning the transport of supplies and troops during the American War. Germain, who was certainly in a position to know, thought that the entire administrative organization of the British government during the war was hampered by a 'natural sloth'. Although no single set of factors can explain this situation, it appears reasonable to conclude that a large part of the blame can be attributed to the fact that the chain of command led from the Cabinet, where decisions were made, through a bureaucratic jungle to the Navy Board, where the Cabinet's decisions were put into effect. The lethargic nature of the higher central administration of the transport service resulted in expeditions sailing late, troops overseas going

[1] PRO, ADM/1/4136, f. 29; T/29/47, ff. 74, 117; NMM, ADM/B/196, June 20, 1778.

on short rations, badly needed army reinforcements and equipment arriving at their destinations too late to be of use in the campaigns for which they were intended, and warships not being repaired because of a lack of necessary naval stores in the overseas dockyards.

CHAPTER II

The Navy Board

DURING the American War the Navy Board was in large part responsible for the success or failure of Great Britain's efforts to provide its fighting forces in North America with adequate supplies. Other agencies—particularly the Admiralty—could and did establish policies in this area, but it was left to the Navy Board to implement them. The powers and responsibilities of the Navy Board were enormous, for to it was entrusted the task of putting into effect those orders of the government that involved the maritime transport of troops, naval stores, military clothing, and certain other types of military equipment; and after 1779 the transport of army provisions to the troops overseas was also placed under its jurisdiction. In short, the speed with which supplies reached Britain's forces overseas depended in large measure on the efficiency with which the Navy Board performed the duties that had been assigned to it.[1]

Throughout the American War the membership of the Navy Board was limited to the 'Principal Officers and Commissioners of the Navy' who were resident in London. At the end of the war the Board consisted of the Comptroller of the Navy, two Surveyors of the Navy, the Clerk of the Acts, the Comptroller of the Treasurer's Accounts, the Comptroller of the Victualling Accounts, the Comptroller of the Storekeeper's Accounts, and three Extra Commissioners of the Navy. There were as well a number of Commissioners of the Navy in charge of various Royal dockyards in the Out-Ports and overseas who did not sit

---

[1] For a general account of the workings of the Navy Board during the American War, see Roland Greene Usher, Jr, *The Civil Administration of the British Navy During the American Revolution*, 50–120.

on the Navy Board and were inferior in rank to the members of that body.[1]

Although the Navy Board was subordinate to the Admiralty, it nevertheless enjoyed a great degree of independence. This relative independence can be attributed in part to the fact that the Navy Board was a far older institution than the Board of Admiralty. The office of Clerk of the Acts has been traced back as far as the reign of King John, when William de Wrotham was appointed to that office in 1214. The other Principal Officers of the Navy were established in the reign of King Henry VIII.[2] The Navy Board jealously guarded its ancient rights and privileges from any encroachments by the Admiralty, and whenever a strong-minded and aggressive man, such as Sir Charles Middleton, held the office of Comptroller, the Board sought to extend its authority at the expense of the Admiralty.

On many different occasions during the American War the Admiralty found it difficult if not impossible to control the Navy Board. For instance, in 1777 the Treasury conducted negotiations with the Navy Board concerning the latter's purchase of a ship called the *Resolution*. When the two boards could not agree on the value of the vessel, the Treasury attempted to use the Admiralty to bring pressure to bear on the Navy Board; but on 13 February 1777 it received a letter from the Admiralty stating 'that the Lords of the Admiralty are restrained from interfering with the Navy Board in the prices they give for the purchase of any stores &c.'.[3]

The Navy Board not only was able to resist pressure from the Admiralty, but it also attempted on occasion to encroach on the authority of the Admiralty. In 1781 the Navy Board, led by Sir Charles Middleton, challenged the Admiralty's right to make appointments in the dockyards. The Board maintained that dockyard appointments fell within its jurisdiction and that the malpractice at the yards could never be brought under control

[1] Usher, ibid., 56, 119–20.
[2] PRO, C/66/3776, no. 5; Usher, op. cit., 38; A. W. Johns, 'The Principal Officers of the Navy', *Mariner's Mirror* (Jan., 1928), xiv, 32; C. S. L. Davies, 'The Administration of the Royal Navy under Henry VIII: the Origins of the Navy Board', *English Historical Review* (April, 1965), lxxx, 268–86.
[3] PRO, T/29/46, f. 25.

until the Board had complete control over the hiring and dismissal of all dockyard personnel. The Admiralty, however,
insisted that the Navy Board's authority was limited to the right
to make recommendations concerning appointments to the
Admiralty. The Admiralty thought that the Navy Board,
because of its involvement in the administration of the dockyards, was not competent to make unbiased selections of
personnel and that these could only be made by the Admiralty.[1]
Lord Mulgrave, a Lord of the Admiralty, even went so far as to
suggest that the Admiralty ought to reduce the powers of the
Navy Board over the dockyards.[2] After several months the whole
question was dropped without either side retreating from the
positions taken during the dispute. What is important about
this affair is that the Navy Board was able to challenge the
Admiralty's right to one of its most important sources of patronage, while the Admiralty was unable to force the Navy Board
to revoke its claim to the control of dockyard appointments.[3]
During the American War the Navy Board also claimed the
right to issue protections from impressment to seamen employed
on board ships of the transport service and ships employed by
contractors to carry naval stores for the use of the King's service.
The Admiralty strongly resisted this innovation, but found itself
unable to make the Navy Board renounce its claim.[4] Thus it is
clear that during the American War the Navy Board, under the
leadership of Sir Charles Middleton, could be both assertive
and recalcitrant in the way in which it exercised authority over

---

[1] NRS, *Barham Papers*, ii, 6, 14–15, 24–31; NRS, *Sandwich Papers*, iv, 377–80.

[2] NRS, *Sandwich Papers*, iv, 380–1.

[3] The question of appointments in the dockyards was complicated by the fact
that these appointments formed a very important part of the government's
parliamentary patronage. For example, see I. R. Christie, 'Private Patronage
versus Government Influence: John Buller and the Contest for Control of Parliamentary Elections at Saltash, 1780–1790', *English Historical Review* (April, 1956),
lxxi, 251–2. However, M. J. Williams after making an exhaustive study of the
appointments made by the Earl of Sandwich has come to the conclusion that
'. . . any indictment of Sandwich for filling the dockyards with irregularly appointed
officers for reasons of political expediency is completely baseless'. See M. J.
Williams, *The Naval Administration of the Fourth Earl of Sandwich; 1771–82*, pp. 278,
281, 282.

[4] Usher, op. cit., 91–9. For a detailed account of the Navy Board's relations
with the Admiralty, see Usher, ibid., 81–101.

a domain which encompassed virtually the entire civil establishment of the Royal Navy.

The powers and responsibilities of the Navy Board during the American War were even more extensive than has been indicated. The Commissioners for Enquiring into Fees in the Public Offices found that 'The duty of the Navy Board is, under the direction of the Lords Commissioners of the Admiralty . . . to transact to the best advantage all affairs tending to the well-being and regulation of the Civil Establishment of Your Majesty's Navy, and all subordinate instruments thereof'. Thus, the Board was responsible for building, equipping, fitting-out, and repairing all the King's ships. It administered the Royal dockyards; all naval officers;[1] the vessels employed in the Impress Service; and certain inferior sea officers such as pursers, gunners, and carpenters. It contracted for and administered all naval stores and equipment except ordnance, food, and medicines. It hired, fitted-out, and administered all shipping required to carry troops, naval stores, camp equipage, and certain other forms of army equipment, and after 1779, army provisions. In addition, the Board prepared the naval estimates, directed the expenditure of most naval monies, audited and certified all naval accounts, and directly supervised the payment of ships crews at Deptford and Woolwich Dockyards and the payment of half pay at the Navy Pay Office.[2]

The Comptroller of the Navy was the most important and powerful member of the Navy Board. The Comptroller was authorized 'to conduct the general business of the board . . . to attend the great officers and offices of state, and, on some occasions, the cabinet council; to carry their orders, which are frequently secret, into execution, and in short to see every part of the business of the [navy] office properly executed'. In addition, he 'superintended the Offices particularly committed to his charge, namely the Office for Bills and Accounts, for Foreign Accounts, and for Payment of Seamen's Wages; to controul the

---

[1] Naval officers were civilian officials who issued stores to the King's ships in ports which were not the seat of a Royal Dockyard.

[2] Usher, op. cit., 55–6; Parliamentary Papers, *The Fifth Report of the Commissioners on Fees, &c. of Public Offices* (n.p., 1806), 168; Williams, op. cit., 24; PRO, C/66/3776, no. 5.

payment of half pay at the Pay Office, payment of artificers and labourers at Deptford and Woolwich Yards, and of ships paid off at these Ports; to visit the said Yards weekly, and the more distant Yards when occasion requires'. The Comptroller of the Navy received, as did every other member of the Navy Board, a basic salary of £500 a year. After 1779 he was paid an additional £300 a year for administering the army victuallers. According to the Commissioners for Enquiring into Fees in Public Offices, Sir Charles Middleton in 1784 had an income from public sources, including emoluments and allowances, of £950 10s 0d a year. But this figure does not take into account his half pay as a captain in the navy, his premiums on clerks, allowances for coals, candles, and for visiting dockyards. In 1786 Middleton put his income from all government sources at '£1499 with a house and taxes'.[1] In addition, all members of the Navy Board received refunds from the Treasury on taxes withheld from their salaries.[2] But Middleton thought that 'The profits annexed to this [the Comptroller's] office are trifling when compared with the labour and trust belonging to it, are barely equal to its necessary expenses. [And] ... as soon as I remove from it I shall think it an act of justice to my successor as well as to the benefit to the King's service to recommend an increase to his salary and to distinguish him otherwise.'[3]

Captain Maurice Suckling was appointed Comptroller of the Navy in April 1775, and held office until his death on 14 July 1778. Before becoming Comptroller, Suckling had served thirty-one years as an officer of the Navy. He was commissioned a lieutenant in 1744 and served throughout the Seven Years War in the West Indies and Europe. Not much is known of his career as Comptroller, but he appears to have been a capable administrator until his activities were curtailed by declining health in the months before his death. Although his last months as Comptroller were marred by sickness, Suckling served the Navy well by presiding over the largest trans-Atlantic troop movement known before the twentieth century and by bringing

[1] NRS, *Barham Papers*, ii, 235, 236; Parliamentary Papers, op. cit., 168, 261.
[2] PRO, T/29/48, f. 233; T/29/49, ff. 127, 263; T/29/50, f. 204; T/29/52, f. 135; T/64/200, pp. 7, 33.
[3] NRS, *Sandwich Papers*, iv, 373.

his nephew, Horatio Nelson, into the Navy and acting as his patron.[1]

Charles Middleton replaced Suckling as Comptroller of the Navy in August 1778. He held the office until March 1790, and on 23 October 1781 he was created a baronet for his work during the American War. In his long tenure as Comptroller, Middleton became one of Britain's greatest naval administrators of the eighteenth century, perhaps second only in importance to Lord Anson. Before Middleton became Comptroller of the Navy, he had served thirty-three years as an officer of the Royal Navy in Europe and North America. In 1745 he was commissioned a lieutenant in H.M.S. *Chesterfield*, and in 1758 he became a post captain. At the end of the Seven Years War, Middleton went on half pay until 1775, when he was appointed to command a guardship at Chatham. At the time of his appointment to the comptrollership he was in command of H.M.S. *Jupiter*, another guardship.[2]

As Comptroller Middleton was a hard-working and thorough administrator, capable of a sustained effort in the pursuit of long-term objectives. His ideas of administration were considerably in advance of those held by most of his contemporaries. One official of the Navy Board wrote of him: 'the comptroller, is a man [as] indefaticable & able as any in my time. The load of business he goes through at the Board, at the treasury, admiralty, & his house, is astonishing, & what I am confedent no other man will be able to exceed [it]. There is talk of him leaving us for a flag, if he does we are ruined.'[3] And one historian has written:

In Middleton and Sandwich the coming age confronted the *ancien régime*. One was the head of a great Whig family; the other the son of

---

[1] *Dictionary of National Biography* (London, 1894), xl, 90; ibid., lv, 146; Add. MSS. 38308, ff. 81, 113.

[2] *Dictionary of National Biography* (London, 1894), xxxvii, 341; *Barham Papers*, i, ix–xix.

[3] SP, 151, Gregson to Shelburne, An Acc[ount] of the members of the Navy Board, [undated]. Robert Gregson, Chief Clerk in the Office of the Clerk of the Acts, for money and hatred of Lord Sandwich, throughout the American War sent Lord Shelburne copies of official documents from the files of the Navy Board and accounts of office gossip. Much of what Gregson related to Shelburne was malicious in nature and should be judged accordingly.

a Scots Customs collector, with two generations of Aberdeen pro-
fessors behind him. Sandwich was a political jobber, for whom
public service was to a considerable extent a matter of pushing one's
friends and interests; Middleton a professional seaman and public
servant, and a censorious advocate of administrative reform and of
professionalism and integrity in government. The new Comptroller
was . . . a forerunner of the administrators who were soon to convert
the archaic racket called government into the efficient instrument
which transformed Victorian England.

Middleton's principles of public service are best summed up in
his belief that 'right measures will always make there own way,
if supported with integrity and disinterestedness'.[1]

The picture of Charles Middleton that emerges from his
writings is one of a country gentleman, called in a time of need
from rural pleasures to the service of his King, without regard
to emoluments.[2] There was, however, another side to his
character. He was nakedly ambitious and a bureaucratic
imperialist. 'The comptroller', Middleton told Lord Shelburne,
'is first in consequence though not in rank in the sea line to the
First Lord of the Admiralty', therefore, Middleton concluded
that the Comptroller ought to be a member of the Board of
Admiralty in order to give that body a degree of professionalism
which would end delays in the transmission of correspondence
and orders between the Admiralty and the Navy Board. During
Middleton's tenure as Comptroller the Navy Board took over
the management of the Treasury's transport service. Middleton
wished as well for the Navy Board to assume control of the
Victualling and Ordnance Boards' shipping because he thought
this was the only way to have a rational policy for the procurement of shipping for government service. At the same time
Middleton advocated transferring to the Navy Board from the
Ordnance Board, which was notoriously inefficient, the responsibility of supplying the Navy with ordnance.[3] Each of these
proposals had administrative merit, but at the same time it
appears that Middleton's answer to inefficiency in those

[1] Piers Mackesy, *The War for America, 1775–1783* (London, 1964), 164.

[2] NRS, *Barham Papers*, passim.

[3] SP, 151, Middleton to Shelburne, June 28, 1782, Middleton to Shelburne,
Sept. 9, 1782; NRS, *Sandwich Papers*, iv, 418–19.

governmental departments having contact with the Navy Board was to annex that part of the other organization which dealt with naval affairs.

Middleton spent a great deal of time deriding his superior, Lord Sandwich, for jobbery, and one of his favourite expressions was 'measures are more likely to support your Lordship's administration than men'. But Middleton was not without connexions himself, being closely related to that clan of Scottish jobbers and political manipulators—the Dundases. He also was not above promising his vote and his influence at India House to Sandwich, and he repeatedly solicited from the powerful and the mighty appointments for his relatives.[1]

Despite these faults, Charles Middleton was a great Comptroller of the Navy. A good case can be made for the view that the administrative groundwork laid by Middleton when he was Comptroller made possible the victories over the French in the years 1793–1802. Without a doubt the transport service would not have functioned as well as it did during the American War without his supervision and management.

The second most important member of the Navy Board was the Clerk of the Acts. The major part of his duty was to

receive, arrange, register, and keep safe all orders and letters from the Admiralty, Treasury, and from the various correspondents of the Navy Board . . . to keep a register of all proceedings of the Board, whether by correspondence or conference; to forward directions pursuant to orders from the Admiralty or Navy Board, to the Officers of the different Dock Yards, and other Officers, for the equipment, victualling and storeing of the ships and fleets, and for the entry of Warrant Officers; to frame, from the Board's Minutes of Agreement, all contracts for ships stores and charter parties; to enter them, and forward copies thereof, signed by him, to the Officers of the Yards, or such other persons as are to see to the execution of same.

In addition, the Clerk of the Acts Office kept track of all financial instruments issued by the Navy Board and was the custodian of log books, journals, and other such records deposited with the Board. According to the Commissioners for

[1] NRS, *Sandwich Papers*, ii, 289, iii, 181; NRS, *Barham Papers*, i, viii–ix; NMM, SAN/T/5, May 23, 1776; Add. MSS., 38205, ff. 235–6, 249; Add. MSS., 38209, ff. 135–6; Williams, op. cit., 280.

Enquiring into Fees in the Public Offices, in 1784 the Clerk of the Acts received from public sources £836 10s 0d plus 'The usual Allowances when visiting the Yards, Coals and Candles for his use, and Premiums with Clerks'.[1]

Throughout the American War the Office of Clerk of the Acts was held by George Marsh, 'a man', in Robert Gregson's opinion, 'totally unfit for employment, as he can neither read, spell, nor write'. This can hardly have been true for even in the eighteenth century no illiterate could make his living for nineteen years as a clerk. George Marsh started his climb to a position on the Navy Board in 1744 as a clerk in Deptford Dockyard. After holding clerical appointments in a number of different dockyards and departments of the Navy Office, in 1763 he became private secretary to Lord Egmont, who was then First Lord of the Admiralty. In November 1763 Marsh was made a commissioner on the Victualling Board and held that position until October 1772 when he became a Commissioner of the Navy.[2] Marsh was trained as a clerk and had spent his whole life either as a clerk or as a secretary until his appointment to the Victualling Board in 1763.

The Comptroller of the Victualling Accounts had charge of examining and balancing the accounts of the Victualling Board, the pursers, and all others concerned with provisioning naval personnel. He also supervised the payments in 'his turn' at the Pay Office in London and at Deptford and Woolwich Dockyards. In 1784, according to the Commissioners for Enquiry into Fees in the Public Offices, the Comptroller of the Victualling Accounts earned £836 10s 0d a year plus 'Coals and Candles for his use, Premiums with Clerks, 13s 6d a day with Coach-hire when attending Payments in Town, and 40s a day when at Deptford'.[3]

William Palmer, who held the office of Comptroller of the Victualling Accounts from 1773 to 1796, began his career in 1757 as a clerk in the Slop Office and in 1760 he became a clerk in the Clerk of the Acts Office. On 9 September 1763 Palmer

[1] Parliamentary Papers, op. cit., 169, 260–1.

[2] Parliamentary Papers, ibid., 194; SP, 151, Gregson to Shelburne, An Acc[ount] of the members of the Navy Board, [undated].

[3] Parliamentary Papers, op. cit., 171, 260–1.

was appointed Clerk of the Survey at Deptford Dockyard, and on 15 August 1771 he became Clerk of the Cheque at Portsmouth Dockyard and held this post until he was appointed a Commissioner of the Navy. According to Robert Gregson, William Palmer as a member of the Navy Board did 'very little in the Board & is very fond of giving his opinion on matters that are very [small]'.[1] It is clear that Palmer was without practical experience in either seamanship or warfare.

The Comptroller of the Treasurer's Accounts audited the accounts of the Treasurer of the Navy, prepared for Parliament estimates for the Ordinary of the Navy and accounts of the Debt of the Navy, and performed a number of other tasks involving accounting and auditing. In 1784 this official received, according to the Commissioners for Enquiring into the Fees in Public Offices, an income of £836 10s 0d plus 'Coals and Candles for his use, [and] Premiums with Clerks'. Timothy Brett held the Office of Comptroller of the Treasurer's Accounts from 1761 until 23 September 1782 when George Rogers assumed the office. Before becoming Comptroller of the Treasurer's Accounts, Brett appears to have served as an Extra Commissioner of the Navy from 1757 to 1761, but before this time nothing is known of his career.[2]

It was the duty of the Comptroller of the Storekeeper's Accounts 'to attend that the several Store Keepers and other Officers of Your Majesty's Dock Yards, keep the accounts of the receipt and issue of stores, according to the order and method directed by their instructions'. This official audited and generally kept track of all stores issued in the naval service. In addition, he supervised 'in his turn the payment of ships and recalls at the Pay Office in London, and the payment of Deptford and Woolwich Yards'. Attending these payments was so time-con-

---

[1] Parliamentary Papers, ibid., 196; SP, 151, Gregson to Shelburne, An Acc[ount] of the members of the Navy Board, [undated]; Usher, op. cit., 65.

[2] Usher, ibid., 65; Parliamentary Papers, op. cit., 170–1, 195–6, 260–1; *Court and City Register for the Year 1757* (London, n.d.), 206; *Court and City Register for the Year 1762* (London, n.d.), 213. Timothy Brett, coming from a naval family, might have had a greater knowledge of naval affairs than is apparent. His father and two brothers held commissions in the Royal Navy. See Sir Lewis Namier and John Brooke, *The History of Parliament: The House of Commons, 1754–1790* (London, 1964), ii, 114–15.

suming that Gregson noted that the 'Compr of the storekeepers
accounts . . . is very seldom at the board. Perhaps not 20 times
a year'. In 1784 the Comptroller of the Storekeeper's Accounts
received an income of £836 10s 0d and 'Coals and Candles for
his use, 40s a day Traveling Expences when attending the Payments of Ships and Yards, and 13s 6d a day when at Board-street;
also Premiums with Clerks'. William Bateman held the office of
Comptroller of the Storekeeper's Accounts from 1762 to 1783.
Before assuming this office he appears to have been an Extra
Commissioner of the Navy for five years, but little is known of
his previous career.[1]

The Surveyor of the Navy supervised the designing, construction, fitting, refitting, and repair of the King's ships and of 'all
buildings proposed to be erected in any of the Dock Yards; to
settle the manner in which the works of all new docks, wharfs,
building slips, and other buildings, are to be carried on'. The
Surveyor controlled the issue of boatswains' and carpenters'
stores to ships both in Britain and overseas, and he also supervised the sale of old or unwanted stores and ships in order 'that
the same be made to the most advantage'. A Surveyor of the
Navy in 1784 received an income of £926 10s 0d and 'When
visiting Yards in the River 35s a day. When . . . [visiting dockyards other than on the Thames] 40s a day besides Chaise-hire;
also Premiums with Clerks, and Coals and Candles for his use'.[2]

During the American War the office of Surveyor of the Navy
was held jointly by Sir John Williams and Edward Hunt.
Evidently it was the policy of the government to appoint men
to the surveyorship who had had experience as shipwrights in
the King's dockyards. Both Williams and Hunt had worked in
this capacity, and their successor, John Henslow, had spent more
than thirty years working in the King's dockyards before becoming Surveyor of the Navy in 1784. Williams seems to have
served for some years as the Master Shipwright at Sheerness
Dockyard before his appointment as a Commissioner of the

[1] Parliamentary Papers, op. cit., 171–2, 260–1; SP, 151, Gregson to Shelburne,
An Acc[ount] of the members of the Navy Board, [undated]; *Court and City
Register for the Year 1762* (London, n.d.), 213; *Court and City Register for the Year 1757*
(London, n.d.), 205.
[2] Parliamentary Papers, op. cit., 168–9, 260–1.

Navy on 31 July 1765, and on 27 September 1771 he was knighted. But during the American War, his old age seems to have made him ineffectual. Gregson stated that Williams was 'totally unfit for business & has been so for some years'. It thus appears that Hunt, who had also served as Master Shipwright at Sheerness, was made a second Surveyor of the Navy in 1778 in order to carry Williams.[1]

During the American War three Extra Commissioners of the Navy sat on the Board. Two of them were obviously appointed to alleviate the crushing burden of business placed on the Navy Board by the war. In 1784 an Extra Commissioner of the Navy received an income of £836 10s 0d and 'Coals and Candles for his use, 13s 6d a day Coach-hire when attending Payments in Broad-street and Premiums with Clerks'.[2]

Sir Richard Temple was the only Extra Commissioner to serve during the American War who had been appointed before the war began. He was neither a seaman nor a navy officer. Temple, who was born on 1 June 1731, succeeded to the baronetcy on 15 November 1761 and became an Extra Commissioner of the Navy in 1761. He also held the office of Comptroller of the Cash in the Excise Office at a salary 'for himself and 2 clerks, [of] £800'. His job at the Navy Office was to keep

an account of all the papers and letters that were referred to particular offices, and [he] checked their returns. These were so immense and had been so little attended to, as to have occasioned great delay and much unnecessary disappointment. This arrangement, with an entire new set of returns, was found in its consequences extremely useful.[3]

[1] Parliamentary Papers, ibid., 192–3; *Annual Register*, viii, 166; *Court and City Register for the Year 1765* (London, n.d.), 228; *Court and City Register for the Year 1764* (London, n.d.), 226; WM. A. Shaw, *The Knights of England* (London, 1906), ii, 293; SP, 151, Gregson to Shelburne, An Acc[ount] of the members of the Navy Board, [undated]; Usher, op. cit., 61–2; Williams, op. cit., 280, NRS, *Barham Papers*, ii, 179; *Royal Kalendar* (London, 1779), 136.

[2] Parliamentary Papers, op. cit., 260–1.

[3] NRS, *Barham Papers*, ii, 238; Usher, op. cit., 67; *Gentleman's Magazine*, lvi, 1003; *Royal Kalendar* (London, 1778), 120. There is a possibility that Sir William Temple obtained his post at the Navy and Excise Offices through the influence of Earl Temple to whom he was remotely related. See G. E. C[okayne], ed., *Complete Baronetage* (Exeter, 1900–1906), i, 83–4; G. E. C[okayne] and Geoffrey H. White, eds., *The Complete Peerage* (London, 1953), xii, 657–8.

Captain Edward Le Cras, before being appointed an Extra Commissioner of the Navy in January 1778, served as an officer of the Navy for thirty-nine years. He was commissioned a lieutenant in 1739, became a master and commander in 1748, and was made a post captain on 4 February 1755. Just before becoming a member of the Navy Board he had commanded H.M.S. *Russell*. As a member of the Navy Board during the American War, Le Cras checked such records as captains', lieutenants', and masters' logs and journals to see that they were kept correctly and also superintended the supplying of stores to ships in Britain and overseas. According to Gregson, he also did 'a good deal of the business respecting the shipping for transports & army victuallers', and 'attends, besides, one month in every three, the comptrolling, payments and recalls of seamen's wages in Broad-street, and the ships and yards at Deptford and Woolwich'.[1]

Captain Samuel Wallis, with the exception perhaps of Sir Charles Middleton, was the most famous man to serve on the Navy Board during the American War. He was commissioned a lieutenant in the Navy on 19 October 1748. After serving throughout the Seven Years War, he was appointed to command H.M.S. *Dolphin* in June 1766. While in command of this vessel, he became a well-known explorer of the Pacific Ocean and discovered numerous islands in the Low Archipelago and Tahiti in the Society Islands. When Wallis was made an Extra Commissioner of the Navy in November 1780, he was in command of H.M.S. *Queen* in the English Channel. Wallis appears to have been appointed to the Navy Board to 'be particularly employed in the transport line'. His duties consisting mainly of managing

the fitting and refitting of transports, storeships, and victuallers; to keep an exact account of their names, tonnage, number of men, guns, &c. and the services on which they were employed, with the agents names whom they were under, and every other particular relative thereto; to superintend the transports employed in transport-

---

[1] PRO, ADM/106/2596, Nov. 19, 1777; [NMM], *The Commissioned Sea Officers of the Royal Navy, 1660–1815* (n.p., 1954), ii, 543; SP, 151, Gregson to Shelburne, An Acc[ount] of the members of the Navy Board, [undated]; Usher, op. cit., 67; Parliamentary Papers, op. cit., 198–9; NRS, *Barham Papers*, ii, 238.

ing stores from one yard to another, and see that they were properly employed, and the storeships carrying stores to East and West Indies and America . . . to assist in examining into Midshipmen's qualifications for being Lieutenants; to attend the claims of run men for relief, and in turn the payments in Broad-street.[1]

The majority of the members of the Navy Board during the American War were without any practical experience in either seamanship or warfare. Only the Comptroller and two of the Extra Commissioners were navy officers who had served on active duty, while the two Surveyors, Sir John Williams and Edward Hunt, appear to have had the experience needed to solve questions of ship construction. But the other members of the Board—George Marsh, Timothy Brett, William Palmer, William Bateman, and Sir Richard Temple—had not had any practical, first-hand naval or military experience. All were bureaucrats of long standing, but a detailed knowledge of naval administrative and accounting procedures did not equip them to solve a problem such as how best to transport a regiment of troops across the Atlantic.

The conduct of all Navy Board business requiring a practical knowledge of seamanship fell to those commissioners capable of handling it, while the others appear to have been mere spectators. Gregson described affairs at the Navy Office as follows: 'the whole of the weight of business falls upon a few, & of those few, chiefly upon the Comptroller & Secretary [Assistant to the Clerk of the Acts] who have piles of papers before them to read a foot high, to digest, & minute, while two or three others at the Bd are looking on or reading newspapers'.[2] Sir Charles Middleton thought this state of affairs resulted from the fact that 'the appointments that have gradually taken place have precluded the seamen from every one of the established offices', and that 'This improper arrangement has made it necessary, in time of war, to call assistance of sea officers under the title of extra commissioners'. Throughout the American War Middleton complained bitterly about the lack of seamen on the Navy

---

[1] *Dictionary of National Biography* (London, 1899), lix, 148–9; PRO, T/29/49, f. 263; Parliamentary Papers, op. cit., 199.

[2] SP, 151, Gregson to Shelburne, An Acc[ount] of the members of the Navy Board, [undated].

Board and once suggested that Captain Richard Kempenfelt be appointed to the Board because 'As it now stands I cannot be one hour absent while the Board sits'.[1] The Admiralty, however, did not fully understand the importance of the role that the Extra Commissioners played in the conduct of the affairs of the Navy Board, for in the summer of 1779, when the Franco-Spanish fleet was in the English Channel off Plymouth and the Navy Board was working around the clock to get every ship possible ready for sea, Sandwich insisted, over Middleton's vehement protests, on sending Le Cras, the only person other than the Comptroller on the Board at that time who was a professional seaman, to Plymouth to settle a problem which could have been handled by any other high-ranking official with a degree of common sense.[2]

The way in which the Navy Board conducted its business compounded the problems caused by the lack of commissioners who had had training in seamanship and warfare. During the American War the Board met six times in a week. The meetings started at ten in the morning and generally lasted until the late afternoon or early evening. The proceedings were taken down in minutes by the Assistant to the Clerk of the Acts who acted as secretary to the Board. In 1784 the Assistant to the Clerk of the Acts had a basic salary of £300 a year, but with the addition of fees and allowances he received a total of £1076 16s od. It was from the minutes kept by this official that the Board's clerks drew up the charter parties, contracts, letters, navy bills, and orders required by the resolves of the Navy Board. The Board 'proceed[ed] by Common Council, and agreement of the most voices', and all financial instruments, orders, warrants, contracts, charter parties, and the like had to be signed by three commissioners.[3] A study of the minutes reveals that no attempt was made to put matters in some form or order before they were presented to the Board for its decision.[4] According to Middleton, this random presentation led to 'a very great number of different

---

[1] NRS, *Barham Papers*, ii, 159; NRS, *Sandwich Papers*, iii, 42–3, iv, 369
[2] For an account of this episode, see A. Temple Patterson, *The Other Armada* (Manchester, 1960), 187–8.
[3] Parliamentary Papers, op. cit., 168, 173, 260–1, PRO, C/66/3776, no. 5.
[4] PRO, ADM/106/2593–611.

subjects before a board thus constituted, in which a great part of the commissioners had very little interest, but could, at any time, delay business by raising doubts and starting objections, even while occasion pressed, and necessity called for immediate decision that matters might not be retarded, nor suffered to run irretrievably into arrear'. Middleton went on to say:

The whole continued to be transacted at one table, with the same irregularity, as matters came by chance before us. No means had been taken for dividing the business nor any provision made for despatch and economy in carrying it on. Some members were over-loaded with business, while others came and went as best suited their own conveniency; and it fell of course to my share to bring things to some conclusion out of this indigested heap before the day ended, be it right or wrong. The natural consequences were,—hasty decisions, accounts passed with little examination, and a perplexing variety of opinions on the most simple subjects.

Middleton considered this 'irksome situation' to be 'intoler-able', but although the Board was conducting business with 'upwards of 2000 correspondents' and was overwhelmed with work, it resisted attempts to change its traditional methods of conducting affairs.[1]

Despite these unfavourable circumstances vast numbers of orders, letters, reports, warrants, invoices, and other papers issued from the Navy Board in the course of a single day. It could not be otherwise, for it took 'unremitting attention' to keep the administrative machinery of the Royal Navy in motion, while the procuring, fitting-out, loading, and dispatch of the transports needed for a major troop movement alone required the issuing by the Navy Board of hundreds of orders and instructions. Before even a single storeship could be dispatched, the Board had to send out more than half a score of orders, instructions, and letters.

Some conception of the difficulties encountered by the Navy Board in its routine operations can be obtained from a brief account of its attempts to dispatch the *Mellish* to Canada. On 6 July 1776 the Admiralty ordered the Board to provide a vessel to transport army clothing to Canada. The Board did not

---

[1] NRS, *Barham Papers*, ii, 236–7; PRO, T/29/50, ff. 27, 40.

act on this matter until it was informed on 12 July that the *Mellish*, a transport which was fitted to carry horses and loaded with forage, had arrived at Deptford. The Board then ordered the Deptford officers to unload the forage 'immediately' so that the *Mellish* could take the clothing on board. On 16 July the Board issued orders to the Deptford officers to 'lay a platform on board the Mellish transport for more convenient stowage of the stores she is to take in', and on 22 July it directed the Victualling Board to furnish the *Mellish* with enough provisions for twenty soldiers. The next day the Board ordered that the forage taken out of the *Mellish* be sold by the officers of Deptford Dockyard, who were also instructed to 'send in an account of the produce'. On 29 July the officers at Deptford Dockyard informed the Board that the *Mellish* would be ready to proceed the next day, and on 8 August the Board asked the Admiralty what orders should be given to her master. The following day the Board proposed that a navy petty officer be put in command of the *Mellish*, and on 10 August in accordance with directions received from the Admiralty, it directed its Agent for Transports at Deptford to order the *Mellish* to proceed to Spithead. On 12 August the Board issued a warrant appointing Samuel Horsenail, a navy petty officer, to take charge of the ship. At the same time orders were issued to the master of the *Mellish* to feed Horsenail. On the same day the Board informed the Admiralty that the clothing for Canada and twenty troops had been embarked. On 14 August the Admiralty directed the Navy Board to provide 'Mr Southouse & family [with] a passage to Quebec on board the Mellish transport', and on 15 August the Board gave orders for the Southouse family to be received on board. Meanwhile the *Mellish* had proceeded to Blackwall en route to Spithead, but it appeared to the Navy Board that she was staying at Blackwall longer than necessary. Consequently, on 16 August the owners of the vessel were told 'That we [the Navy Board] have ordered her to be protested against for delay & shall mulct her of Freight from this day until she proceeds from thence'. On 21 August the Navy Board ordered the owners of the *Mellish* 'to provide another master & mate for the Mellish transport, the present ones having declared that in case of her being attacked . . . they would not defend her'. Meanwhile

Horsenail was ordered by the Board on 23 August to take an inventory of the ordnance stores on the *Mellish* which were supplied by the owners and to send an account of this inventory to the Board. Horesnail did this on 30 August. The *Mellish*, having in the meantime arrived at Spithead, was ordered by the Board on 23 August to place herself under escort of H.M.S. *Richmond* for the voyage to Canada. All this trouble was to no avail, for the *Mellish* parted company with H.M.S. *Richmond* en route to Quebec and was captured by John Paul Jones off Cape Breton on the morning of 12 November.[1]

The capture of the *Mellish* did not end the Navy Board's concern in the matter, for the question had to be resolved, whether or not to pay compensation to her owners for the loss of the vessel. At a meeting of the Board on 20 March 1777 it was decided that she had not been lost through the negligence of her owners, master, or crew, and that therefore her owners would receive from the government in navy bills the assigned value of the vessel less the wear and tear she had received while in the service of the Navy Board. Even now the Board's involvement with the *Mellish* was not over, for in May 1777 a petty officer belonging to H.M.S. *Richmond*, who had been on board the *Mellish* at the time of her capture, arrived in London and requested that he be paid his wages and the expenses he had incurred by being captured. The Board resolved on 5 June that the petty officer could not be paid his wages or expenses at this time because his name was still on the books of H.M.S. *Richmond*. As a consequence he could not be paid until that ship was paid off.[2] Eleven months after first receiving the order from the Admiralty to supply a vessel to transport army clothing to Canada, the Navy Board was able to bring the matter to a close.

The problems of the *Mellish* were typical of those presented to the Navy Board by the hundreds of other ships in the transport service. At times the Board was faced with the task of having simultaneously to procure, fit-out, load, and dispatch

[1] NMM, ADM/N/247, July 6, 1776; ADM/B/193, Aug. 12, 1776; PRO, ADM/106/2594, July 3, 12, 16, 22, 29, Aug. 8, 9, 10, 12, 15, 16, 21, 23, 31, 1776; NRS, *Sandwich Papers*, i, 172; Samuel Eliot Morison, *John Paul Jones: A Sailor's Biography* (London, 1959), 79–80.

[2] PRO, ADM/106/2595, March 20, May 22, 26, June 5, 1777.

scores of vessels such as the *Mellish*. The Navy Board also had to administer the entire civil establishment of the Royal Navy. In view of the staggering load of business and the slap-dash methods employed to conduct affairs at Crutched Friars, it is to the great credit of the Commissioners of the Navy that the responsibilities of the Board directly related to military operations did not fall hopelessly into arrears during the American War.

In order to keep up with the operational demands of the war the more hard-pressed members of the Board, such as the Comptroller, had to delegate most of their routine responsibilities to the clerks in the Navy Office. Middleton observed that: 'In this way of managing business many material branches are of a necessity entrusted to clerks', and 'custom had transferred all business of accounts to the head clerks'; and he even went so far as to say that he was not able 'to examine further into the business of his own Offices for Bills and Accounts and for Seaman's Wages than a general view of what is brought before him to sign'.[1] A study of the minutes of the Navy Board also reveals that a great deal of the work assigned to Samuel Wallis concerning the transport service was done before his appointment to the Board in 1780 by Thomas Davies, Chief Clerk in the Comptroller's Office for Bills and Accounts.[2] It is thus clear that a great deal of routine, but important, business was left almost without supervision in the hands of the Navy Board's clerks.

During the American War the Navy Board was one of the biggest bureaucracies in the world. In 1784 it was one of the few organizations which employed a staff of 100 clerks in one office. Each member of the Board had a number of clerks assigned to him who were employed in carrying out the tasks for which he, as a Commissioner of the Navy, was particularly responsible. Thus, in 1784 the Comptroller of Storekeeper's Accounts had nine clerks engaged in checking accounts related to the issue of stores, and the Comptroller of Treasurer's Accounts had twenty clerks in the Ticket Office working on

[1] NRS, *Barham Papers*, ii, 226, 240–1; Parliamentary Papers, op. cit., 192.
[2] PRO, ADM/106/2593–602.

such projects as checking ship's books.[1] This system of assigning clerks to offices under the control of individual members of the Navy Board resulted in more than half the clerks belonging to the Navy Board being employed in checking and auditing accounts which were so far in arrears that they had no relation to the American War. As a consequence all current business of the Board was thrown on the clerks under the direction of the Comptroller of the Navy, Clerk of the Acts, and Extra Comissioners who were not engaged in auditing tasks. This in turn meant that while some clerks attended the Navy Office only five hours a day, others were overloaded with work and had to put in a considerably longer work day. For example, Richard Alexander Nelson, Seventh Clerk in the Clerk of the Acts Office had the following duties:

to make out and enter all warrants for Cooks to ships; to collect and regulate the papers of Midshipmen who pass examination for Lieutenants; to make out and enter their certificates of qualifications; to keep a book of all post letters inwards; to cheque and enter the accounts of the Purveyors and Messengers journies; to indorse and put away all letters to the Board, excepting those on Transport and Army Victualling service, and to assist the correspondence of Office, part of which relates to Transports and Army Victualling business.

Nelson found that in order to carry out these tasks he had to attend the Navy Office 'from ten or eleven till the business of the day is finished': in wartime this meant attendance in the evening.[2]

Despite the obvious administrative handicaps under which the Navy Board laboured, the affairs of the transport service during the American War never fell hopelessly into arrears. On the contrary, under Middleton's guidance the Board was able to surmount its internal administrative problems to such an extent that it was able to increase the scope of the transport service to meet the demands placed upon it by the spread of the conflict from North America to the West Indies, India, and Europe, following the entry of the European powers into the war.

[1] Parliamentary Papers, op. cit., 262–5.
[2] Parliamentary Papers, ibid., 231.

CHAPTER III

The Lower Chain of Command

THE ABILITY of the transport service to support the British military effort during the American War depended in large part on the subordinate officials of the Navy Board. These officials, under the direction of the Navy Board or the commanders-in-chief overseas, supervised the ships of the transport service. They were responsible for transmitting the orders of the Navy Board and the overseas commanders-in-chief to the masters of the various ships and making sure that these orders were carried out. Also they saw to it that the owners of ships under charter to the Navy Board kept their vessels properly manned, equipped, and repaired in accordance with the terms of the ships' charter parties.

Through the exercise of the 'power of the purse' the Navy Board made the owners and the masters of ships under charter comply with the terms of its charter parties and obey the Board's orders. To ensure the good conduct of master and owner it was the policy of the Board to withhold a major part of a vessel's freight until the service for which it had been chartered was completed.[1] If there was any misconduct on the part of a ship's master or a breach of a ship's charter party, the Board would place a mulct upon the freight of the offending ship. On 30 December 1776 the Board resolved that because of complaints

against several transport ships employed in his Majesty's service, on account of delays, breach of orders, or other neglects of duty, in relation to their charter parties . . .

That it is very proper and necessary to make mulcts from the freight of such ships as are protested against for breach of their Charterparties, not only as a punishment upon them on account of

[1] See below, p. 86.

the detriment sustained by the public service, but also as a distinction between those who do, and those who do not comply with the terms of their Charter.

That in making these mulcts the following mode (being the most equitable the Board can think of) be observed. Viz. Every ship protested against for want of men in such cases when the service is not immediately delayed upon her account, shall be mulcted for the deficiency in her complement, to be reckoned upon the medium for the time she may be found to be deficient, and at the rate of £2 10s 0d ℔ man ℔ month for wages, and one shilling ℔ day for provisions, but when the service is stop'd or postponed on account of the deficiency or delay of any particular ship or ships, the mulct to be made in such case must be the whole freight of such ship or ships for the whole time the service is delayed.

On 2 September 1777 the mulct was raised from £2 10s per month for each seaman missing under the number called for by the ship's charter party to £3 per man per month.[1]

When an official of the transport service discovered an act of abuse, neglect, or disobedience by the owner or master of a vessel under charter to the Navy Board, the vessel in question was 'protested' against. The official went before a notary public and had a sworn statement setting forth the nature of the neglect drawn up and notarized. This statement was then transmitted to the Navy Board and served as the basis upon which the freight of the vessel in question was mulcted.[2] The ability to protest against and mulct the freight of a vessel for neglect of duty and nonperformance of the terms of its charter party placed in the hands of the Board a powerful weapon for enforcing its commands. The effectiveness of this weapon, however, was entirely dependent upon the ability of the subordinate officials of the transport service.

The most important officials of the transport service were the agents for transports. They were usually appointed by the Admiralty on the recommendation of the Navy Board.[3] On

---

[1] PRO, ADM/106/2594, Dec. 30, 1776; ADM/106/2596, Sept. 2, 1777; SP, 151, Navy Board to Admiralty, Aug. 30, 1782.

[2] E.g., ADM/49/2, ff. 183–4.

[3] E.g., PRO, ADM/106/2593, Aug. 11, 1775; NMM, ADM/N/244, Aug. 12, 1775; ADM/B/191, Jan. 8, Feb. 21, 1776; ADM/B/194, Feb. 11, 1777; ADM/B/198, April 5, 1779.

several occasions, however, military and naval commanders overseas appointed agents for transports.[1]

During the American War men appointed to this office invariably held the rank of lieutenant in the Navy at the time of their appointment, and in most cases they were senior lieutenants who had been commissioned during the Seven Years War. For example, the three officers who held the position of Principal Agent for Transports during the American War— Henry Chads, Thomas Tonken, and John Bourmaster—were commissioned as lieutenants on 7 March 1759, 6 April 1757, and 19 October 1759, respectively.[2] They were thus usually men of considerable naval experience. An agent for transports holding the rank of lieutenant in the Navy was paid 'fifteen shillings a day with a servant in addition to his half pay [as a lieutenant], while he is so employed'. The half pay of a lieutenant of the Navy was 3s per day. For example, the Board paid Lieutenant Stephen Harris, its agent for transports at Cork, a salary of £273 15s 0d per year and an allowance for his servant of 19s per month.[3] If an agent for transports was promoted from lieutenant to master and commander, his salary was increased from 15s per day to a guinea per day.[4] On occasion the Board allowed its agents for transports 5s per day in periods of unemployment. The only fees or emoluments that appear to have been taken by agents for transports were the 'five or six guineas' received from shipowners by Lieutenant Stephen Harris, until the Navy Board forbade it, for issuing certificates certifying that victuallers were fit for service.[5]

[1] E.g., PRO, ADM/49/2, f. 2A.

[2] [NMM], *The Commissioned Sea Officers of the Royal Navy, 1660–1815* (n.p., 1954), i, 87, 156; iii, 922.

[3] NMM, ADM/N/248, April 7, 1779; PRO, T/1/545, Admiralty to Treasury, April 14, 1778; T/1/575, Navy Board to Treasury, Nov. 1, 1782.

[4] By looking up the salary granted to Captain James Randell who served as a principal agent for transports with the rank of master and commander during the Seven Years War, the Navy Board arrived at the sum of one guinea as the salary of an officer serving as an agent for transports who also held the rank of master and commander. NMM, ADM/B/199, May 22, 1779; ADM/N/248, March 22, May 25, 1779; PRO, ADM/106/2600, May 26, 1779.

[5] PRO, ADM/108/1C, May 31, June 1, 1782; ADM/106/2596, Sept. 4, 1777; ADM/106/2609, July 24, 1782.

The position of agent for transports could not have been a very distinguished appointment for an eighteenth-century navy officer, for there was very little opportunity to win prize money, glory, or fame. Out of approximately twenty officers employed as agents for transports during the American War, only two —John Bourmaster and John Knowles—were ever promoted to flag rank;[1] and Walter Young was the only agent for transports to obtain any degree of notoriety. After leaving the transport service in 1779, Young became Sir George Rodney's flag captain and was thought by some to have been instrumental in formulating the tactics by which Rodney defeated the Spanish fleet during the relief of Gibraltar in 1780.[2] The achievements of Bourmaster, Knowles, and Young were exceptional for many agents for transports never became post captains.[3] The office of agent for transports, however, had the advantage of bringing its occupant into close contact with many high-ranking officials, and this proximity to the holders of power probably greatly facilitated promotion from lieutenant to master and commander. At the end of 1775, Lieutenant William Cumming, Agent for Transports, brought Lieutenant General Thomas Gage to England in the transport *Pallas*. Upon attending the Navy Board, Cumming was informed 'that they had no further commands for him at present as agent', but on 29 December 1775 the Board received a letter from Gage 'recommending Lt. Cumming to the Boards protection as a faithful & diligent Officer'. Cumming was reappointed as agent for transports the next day. Lieutenants Benjamin Hill and Thomas Haynes were promoted to the rank of master and commander by the Earl of Sandwich on the recommendations of the Landgrave of Hesse and the Duke of Brunswick 'for their care and attention in embarking and conducting of the troops of those princes to America as agents for transports'. Lieutenant John Bourmaster won the praise of General William Howe by saving two transports in Boston Bay from capture and in June 1776 Bourmaster,

---

[1] [NMM], *The Commissioned Sea Officers*, i, 87; ii, 526.

[2] See W. M. James, *The British Navy in Adversity* (London, 1926), 192; NRS, *Barham Papers*, i, xli, xliii. However, Young's role in the formulation of Rodney's tactics has largely been discredited by historians.

[3] [NMM]. *The Commissioned Sea Officers*, passim.

at the request of Howe, was appointed Principal Agent for Transports and promoted to master and commander.[1]

From the point of view of professional advancement, the drawback to serving as an agent for transports was that the position turned a navy officer into a specialist in the management of merchant shipping and if he afterwards obtained a command he was liable to be removed from it at a moment's notice if his particular expertness was in demand. On this ground Captain Kelly was removed from the command of H.M.S. *Blast* by Admiral Sir George Rodney on 8 April 1782. On 30 June 1781 Rodney also transferred Captain Thomas Walbeoff, a former Agent for Transports, from command of H.M.S. *Port Royal* to help prepare transports at Jamaica to carry wounded men to England and prisoners of war to France for exchange.[2] The specialized skills which Kelly and Walbeoff possessed, although the cause of their removal from commands, were what made the agents for transports of such importance to the conduct of the transport service.

The Navy Board employed agents for transports in three different types of services. Throughout the war there were always a number of agents for transports stationed at various ports in the British Isles which were major depots and naval bases. A second group of agents travelled with and superintended flotillas of transports and victuallers as they made their way back and forth across the Atlantic. The third group was stationed overseas. The officers in this last group, based mostly at New York, supervised the transports and victuallers serving in America and the West Indies.

Agents for transports were stationed permanently at Deptford, Portsmouth, and Cork and were directly under the command of the Navy Board. Deptford Dockyard was the major base for measuring, fitting, and storing transports, victuallers, and storeships. Once the ships of the transport service had been made ready for sea by the officers of the Deptford Dockyard,

---

[1] PRO, ADM/1/4131, f. 3; ADM/106/2593, Dec. 5, 29, 30, 1775; NMM, SAN/T/8, April 28, 1777; Robert Wilden Neeser, ed., *The Dispatches of Molyneux Shuldham* (New York, 1913), 259.

[2] NYHSC, *Letter-Books and Order Book of George, Lord Rodney*, ii, 658–9, 810. For another example see PRO, ADM/1/486, f. 244.

they were usually dispatched to other ports for loading. The orders for their further movements were normally sent through the agent at Deptford.[1] In addition to transmitting orders and instructions to transports, this agent furnished the Navy Board with information about transports and victuallers in the Thames.[2] The agent was also called upon to settle problems of cargo stowage.[3]

The agent for transports at Deptford spent considerable time and energy preventing 'abuses' and making the masters and owners of transports follow the orders of the Navy Board. Lieutenant Walter Young who served as agent for transports at Deptford for several years reported on 13 May 1779 that the masters of a number of victuallers which were refitting had attempted to bribe him in order to allow them to carry private cargoes to Cork. On 29 June 1779 Young reported that Walter Paterson, Governor of St John's (Prince Edward Island), had appeared at Deptford and informed the owner and master of the transport _Æolus_ 'that Lord George Germain had ordered this ship particularly for his use, and when the clothing was on board, he was to fill up the ship with what goods he thought proper; but, that things might be carried on smoothly, he offered the owner £50, provided he—the owner and master—would aid and assist him therein'.[4]

From November 1778 until the end of the war the Navy Board stationed an agent for transports permanently at Portsmouth, because most of the convoys proceeding overseas were formed at the Spithead anchorage, and because in the last years of the war the Board maintained its largest provision depot in England at Cowes. Before this appointment was made, the business of the transport service there was conducted either by the officers of Portsmouth Dockyard, by agents accompanying various flotillas of transports which happened to be at Spithead, or by Young, whom the Board on various occasions sent there

---

[1] E.g., PRO, ADM/106/2594, July 1, Nov. 25, 1776; ADM/106/2597, March 11, 1778.

[2] E.g., PRO, ADM/106/2607, Feb. 28, 1782.

[3] E.g., PRO, ADM/106/2598, Aug. 13, 1778; ADM/106/2600, June 9, 1779.

[4] NRS, _Barham Papers_, i, 50–2. For other examples see PRO, ADM/106/3529, Sept. 1, Dec. 8, 1780, Feb. 16, 1781.

from Deptford to deal with specific problems. On 28 November 1778, however, the Navy Board put an end to these *ad hoc* arrangements when it 'Gave orders to Lt [Robert] Parrey to continue at Ports[mouth]'.[1]

As permanent agent, one of Lieutenant Parrey's major tasks was that of transmitting to the Board detailed reports on the state of the transport service's shipping in the Portsmouth area. On 16 January 1779 he received orders 'to report . . . from time to time when the transports at Ports. are ready for service'. The Board, however, must have found Parrey's occasional reports inadequate, for on 1 November 1779 it directed him 'to send us weekly an account of the transports, transport victuallers, & storeships at Spithead, in Ports. Harbour, or [in] that neighbourhood, in the following form viz. ships—masters—tons—guns—men—where—in what service'. On 19 February 1780 Parrey was instructed to include in his reports the number of flat-bottom boats and bateaux on board each transport at Portsmouth, and later in the year he was ordered to report the dates when transports and victuallers then refitting at Portsmouth would be complete and ready for service. The Board's appetite for information seems to have been insatiable, for on 25 May 1781 it ordered Parrey to 'send . . . an exact list of storeships & transports which sailed with the different convoys and to do so with all [which] shall sail in future'. On 8 January 1782 Parrey was required 'to make a column in his weekly return for storeships arriving at Spithead mentioning the time they arrive', and on 10 April 1782 he was ordered to send reports to the Navy Board on the state of 'coppered transports lying at Spithead & their destinations'. On 11 September 1782 he was ordered to indicate 'in his list[s] of transports such as are fitting for troops and such as are fitting for provisions'.[2] During the time that Parrey was agent for transports at Portsmouth, he sent to the Board masses of detailed information on the state and

---

[1] PRO, ADM/106/2597, April 16, 1778; ADM/106/2598, July 30, Nov. 28, 1778.
[2] PRO, ADM/106/2599, Jan. 16, 1779; ADM/106/2601, Nov. 1, 1779; ADM/106/2602, Feb. 19, 1780; ADM/106/2604, Nov. 22, 1780; ADM/106/2605, May 25, 1781; ADM/106/2607, Jan. 8, 1782; ADM/106/2608, April 10, 1782; ADM/106/2609, Sept. 11, 1782.

movements of ships of the transport service in the Spithead area. The progressively more elaborate nature of the returns demanded from Parrey is indicative of an increasing sophistication and expertness derived from war experience on the part of the professional administrators on the Navy Board.

The agent for transports at Portsmouth was not only a source of information to the Navy Board, but he was also an instrument for enforcing the orders and directions which it issued to the masters of transports and victuallers. For example, on 28 December 1779 he was sent orders to examine the journals of a number of transports which had arrived at Spithead from Deptford to see if 'they have loitered away time on the passage', and on 20 November 1780 he was ordered to direct the master of the *John & Bella* to put in writing his reasons for disobeying orders. At this time Admiral Sir Samuel Hood, who was attempting to form a convoy for the West Indies at St Helens, was sending the Admiralty complaints that the transports belonging to the convoy were arriving late at St Helens and thus preventing his departure for the Caribbean. On 27 November 1780 the Admiralty transmitted Hood's complaints to the Navy Board, which in turn ordered Parrey 'to make inquiry & report the reasons of their [the masters of the transports] disobedience & to use every means in his power to hasten the ships to St. Helens'.[1]

In addition to his duties relating to transports and storeships at Portsmouth and Spithead, Parrey had to supervise the loading and dispatching of victuallers at Cowes, a task which required that he commute between Cowes and Portsmouth.[2] In 1781, however, the Board began to relieve Parrey of some of his responsibilities at Cowes by delegating this task to other agents for transports on a more casual basis.[3]

When the Navy Board assumed the responsibility for the transport of army provisions in the spring of 1779, an agent for transports was permanently stationed at Cork, which was the major depot for the shipment of army provisions from Ireland.

[1] PRO, ADM/106/2601, Dec. 28, 1779; ADM/106/2604, Nov. 20, 1780; NRS, *Letters written by Sir Samuel Hood*, 2–3, 5–7.
[2] E.g., PRO, ADM/106/2602, April 26, 1780; ADM/106/2603, June 29, 1780.
[3] E.g., PRO, ADM/106/2605, Aug. 21, 1781.

On 3 April 1779 Lieutenant Stephen Harris, an agent for transports, attended the Board and was ordered to proceed to Cork
and take charge of the victuallers there. In addition he was
instructed 'to see that the transports were cleared of their ballast
before they begin to load & to take particular care that the
Holds & between decks are stored to the best advantage leaving
no more room for the ships stores than is absolutely necessary'.
Harris was further instructed

> to give constant attendance whilst the ships are loading & during
> that time employ one of the most skilful masters of the transports or
> any other proper person you can confide in at an allowance of two
> shillings & six pence per day to assist in going from ship to ship to
> see that the utmost advantage is taken for the benefit of the public
> in stowing them & when the whole are loaded to deliver them into
> the charge of Lieut. [Archibald] Dow who is furnished with our
> instructions for his further proceedings.

The Navy Board issued additional instructions to Harris on
30 April 1779, when it ordered him 'not to suffer any [cargo] to
be carried from Cork without our special orders, & to report to
us any misconduct in the masters to the prejudice of the
government'. Despite the best efforts of Harris, a number of
irregularities occurred on board the victuallers at Cork. On
23 October 1779 Harris protested against Paul White, master of
the victualler *Saville*, 'for not filling the Fore Hold, but leaving
a space, which could have received five or six tons of dry
Provisions, & filling it with wet [provisions] of his own'.[1] The
situation did not improve, and by March 1780 so much private
cargo was being shipped on board the victuallers that Harris
had the following warning printed in the Cork newspapers:

> To the Merchants of the city of Cork and whomever it may con-
> cern Lieutenant Harris of His Maj. Navy, Agent for Transports,
> hereby acquaints the merchants of this city that should any of the
> Masters of the Navy Victualling Transports under his directions
> take on board provisions or any other merchandize on freight or
> otherwise they will be proceeded against, & the goods found on
> board [will be used to] reimburce the loss the Government may
> sustain by the Tonnage such goods may occupy. He thinks it

---

[1] PRO, ADM/106/2599, April 3, 30, 1779; T/64/200, p. 13, 46–7.

necessary to give this notice as some merchants have appeared to be unacquainted with the impropriety of taking freight on board vessels in the King's Service.[1]

The practice of carrying private cargoes was not the only misconduct by the masters of the victuallers at Cork that caused difficulty for Harris. On 14 July 1779 he informed the Board that the victualler *Betsy* had been lost when her mate, in the absence of the master, ran the ship aground. On 12 August 1780 a convoy of thirty-two victuallers, one transport, forty-one ships loaded with oats for the army, and twenty-five merchant ships had been assembled with great difficulty in the Cove of Cork awaiting a fair wind for America. The commander of H.M.S. *Charon*, the escort, had given orders for the ships to be ready to sail as soon as the wind turned fair. On the night of 12 August, however, many of the masters of the victuallers took their ships' boats and went to Cork for an evening of pleasure, and by the time they had returned the wind had turned fair and the convoy had sailed. Harris protested against four of the victuallers, and when the Board received the protests it informed the owners of these ships that they were 'answerable for the consequences' of the masters' dereliction of their duty.[2]

One of Lieutenant Harris's most important duties was to select victuallers recently returned from overseas which were suitable for immediate reemployment. For instance, on 1 January 1782 he was directed by the Board that 'in case there should not be a sufficiency of transports amongst those returned from Quebec that are fit for service or can be made so at Cork or Waterford, to complete the 6000 tons (ordered to be detained) from the fleet expected from New York'. Cork, because it was the port where victuallers were selected for immediate redeployment, became the place where these ships were put into condition for further service. Thus, Harris, in addition to his other duties, had to supervise the repairing and refitting of numerous victuallers.[3]

---

[1] SP, 146, Stephen Harris to Navy Board, Feb. 26, 1780; PRO, ADM/106/2602, March 7, 1780.

[2] PRO, ADM/49/2, f. 50; T/64/200, p. 27.

[3] PRO, ADM/106/2607, Jan. 1, 1782. For an account of the process of refitting, see below, p. 117.

By stationing agents for transports permanently at Cork, Deptford, and Portsmouth, the Navy Board was able to obtain a high degree of coordination and control over the movement of the shipping in its service. This gave the Board the ability to arrange matters in such a way that, when a group of ships came into port at any of these three places, orders for their further employment would be waiting. For example, Lieutenant Robert Parrey was directed on 22 December 1780 to order the masters of the transports carrying the 4th, 5th, and 49th Regiments to place themselves under escort of H.M.S. *Leander*, proceed to Cork, and upon their arrival at that port report to Lieutenant Stephen Harris. At the same time that it issued these directions to Parrey, the Board ordered Harris at Cork to prepare for the disembarkation of three regiments and to have the transports 'complete their water' and place themselves under the command of Lieutenant Grosvenor Winkworth. On 19 June 1781 the Board dispatched orders to an agent for transports in command of a group of transports and victuallers at Leith to proceed to the Downs, and on his arrival there to send those vessels under his command fit for service or in need of only a 'small refitting' to Portsmouth. Those ships in need of major repairs were to be sent to Deptford. At the same time as the Board dispatched these directions to Leith, it issued directions to Lieutenant Robert Parrey at Portsmouth and Lieutenant George Teer at Deptford to 'lose no time in getting them refitted'.[1]

During the American War agents for transports were assigned by the Navy Board to supervise flotillas of transports and victuallers. They travelled with the ships under their command and provided the Board with a means of maintaining control over the shipping under charter to it. Before his departure overseas with a group of transports or victuallers, an agent for transports usually attended the Navy Board and was issued his instructions and warrant. For instance, on 5 April 1779 Lieutenant Archibald Dow attended the Board, received his warrant, and was ordered to go to Cork and take charge of a group of ships bound for North America. During the voyage he

---

[1] PRO, ADM/106/2604, Dec. 22, 1780; ADM/106/2605, June 19, 1781.

was to be under the command of the commander of the naval escort. Upon reaching New York, Dow was directed to unload the ships and arrange for a convoy back to Cork as quickly as possible. In addition, he was ordered to send at 'every opportunity' reports back to the Board and if any of the ships remained in America he was required to inform the Board and to direct their masters to report to the first agent for transports they encountered. Upon his return to Cork from New York, Dow was to report to Lieutenant Stephen Harris for further orders.[1] After receiving his instructions from the Board, an agent for transports in command of a group of transports was then issued by either a naval officer or a dockyard with 'the usual colours & stores supplied to Agents for Transports', these being a set of signal flags and lanterns, and an eighteen-foot cutter which the seamen from the transports under his command were expected to man.[2]

One of the major tasks of an agent for transports in command of a flotilla of ships was to decide what cargo each ship should carry. For example, in August 1775, Lieutenant Thomas Tonken, the agent for transports in charge of the transports which were to carry the troops from Cork to North America for the attack on Charleston, South Carolina in 1776, decided that the transports *Argo*, *Mercury*, *Chatham*, *Venus*, *Betsey*, *Juliana*, and *John & Christopher* were not capable of stowing flat-bottom boats. He thought, however, that the transports *Grosvenor*, *Grand Duke of Russia*, and *Harcourt* were each capable of stowing two flat-bottom boats and that the transports *Enterprize*, *America*, *Ocean*, *Whitby*, and *Peace & Plenty* could each stow one flat-bottom boat.[3] Agents for transports in charge of a group of transports were also responsible for the embarkation and distribution of troops on board the ships under their command. In the winter of 1776–77 transports were sent to the Dort to embark 1850 German troops. These troops were under the direction of Colonel Charles Rainsford, one of the Commissaries in Ger-

[1] PRO, ADM/106/2599, April 5, 1779; T/64/200, pp. 14–16.
[2] PRO, ADM/106/2593, Nov. 14, 23, 1775; ADM/106/2595, Feb. 14, May 13, 1777; ADM/106/2597, March 9, 1778; ADM/106/2599, Feb. 3, 1779; ADM/106/2604, Oct. 14, Nov. 14, 1780; ADM/106/2608, May, 28, 1782.
[3] PRO, ADM/106/3402, p. 327.

many assigned to muster foreign troops into the British service and to conduct them to the place of embarkation for America. On 12 February 1777 George Marsh, Clerk of the Acts, sent Rainsford a list of the transports which were to be employed to carry these German troops. On 18 February 1777 the Board issued orders to Lieutenant William Cumming to proceed to the Dort with thirteen transports under his command and embark the Germans and carry them to Spithead. Lord Suffolk, Secretary of State for the Northern Department, ordered the Admiralty on 23 February 1777 to issue directions to Cumming 'to make any changes in the appropriation of vessels that Col. Rainsford may find expedient; for though nothing can be better upon paper than the proportions assigned by the Navy Board to the different corps of infantry, many delays and disappointments may happen . . . that may induse his Maj. Commissary [Rainsford] to recommend a change of plan new to your agents'. On his arrival at the Dort Cumming found that instead of 1850 troops there were 1985, plus 120 women, to be embarked on board the 3911 tons of transports under his command. Therefore, at the beginning of March, Cumming informed the Board that he required an additional ship in order to embark all the German troops and their women at the rate of two tons per man. The Board on 11 March ordered him to 'contrive to bring the [troops] . . . in the ships he now has . . . to Spithead, where he will find the Polly of 240 tons to receive the overplus'. By the end of March, Cumming had 'contrived' to embark all the troops on board the transports under his command in 'as equal distribution as I can make, according to this Tonnage and conveniences of the ships', and he informed Colonel Rainsford that 'When I get to Portsmouth I will allot the Polly . . . either to the Chassers or Artillery & the sick, as is most agreeable to the colonel'.[1] The difficulties that Tonken and Cumming encountered in the stowing of flat-bottom boats and embarking troops were common in the daily conduct of the transport service.

---

[1] NYHSC, *Transactions as Commissary for Embarking Foreign Troops in the English Service from Germany with copies of Letters relative to it. For the years 1776–1777. By Charles Rainsford*, 345, 351–3, 370–1, 373–4, 384, 413; PRO, ADM/106/2595, Feb. 18, March 11, 1777; Add. MSS., 23649, f. 2.

Agents for transports in charge of a flotilla of transports or victuallers were required to report to the Navy Board any irregular or negligent acts by ships' masters. On 30 September 1778 Lieutenant Collingwood reported that the transport *Fathers Desire* had sailed without waiting for convoy, and on the next day the Board informed him 'that we will take proper notice of the misconduct of the master'. Lieutenant Dickinson informed the Board on 20 May 1779 that the masters of the transports *Countess of Darlington* and *Good Intent* had refused to pay a light duty. After Lieutenant Bradley had written from Plymouth on 2 September 1781 that the master of the transport *Ann* was a drunkard, the Board on 5 September informed the ship's owner 'that if he does not immediately send another master & mate to her we shall put a heavy mulct upon her'.[1]

Agents for transports were required to inform the Board of any ship which became separated from a convoy. These reports also stated whether or not the master of the ship was at fault for not keeping company. Thus, the Board on 30 July 1781 directed Lieutenant Bradley to inform it why the victuallers *Pomona* and *Esther & Ann*, which had been captured while en route between New York and Cork, 'came to be separated from the convoy and whether in his opinion the same could be avoided or that the masters were any way blameable on that occasion so that the Government should not pay for the value of the ships'. On 22 May 1782 Lieutenant John Shortland informed the Board that he had arrived at Spithead from Gibraltar with the transports *Vernon*, *St Ann*, *Antigallican*, and *Mercury* and that the transports *Royal Britain*, *Thompson*, and *Valiant* were captured off Gibraltar. In reply to the Board's question of whether or not the loss of the three transports had resulted from the neglect of their masters, Shortland on 28 May replied: 'In respect to the masters behaviour of the three transports captured, no blame can be charged to them, as they sustained the fire from the Enemy for 3 glasses and I was informed by one of the armed ships that when they passed them the Royal Britain['s] main-

[1] PRO, ADM/106/2598, Sept. 30, 1778; ADM/106/2600, May 21, 1779; ADM/106/2606, Sept. 5, 1781.

masts went over the side.' The Board, however, was not satisfied with this report, and it ordered Shortland to 'send us an extract of his Journal from his sailing to these ships being captured', which he did on 1 June 1782.[1] Thus, the Board's policy of assigning an agent for transports to flotillas of transports and victuallers provided it with an effective means of insuring that masters of the ships under charter to it would comply with its regulations.

Throughout the American War a number of agents for transports were assigned to the British forces in America. On 22 February 1776 the Admiralty directed the Navy Board to order all agents for transports to place themselves under the command of the naval commander-in-chief upon their arrival in America. The next day the Admiralty dispatched orders to Admiral Molyneux Shuldham, the commander-in-chief of British naval forces in North America, directing him to take command of all ships of the transport service in American waters and to employ these vessels in support of the army. This order remained in effect throughout the war, although Generals Howe and Clinton both thought that the transports should be under the control of the army. In June 1776, at the request of General Howe, Shuldham appointed Captain John Bourmaster to the post of Principal Agent for Transports in America.[2] With the assistance of a number of lesser agents, he became responsible for controlling, under the naval commander-in-chief, all ships of the transport service in American waters.[3]

The principal agent for transports in America and the agents under his command, although originally responsible only for shipping of the transport service, gradually assumed control over most of the shipping in the service of the British forces in North America and the West Indies. In December 1781 Admiral Robert Digby, upon discovering that the shipping at New York under charter to the Victualling Board was not being properly

---

[1] PRO, ADM/49/2, ff. 130, 132; ADM/106/2605, July 14, 30, 1781.

[2] NMM, ADM/N/245, Feb. 22, 1776; Neeser, op. cit., 63, 259; HMC, *Stopford–Sackville MSS.*, ii, 35; PRO, ADM/1/484, ff. 627–9; William B. Willcox, *Portrait of a General: Sir Henry Clinton in the War of Independence* (New York, 1964), 355.

[3] Roland Greene Usher, Jr., *The Civil Administration of the British Navy During the American Revolution*, 265–7.

conducted, directed that it be placed under the command of an agent for transports.[1] It appears that the agents for transports were also given control of the Victualling Board's shipping in the West Indies.[2] The agents for transports also became involved with the Ordnance Board's shipping in America.[3]

By 1781 the principal agent for transports in America, Captain Henry Chads, had assumed control over most of the ships, vessels, and small craft belonging to the British army. The Navy Board did not fully approve of its agents for transports in America assuming control of army shipping, for on 15 June 1779 it informed Lieutenant Andrew Sutherland, Agent for Transports, that 'We approve of his extracting himself from the office of hiring transports for Gen. Campbell, & that it has been transferred from him to the Quarter Master General'. Nevertheless, the principal agent for transports was the 'Sole Agent for all Ships and Vessels which shall come Freighted by Government and Consigned to His Excellency the Commander in Chief [of the army], and of all as may be chartered by his order'. On 17 August 1781 Chads had under his direction at New York fifty-three dispatch boats, armed vessels, and other craft in the service of the Quarter Master General's Department, as well as twenty-one schooners and sloops belonging to the Commissary General's Department and seventeen vessels under charter to the Barrack Master General's Department.[4] This was a large responsibility. With control over most of the auxiliary small craft and vessels, as well as ships of the transport service in American and West Indian waters, the office of principal agent for transports became a position of great importance, for he and his subordinates became the chief experts in the British forces on all matters relating to shipping.

The agents for transports in America and the West Indies, by virtue of commanding most of the shipping attached to the British forces, played a major role in the conduct of military operations. Agents for transports were so deeply involved in the

[1] PRO, ADM/49/7, ff. 68–9.   [2] E.g., PRO, ADM/108/1C, Dec. 18, 1782.
[3] HMC, *American Manuscripts*, iii, 410.
[4] PRO, ADM/106/2600, June 15, 1779; T/1/573, Jan. 7, May 14, 1782; T/64/112, ff. 9, 39; NYHSC, *Proceedings of a Board of General Officers of the British Army at New York, 1781*, pp. 62–71.

THE LOWER CHAIN OF COMMAND

conduct of amphibious operations that in October 1781 they
were employed to spread a rumour in New York to deceive the
Americans into believing that the British were going to launch
an amphibious attack up the Hudson River towards the Highlands. Four agents for transports accompanied the British force
that attacked Newport, Rhode Island, in December 1776. When
General Sir William Howe's army invaded Pennsylvania in the
summer of 1777, the agents for transports played a key role in
the operation. The expedition was carried to the Head of the
Elk by a fleet consisting of 265 vessels. The transports, storeships, and victuallers employed in this operation were formed
into six divisions each under the command of an agent for
transports. The agents for transports were, in turn, under the
direction of Captain John Bourmaster, Principal Agent for
Transports, who took his orders from the commander of the
naval escort on board H.M.S. *Nonsuch*.[1]

On 26 December 1779 Sir Henry Clinton, with 7500 troops
in eighty-four transports and other vessels, escorted by a naval
force under command of Admiral Marriot Arbuthnot, sailed
from New York to invade South Carolina. The transports were
under the command of Captain Thomas Tonken, who had
succeeded Bourmaster as principal agent for transports, assisted
by three other agents for transports. The voyage was a stormy
one, and a large number of transports were damaged or lost.
The transport *Ann* with Hessians on board was dismasted and
drifted all the way to St Ives in Cornwall. While at sea on
16 January 1780 Tonken had to remove four companies of light
infantry from the transport *George*, which was sinking, and distribute the troops among the other transports. On 19 January
the agents for transports had to distribute among the ships of
the fleet eighty men, women, and children belonging to the
artillery who had been rescued from the transport *Russia*

[1] *Diary of Frederick Mackenzie: Giving a Daily Narrative of His Military Service as an
Officer of the Regiment of Welch Fusiliers during the Years 1775–1781 in Massachusetts,
Rhode Island, and New York* (Cambridge, Mass., 1930), i, 120, ii, 675–6; Henry
Cabot Lodge, ed., *André's Journal* (Boston, 1903), i, 55–68; Bernhard A. Uhlendorf,
trans. and ed., *Revolution in America: Confidential Letters and Journals, 1776–1784, of
the Adjutant General Major Baurmeister of the Hessian Forces* (New Brunswick, N.J.,
1957), 93, 97–8.

Merchant before she sank.[1] When the force arrived off the coast
of South Carolina at the beginning of February 1780 Arbuthnot
placed Captain George Keith Elphinstone in charge of landing
the troops and in command of the naval personnel to be
employed in the siege of Charleston. To assist Elphinstone in
this task, the Admiral placed under his command all the agents
for transports in the force. The Admiral also ordered the agents
for transports to warn the crews of the vessels under their command not to loot while working on the shore with the army.
The landing by the British troops on John's Island was conducted under the command of Elphinstone with the assistance
of the agents for transports. Tonken conducted the embarkation
of the troops that crossed the Ashly River above Charleston,
while Elphinstone conducted their disembarkation. During the
siege of Charleston, after the investment of that city by the
British forces, the agents for transports were engaged under the
direction of Elphinstone in transporting stores, equipment, and
munitions from the fleet to the army in small craft manned by
transport seamen.[2] On 14 May 1780 Tonken reported to the
Navy Board that the men belonging to the transports 'have all
been employed in Flat Boats, and Long Boats, carrying men,
provisions, and stores of all kinds. I have been absent from the
ships with three hundred of them for near two months; in short
everything brought on Charles Town Neck for the siege &c.
was by the transport boats.' It was not an idle boast when
Tonken later declared that the men of the transport service 'do
all the business of the army such as crossing them over
Rivers &c.'.[3]

The agents for transports stationed overseas served two

---

[1] James Bain, Jr, ed., 'The Siege of Charleston; Journal of Captain Peter Russel,
December 25, 1779, to May 2, 1780', *American Historical Review* (April, 1899), iv,
479; PRO, CO/5/99, ff. 29, 31; Piers Mackesy, *The War for America, 1775–1783*
(London, 1964), 340; Bernhard A. Uhlendorf, trans. and ed., *The Siege of Charleston,
with an Account of the Province of South Carolina: Diaries and Letters of Hessian Officers
from the von Jungkenn Papers in the William L. Clements Library* (Ann Arbor, Mich.,
1938), 125–7; Harry Miller Lydenberg, ed., *Archibald Robertson, Lieutenant-General
Royal Engineers, His Diary and Sketches in America, 1762–1780* (New York, 1930), 208.
[2] NRS, *The Keith Papers*, i, 135–76; Uhlendorf, *The Siege of Charleston*, 31–3,
173–5, 181, 211, 223.
[3] PRO, ADM/49/2, ff. 216, 229.

masters, for while they were under the operational control of the overseas naval commanders-in-chief, these officers were also directly responsible to the Navy Board for the management of ships under charter to it. In short, while overseas agents for transports were required to report regularly to the Board on the state and condition of the ships under their command, these officers also had to supply the Board with any information that it might require about ships in the transport service in America and the West Indies. In addition, it was their task while overseas to enforce the terms of ships' charter parties and to report any breach of these agreements to the Board.

In the course of the American War agents for transports who were stationed overseas sent thousands of reports to the Navy Board.[1] From time to time the principal agent for transports sent the Board reports showing the deployment of all the transports in North America. For instance, on 9 November 1778 Tonken reported that there were eighty transports with a total tonnage of 21,804 tons in North America deployed in the following manner:

Place	Number of ships	Tonnage
Pensacola	8	2331
Rhode Island	39	9475
Bermuda	2	581
Providence	2	433
New York	15	4767
Condemned at New York	1	256
Prison ships at New York	1	725
Horse transports. Four at New York and one at Halifax	5	1363
Halifax	6	1543
Proceeding to England	1	330
Total	80	21804[2]

The failure of an agent for transports to send proper returns brought prompt censure from the Navy Board.[3]

---

[1] E.g., PRO, ADM/106/2593, July 26, Sept. 5, 1775.

[2] PRO, ADM/49/2, ff. 186–8. For another example, see SP, 145, Abstract of the no. & tonnage of transport vessels in America on 30 Nov. 1777.

[3] E.g., PRO, ADM/106/2601, Dec. 2, 1779; ADM/106/2604, Nov. 23, 1780.

A great number of the reports made by overseas agents for transports to the Navy Board consisted of returns of musters of transports' crews. Under the terms of the charter parties, the owners of transports were required to provide seven seamen for every hundred tons of the ship's burden. This requirement was lowered in 1781 to six seamen per hundred tons of the ship's burden. It was the duty of agents for transports to go periodically on board each of the ships under their command and count the number of seamen in the crew.[1] Any deficiency had to be reported to the Navy Board. The 'masters [of the transports overseas were] most positively assured [by the agents for transports] that the consequences of being short of complement will be a mulct against the hire of the ship'.[2] But despite 'frequent and punchual' musters and the threat of being mulcted, the transports serving in American waters were nearly always short of the complements called for by their charter parties. At the end of 1779, when Captain Johann Hinrichs of the Jäger Corps embarked on the transport *Apollo* at New York, he found that her crew consisted of only nineteen men, although she was supposed to have a complement of twenty-five. The shortage of seamen in the transports in American waters was not always the fault of the masters of the ships, for as Tonken explained to the Board on 17 January 1778, 'tho' most of the ships are short of men, I must in justice to the masters say, that they use every method in their power to keep their ships compleatly mann'd, but from various circumstances it is absolutely impossible. I only beg to give you one instance of encouragement given to seamen by private traders, on the taking of Philadelphia, they gave seamen fifteen guineas a man, a bribe sufficient to make all the seamen in the transports desert.'[3]

Agents for transports stationed overseas transmitted to the Navy Board protests against all acts of negligence and breaches of charter parties committed by masters of transports. On 20 March 1778 Tonken protested against Isaac Amory, master of the transport *Henry*, for not 'getting on board his things &

---

[1] Returns of musters of transports in America are contained in PRO, ADM/49/3, 4, 5, 6.
[2] SP, 145, [Thomas Tonken] to Navy Board, June 9, 1777.
[3] Uhlendorf, *The Siege of Charleston*, 111; PRO, ADM/49/2, f. 179.

fitting his ship after she had hove down notwithstanding Lt. Sutherland & myself constantly pressing him for that purpose ... [and] I hope you will approve & take notice of [this protest] as it will be the means of making other masters be more attentive to their duty'. On 3 January 1781 another agent for transports reported that the transport *Betsey* was lost at Hell Gate when she was run on a rock by her pilot, 'where she remained a tide; during which time ... [the agent for transports] engaged all the assistance in his power, such as boats, anchors, and hawsers, and had his orders been attended to, the ship in all probability would have been saved and unhurt. But ... the master and pilot were both asleep ... when the ship slipped off the rock ... the consequences of which negligence was that the ship suddenly started from that rock and shot over to Long Island shore where she was lost.'[1] During the American War the agents for transports in America and the West Indies transmitted to the Board a never-ending stream of protests against the acts of negligence committed by masters of transports. In addition, at the request of the Navy Board they supplied the information on which the Board based its settlement of claims made by shipowners for services rendered or for compensation for ships which were taken or destroyed while under charter to the Navy Board.[2]

It is thus clear that the agents for transports stationed overseas during the American War, in addition to playing a vital part in the conduct of military operations, also served as a means by which the Navy Board maintained control over the ships of the transport service while they were away from the British Isles. It was the reports, returns of musters, and protests made by agents for transports in America and the West Indies which supplied the Board with the information required to mulct the freight of ships under charter to it which had not complied with the terms of their charter parties.

In addition to agents for transports, the Navy Board employed a variety of civil officials and navy officers to supervise and manage the shipping under charter to it. These men were usually

---

[1] PRO, ADM/49/2, ff. 102–3, 182.
[2] E.g., PRO, ADM/106/2595, June 18, 1777; ADM/106/2600, Aug. 31, 1779.

employed by the Board to supplement the activities of agents for transports or to act when there were no available agents for transports. From time to time the Board appointed masters of transports to superintend a flotilla of transports or victuallers. The Board sometimes placed a group of transports under the command of the master of one of them and then ordered the master to place himself under the command of the commander of one of His Majesty's ships.[1]

The Navy Board also employed the services of officers in command of the King's ships to furnish information on the activities of the shipping in its service. In 1778 the transport *Fanny*, while returning to England from New York, parted from her convoy, was captured, and carried into Brest. And on 23 December 1778 the Board requested that the commander of H.M.S. *Leviathan*, the escort of the *Fanny*'s convoy, 'inform us if the master obeyed his signals, or if he can account for his having parted company from the convoy'. The Board wrote to Captain Robert Fanshawe that the transport *William* 'which came from Jamaica under his convoy is put into Belfast and desir[ed that] he will let us know whether he has any reason to be dissatisfied with the masters conduct in leaving the convoy'.[2] The Board also periodically requested that army officers supply it with information about the conduct of the ships in its service.[3] Unsolicited reports from the King's officers about the misconduct of ships of the transport service were sometimes received by the Board.[4]

The officials of the Royal Dockyards were employed by the Navy Board to supervise and manage shipping in the transport service and were occasionally used by the Board as a means of transmitting orders to transports.[5] They also served as a source of information to the Navy Board on the activities and move-

---

[1] E.g., PRO, ADM/106/2598, Aug. 30, 1778; ADM/106/2599, Jan. 29, 1779; ADM/106/2609, Aug. 5, 1782; T/64/200, pp. 15, 200; NMM, ADM/N/248, Aug. 27, 1778.

[2] PRO, ADM/106/2598, Dec. 23, 1778; ADM/106/2605, July 3, 1781.

[3] E.g., PRO, ADM/106/2605, Aug. 23, 1781.

[4] E.g., PRO, ADM/106/2602, April 18, 1780.

[5] E.g., PRO, ADM/106/250, April 8, 1779, May 5, 1780; ADM/106/2597, June 30, 1778; ADM/106/2598, Sept. 14, 1778.

ments of shipping under charter to it,[1] and it was yet another of their tasks to muster the crews of transports so that they were manned in accordance with their charter parties.[2] The officials of the dockyards thus engaged in much the same activities as did the agents for transports, but most likely when they performed such tasks as mustering transport crews they were filling in for an absent agent.

Another type of official employed by the Navy Board to regulate and supervise the shipping in the transport service were the naval officers stationed at various Out-Ports in the British Isles. The two naval officers of the most importance to the conduct of the transport service were George Lawrence at Deal and T. Foxworthy at Kinsale in Ireland. Lawrence supervised and managed the shipping of the transport service which was in the Downs, while Foxworthy supervised the transports in the Cork area before Lieutenant Stephen Harris was stationed in that port in 1779 as an agent for transports. These two naval officers transmitted Navy Board orders to transports, kept the Board informed of the movements of the shipping in its service, and enforced the Board's orders and the terms of the ships' charter parties.[3]

When ships in the service of the Navy Board were in those British ports, such as Bristol, Liverpool, Glasgow, and Dublin, which were not seats of a Royal Dockyard or which did not have resident naval officers, the Board made use of the services of a number of minor officials. These were usually the overseers assigned by the Board to supervise the construction of King's ships in private yards or the regulating captains of the Impress Service.[4] With the help of officials of this kind, there were few ports in the British Isles to which the Board could not dispatch orders to its ships.

[1] E.g., PRO, ADM/106/250, Feb. 19, 1776, March 1, 1783; ADM/106/2600, Aug. 6, 1779; ADM/106/3385, p. 78.

[2] E.g., PRO, ADM/106/2594, Aug. 6, 1776; ADM/106/2595, May 16, 1777; ADM/106/2598, Dec. 16, 1778.

[3] E.g., NMM, ADM/B/189, May 9, 1775; PRO, ADM/106/250, Feb. 19, 1781; ADM/106/2603, July 14, 1780; ADM/106/2594, Nov. 5, 22, 26, 29, Dec. 6, 1776; ADM/106/279, June 23, 1778.

[4] E.g., PRO, ADM/106/2597, June 11, 1778; ADM/106/2598, July 8, Dec. 24, 1778; ADM/106/2600, May 26, 1779; ADM/106/2602, Feb. 15, 16, 1780; ADM/106/2604, Oct. 23, 1780.

It is clear that the Navy Board had the means to exercise control over the shipping of the transport service. The network of agents for transports both in the British Isles and abroad, officials of the Royal Dockyards, naval officers, and other officials of the Royal Navy extended to wherever the requirements of the war might take the shipping of the transport service. While it is true that abuses were committed by the owners and masters of ships of the transport service, the representatives of the Board were as tireless in their efforts to discover and report abuses as the Board was ruthless in meting out punishments by mulcting the freight of the offending ships. In addition to preventing abuses, frauds, and acts of disobedience, the Navy Board's machinery for supervising and regulating the transport service enabled the Board to get the maximum use out of the ships in its service through centralized control and coordination of the ships in the British Isles. The reports submitted by the agents for transports, the officials of the dockyards, and naval officers enabled the Board to know the location and employment of every ship in Britain in the transport service as well as to plan and coordinate the movements of its vessels. In essence, the methods employed by the Board to administer the transport service were effective, and they greatly assisted that agency in meeting the demands of a world-wide maritime war.

CHAPTER IV

Short-term Procurement of Tonnage

THE MAJORITY of the ships under contract to the Navy Board entered into the service of the government under time charters which ran for an indefinite period of time. Employed as armed transports, storeships, and victuallers, these ships formed the backbone of the transport service. Occasionally, however, the Board chartered ships under short-term agreements for a specific task. In these agreements the Board chartered a ship or cargo space on a ship for a single voyage in much the same way as a merchant contracted for the transport of his goods.

The short-term agreements made by the Navy Board with shipowners for the transport of men and material were of considerable importance for they provided the Board with a means of increasing the amount of tonnage available for employment at any given time. This was a decided advantage, for although the number of troops and the amount of material carried by ships under short-term contract were small when compared to that carried by the transport service, the aggregate amount of cargo carried under these agreements was considerable.

During the American War the Board hired coasters on a short-term basis to transport naval stores between various British ports.[1] Whenever the Board had difficulty in coming to terms with the owners of such vessels over the freight rate, it would simply make use of a transport to do the job;[2] but it rarely employed transports for such purposes because it was usually able to hire coasters at reasonable rates, and used the

---

[1] See PRO, ADM/106/2593–610, passim.
[2] E.g., PRO, ADM/106/2599, Jan. 21, 1779.

existence of the transports as a means of keeping the freight rate of the coasters within reasonable limits.

Of much greater importance were the short-term agreements entered into for the transport of stores and troops overseas. The ability of the Board to procure ships to carry cargoes to overseas ports on a short-term basis depended to a considerable degree on the pattern of the British carrying trade. The Board found it very easy to procure cargo space on ships proceeding to regions where there were plentiful homeward-bound cargoes to be found. On the other hand, it had trouble finding ships that could be hired on reasonable terms to carry goods from England and New York because there was no return cargo. Thus, the Board tended to procure cargo space on outward-bound merchant ships that were proceeding to a few well-defined regions where the exports to Britain required more cargo space than the imports from Britain.

One such region was the West Indies. During the eighteenth century the British West Indies exported vast amounts of sugar and rum, and the transport of these products to Britain demanded the employment of scores of vessels. The West India Committee estimated in April 1778 that in the preceding year 234 ships carrying 76,700 casks of sugar and 12,257 casks of rum entered British ports from the West Indies.[1] Even after supplies of timber and foodstuffs from America were cut off at the beginning of the war, the imports of the West Indies from Britain did not require as much cargo space as their exports. Constantly faced with the problem of finding cargoes for their outward-bound ships, the owners of ships engaged in this trade welcomed the opportunity to carry troops and stores to the Caribbean.[2]

Eighteenth-century British trade with the East Indies was similar to the West India trade in that the East India Company had difficulty finding cargoes for the voyage to the East. Because the Company was unable to find a European product which

[1] West India Committee Minutes, April 2, 1778. See also March 30, 1779; April 19, 1780; March 27, 1781; March 26, 1782; March 25, 1783.
[2] See Ralph Davis, *The Rise of the English Shipping Industry in the Seventeenth and Eighteenth Centuries* (London, 1962), 267–99. According to Richard Pares, 'The profit of owning ships in the West-India trade depended, above all, on the rate of homeward freight'. Pares, *A West-India Fortune* (London, 1950), 231.

could be traded for the produce of India and China, its major export to the Far East was bullion, even though its ships were required by law to carry a certain amount of British goods to the East Indies each year.[1] The East India Company was consequently able to grant cargo space in its ships for the conveyance of the King's stores to India.

While the procurement of cargo space on outward-bound East and West India merchant ships proved to be a fairly simple matter, the Board encountered great difficulties when it attempted to send goods to the Mediterranean, Canada, or America. Before the entry of Spain into the American War in the summer of 1779, the Board shipped several cargoes of naval stores to Gibraltar and Minorca on board merchant ships bound to the Mediterranean.[2] But once Spain had entered the war, the British Mediterranean trade sharply declined, and the Board had to revert to other means for supplying British bases. Occasionally the Board was able to procure cargo space on merchant ships bound to Quebec, Nova Scotia, and Newfoundland,[3] but, because the carrying trade between these regions and Britain was small its use of these facilities was limited and irregular. Because of the danger of capture, the lack of a regular trade between Britain and America during the war, and insufficient return cargoes in those areas under the control of British forces, the Board found it impossible to hire cargo space on ships proceeding to America except by paying excessive freight rates. Thus, most of the men and material sent from Britain to America was carried by the transport service, and except in emergencies the Board rarely hired merchant ships on short-term contracts for this task.

Although never explicitly stated, the Navy Board's policy on the procurement of cargo space on outward-bound merchant ships or on chartering ships for a single voyage is made very

[1] Davis, op. cit., 258. An informative contemporary account of the economics of the China trade can be found in Arthur Harrison Cole, ed., *Industrial and Commercial Correspondence of Alexander Hamilton Anticipating His Report on Manufactures* (Chicago, 1928), 129–61.

[2] E.g., PRO, ADM/106/2594, Aug. 9, 1776; ADM/106/2598, Oct. 21, 1778.

[3] E.g., PRO, ADM/106/2593, July 5, 1775; ADM/106/2599, April 6, 1779; ADM/106/2603, Aug. 3, 1780.

clear by a study of its minutes.[1] The Board attempted to send as many troops and as much cargo as possible in outward-bound merchant ships under short-term agreements to the Mediterranean, India, the West Indies, and Canada in order to release as much transport service tonnage as possible for the run between Britain and America.

The Board appears to have informed shipowners of its desire to hire a ship to carry a cargo overseas either by word of mouth or by advertising. The Commissioners of the Navy were in touch with scores of shipowners and merchants, and it seems that a large number of ships hired were first brought to the Board's attention through personal contacts; but if this method failed to produce a ship capable of performing the service required, the Board advertised, sometimes by posting notices at various places, such as Lloyds Coffee House, which were frequented by merchants, underwriters, and shipowners.[2] But, advertisements in the London newspapers appear to have been the most common method employed. The Commissioners regularly placed advertisements inviting tenders for the transport of cargo on freight in various newspapers such as the *Morning Chronicle and London Advertiser*, *Public Advertiser*, and *St James Chronicle*.[3] These advertisements specified the type of cargo, the place to which it was to be carried, and the day on which bids would be received. For example, on 8 January 1779 the Board ordered that 'Publication be made to treat for the freight for masts and stores to Antigua & Jamaica on the 12th instant', and on 9 January the following advertisement appeared in the *Public Advertiser*:

Navy Office

Jan. 8, 1779

The principal Officers and Commissioners of his Majesty's Navy give Notice That on Tuesday next, the 12th Instant, they will be ready to treat with such Persons as are willing to lett 350 Tons of

---

[1] PRO, ADM/106/2593–2610, passim.
[2] E.g., PRO, ADM/106/2606, Nov. 7, Dec. 26, 1781; ADM/106/2609, Aug. 2, 1782.
[3] Examples of the Navy Board's newspaper advertisements can be found in the British Museum, Burney Collection of Newspapers, vols. 662.b.–728.b.

Shipping, to Carry Masts of 101 Feet long, and other Stores, to Antigua; also for 1050 Tons, to carry Masts of the same Length, and other Stores to Jamaica. The said shipping is to sail with the next Convoy.

This advertisement was repeated in the 11 and 12 January issues of the *Public Advertiser*, and it also appeared in the *Morning Chronicle and London Advertiser* on 9, 11, and 12 January 1779.[1] 12 January 1779 'being the day published to treat for freight of stores to Jamaica & Antigua: several persons atten'd [the Board] and sent in their proposals: Messrs Wilkinson & Deacon being the lowest in their demands were agreed with'.[2]

Most of the short-term agreements entered into by the Board called for the renting of cargo space on a ship. This form of agreement is called a space charter and under it the shipowners are paid according to the amount of cargo received on board. On 6 April 1779 the Board made an agreement with Gregory Olive and Company for their vessel, the *Speedwell*, to carry stores from Plymouth to Newfoundland 'at the rate of £4 ℔ ton, for such quantity as shall be put on board her'.[3] And on 7 October 1779 the Board agreed with the firm of Drake and Long for its ship *James Dawkins* to carry naval stores to Jamaica at the rate of £1 5s per ton 'for such quantity as shall be put on board her'. On 14 October, a week later, however, the Board agreed with the owners of the *Dalling* and *Cato* for these ships to carry naval stores to Antigua 'at the rate of 40s ℔ ton, for such quantity of stores as shall be laden on board them'.[4]

A space charter was not always satisfactory to the shipowners because the freight was paid according to the amount of cargo and did not take into account the time the ship actually spent in her passage. This was an important consideration because in wartime a ship might be forced to spend months on a voyage which in peacetime would take only weeks. On 7 August 1775 the Board agreed with the owners of the ship *Brown Hall* to

[1] PRO, ADM/106/2599, Jan. 8, 1779; *Public Advertiser*, Jan. 9, 11, 12, 1779; *Morning Chronicle and London Advertiser*, Jan. 9, 11, 12, 1779.

[2] PRO, ADM/106/2599, Jan. 12, 1779.

[3] PRO, ADM/106/2599, April 6, 1779.

[4] PRO, ADM/106/2601, Oct. 7, 14, 1779. For other examples of the same type of agreement, see PRO, ADM/106/2593–610, passim.

transport naval stores from Deptford to Halifax at the rate of £1 5s per ton of cargo put on the ship.[1] The *Brown Hall* was loaded at Deptford and ordered to Spithead to join a convoy which was 'not provided for by Charter party'. The ship did not leave England because of delays in assembling the rest of the convoy until late fall and then encountered such adverse weather that she was forced to the West Indies. After spending months in Antigua waiting for escort, the *Brown Hall* finally arrived at Halifax and delivered her cargo in the summer of 1776. Her owners calculated that because of the extra expense incurred on the voyage due to delays, freight should be paid by the month instead of by the amount of cargo and insisted that the Board owed them £2000. The Board thought this amount too large, but conceded that the owners had a case and agreed, on 10 April 1777, to pay £1200.[2]

The Board could avoid disputes of this kind by hiring ships for a single outward-bound voyage where the freight was paid by the month under a short-term time charter instead of on the basis of cargo put on board.[3] The number of such agreements, however, was very small. Consequently, many ship-owners insisted on the payment of demurrage for delays incurred by their ships while carrying cargoes at a flat rate for the amount of cargo received on board the ship.[4]

The most successful series of short-term agreements made by the Board during the American War were those with the London West India merchants for the transport of troops to the Caribbean from 1779 to 1782. Even before the entry of France into the American War and the spread of the conflict to the Caribbean, the Board took advantage of the desire of the West India merchants to procure cargoes for their outward-bound ships by sending naval stores to the Caribbean on board West Indiamen.[5] But the agreements made with the West India merchants for the transport of naval stores to the Caribbean

[1] PRO, ADM/106/2593, Aug. 7, 1775.
[2] PRO, ADM/106/2595, April 10, 1777.
[3] E.g., PRO, ADM/106/2598, July 27, 1778; ADM/106/2599, Jan. 15, 1779.
[4] E.g., PRO, ADM/106/2595, June 30, 1777.
[5] E.g., PRO, ADM/106/2594, Sept. 17, Nov. 30, 1776; ADM/106/2597, March 2, 1778; ADM/106/2598, Sept. 24, 1778.

were of minor importance when compared to the contracts entered into for the conveyance of troops.

The first regiment sent from Britain to the West Indies after the French entry into the war was the 79th (Liverpool) Regiment, which was dispatched to Jamaica on board West India merchant ships in March 1779. It is not clear who first thought of employing West Indiamen as transports, but it appears that Lord George Germain took up the idea with Stephen Fuller, Secretary of the West India Committee, in January 1779. Fuller then consulted with Beeston Long, Chairman of the West India Committee, and Long called a meeting of the West India merchants and the masters of the West India ships at the Jamaica Coffee House on 6 January 1779 to consider Germain's proposal.[1] At this meeting the merchants and shipmasters agreed on the terms under which they would be willing to carry troops to the Caribbean. These proposals were then sent to Germain, who enclosed them with his order to the Admiralty to provide transportation for the Liverpool Regiment to Jamaica. Germain strongly suggested that the merchants' terms be accepted. On 23 January 1779 the Admiralty transmitted to the Board the text of Germain's order and the proposals of the West India merchants.[2]

The West India merchants' terms for carrying the 1169 men of the Liverpool Regiment to Jamaica undoubtedly appealed to the Board. Employment of West Indiamen would mean a saving of at least 2200 tons of transports urgently required for other service, and the vessels in which the merchants proposed to carry the troops to Jamaica were large, well-manned, and heavily-armed ships which were ideal troop transports.[3] On 26 January 1779 the Board agreed with the owners of fourteen West Indiamen that the troops would be carried at the rate of '£6 ℔ head, [and] be victualled in the usual manner as on

---

[1] Add. MSS., 38210, ff. 198–9. Although officials and members of the West India Committee were deeply involved in making arrangements for the transport of troops to the Caribbean on board West Indiamen, it appears from a study of the minutes of the Committee that this body was not officially involved in making these arrangements.

[2] NMM, ADM/N/248, Jan. 23, 1779.

[3] NMM, ADM/N/248, Jan. 23, 1779; Add. MSS., 38210, f. 201.

board transports'. The owners of the ships were allowed demurrage at the rate of 1s per soldier embarked per day for every day which the ships were detained in harbour in Europe. This demurrage was to commence forty-eight hours after the embarkation of the troops. Demurrage was also to be paid at the rate of 15d per day per soldier for 'such detaining in the West India Islands. Personal equipment and personal baggage within reason [would be] freight free. Camp equipage, tents, household goods . . . [would be carried at the rate of] 40s per ton.' The Board would provide beds and bedding, while the ships would 'provide all water casks, good new provisions, bowles, platters, cans, spoons, coals, candles and utensils for cooking and dressing of the victuals', and 'All the troops that are on board . . . [would] be paid for according to a list taken on the day of embarkation [by an agent for transports], upon a certificate thereof being produced, either in ready money or navy bills with £6 ℗ cent added thereto for discount'.[1]

Although satisfactory to both the shipowners and the Board, this agreement was almost cancelled at the last minute when the shipmasters and the officers of the regiment failed to agree on the price to be paid by the army officers for berths in the ships' cabins. The privates and noncommissioned officers were berthed in the hold, but the officers of the regiment thought their rank entitled them to berths in the ships' cabins. The masters stated that they received £30 per person for cabin passengers and would not carry the officers for less, while the officers maintained that they could not afford £30 and would not embark unless they received cabin berths. By 25 February 1779 an 'Accommodation' had been reached through negotiations conducted by Germain and Lord Amherst. The officers agreed to pay the masters of the ships £5, the masters agreed to lower their price to £25, and Germain ordered the naval authorities to pay the masters £20 for each army officer embarked.[2]

The West India ships were supplied with beds, bedding, and canvas ventilators at Deptford Dockyard. The ships then pro-

---

[1] NMM, ADM/N/248, Jan. 23, 1779; PRO, ADM/106/2599, Jan. 26, 1779.
[2] NMM, ADM/N/248, Feb. 26, 1779; PRO, ADM/1/4138, f. 45.

ceeded to Spithead, and on 15 March 1779 the agent for transports at Spithead reported that the Liverpool Regiment had been duly embarked.[1]

The use of West Indiamen to transport the Liverpool Regiment proved so successful that the Board continued to send troops to the West Indies on merchant ships until the end of the war. From 1779 to 1782 the Board made arrangements, which were similar to the one covering the Liverpool Regiment, with the West India merchants for the conveyance of some 7500 troops to the Sugar Islands on merchant ships.[2] These arrangements enabled the Board to use for other purposes 15,000 tons of transports that otherwise would have been required to carry troops to the Caribbean.

At various times during the American War, however, the Board was obliged to enter into other short-term agreements for the hire of ships because it did not have the tonnage available to perform the desired service. In April 1778, for instance,

The Board finding a difficulty to procure Freight for the [naval] stores prepared for Quebeck, the ships . . . which were expected to take them in being full, and hearing that Mr. Schoolbred had a ship bound thither they sent for him to know whether he could take them . . . Upon his attending he offered to carry the said stores at Three Pounds ℔ Ton to be paid in ready money on the whole being taken on board, and would not take them on any other terms. The Board seeing no other mode of sending [the stores] . . . agreed with him on those terms.[3]

Such agreements, however, were of minor importance when compared to the short-term contract entered into by the Board in 1781 for the transport of oats to New York.

The British forces at New York in August 1781 had 3596 horses in service which could not be supported by local supplies

---

[1] NMM, ADM/N/248, March 13, 1779; PRO, ADM/106/2599, March 10, 16, 1779.

[2] For an account of these arrangements, see David Syrett, 'The West India Merchants and the Conveyance of the King's Troops to the Caribbean, 1779–1782', *Journal of the Society for Army Historical Research* (Autumn, 1967), xlv, 169–76.

[3] PRO, ADM/106/2597, April 1, 1778. For another example see PRO, ADM/1/4140, f. 69; NMM, ADM/N/249, Oct. 19, Nov. 24, 1779.

of forage.[1] Therefore, additional forage had to be procured from Rhode Island, Georgia, and Nova Scotia; but these sources proved to be inadequate. The British withdrew from Rhode Island in 1779, the supplies of rice were cut off by the outbreak of guerrilla warfare in the American South, and drought caused the hay crop in New York to fail in the summer of 1780. Thus, in December 1780 Sir Henry Clinton found it necessary to request that 50,000 quarters of oats be sent from Britain to New York.[2]

When Clinton's request for oats arrived in London in March 1781, the Treasury wrote at once telling him that the forage would be immediately dispatched. However, when the Treasury consulted the Navy Board about providing shipping to carry the oats to America, the Board replied that there was no prospect of providing the tonnage required and suggested that this service should be postponed until all the army provisions for the year 1781 had been dispatched.[3] The Treasury, however, could not agree to put off the shipment of the oats until sufficient victuallers became available, and on 27 March 1781 it ordered the Board to hire shipping on whatever terms possible to transport the oats.[4]

On 4 May 1781 the Board informed the Treasury that, although it had advertised for the shipping needed to carry the oats to New York, it had received a bid only from the firm of Mure, Son, and Atkinson. It therefore contracted with this firm for the 10,000 tons of shipping required to transport the oats to America 'at the Rate of Five Guineas ℔ Ton of Thirty six Winchester Bushels payable on producing the bills of Loading in Navy Bills'. The navy bills were to have 'a Discount of £10 ℔ cent added thereto in lieu of payment in money', and Mure, Son, and Atkinson were also to receive demurrage 'at the Rate of twelve Shillings & ninepence ℔ ton ℔ Callendar

---

[1] New-York Historical Society, The Letter Book of Daniel Wier, Commissary General of the British Forces in America, Aug. 11, 1779, NYHSC, *Proceedings of A Board of General Officers of the British Army at New York, 1781*, pp. 89–93.

[2] PRO, T/64/111, ff. 9–10; Bernhard A. Uhlendorf, trans. and ed., *Revolution in America: Confidential Letters and Journals, 1776–1784, of the Adjutant General Major Baurmeister of the Hessian Forces* (New Brunswick, N.J., 1957), 366.

[3] HMC, *American Manuscripts*, ii, 256, 257.

[4] PRO, T/1/564, Navy Board to Treasury, May 4, 1781.

month for the Tonnage each Ship is paid Freight for'. The demurrage was to begin on the day of the first fair wind at Cork after 20 June and to remain in effect until the ships sailed for New York, and to commence at New York on 'the first fair Wind for leaving the Coast after one Month from the arrival of the Convoy' from Europe. In addition, the Board was to compensate the firm for any ship taken or destroyed by the enemy 'at the rate of Ten Pounds ₱ Ton for the Tonnage which she is paid freight for'. The ships were also required to sail under the direction of an agent for transports.[1]

The Board was not fully satisfied with this agreement. It thought the freight too high, but more important, 'the Article of Demurrage may amount to too large Expence unless a Certainty & punctuality of Convoy from America can be depended on for this particular Service'. The Board, therefore, requested the Treasury to direct Clinton to have the ships unloaded immediately upon their arrival. A request was also made to the Admiralty to provide a warship to escort the vessels back to Britain as soon as they had been unloaded. Both requests were complied with.[2] Once again the evidence is clear that such short-term contracts not only released tonnage for other uses, but also enabled the Board to carry out services which would otherwise have been impossible.

The problems faced by the Board in securing cargo space on East India Company ships were very different from those encountered in its efforts to make short-term agreements with individual merchants. Unlike the merchants with whom the Board had dealings, the East India Company was a massive corporate body which, in addition to being a trading organization, was for all practical purposes a semi-independent branch of the British government. The Company ruled large areas of the Indian subcontinent and maintained in India a military establishment of considerable size. Thus, in addition to goods necessary for trade, the ships in the service of the Company had

[1] PRO, ADM/106/2605, May 5, 1781; T/1/564, Navy Board to Treasury, May 4, 1781.
[2] PRO, T/1/564, Navy Board to Treasury, May 4, 1781; T/64/107, p. 63; ADM/1/4288, May 23, 1781; NMM, ADM/BP/2, May 7, 1781; ADM/N/250, May 10, 1781.

to transport to India all the personnel and material needed to maintain itself as a military power in the East. In normal times the Company always had enough tonnage available to fulfil its own commitments as well as to provide free transport to India for the King's stores. But when the American War became a world war and major military operations began in India, the shipping resources of the Company became inadequate. As a result of these developments some transport tonnage had to be used to support the East India Company.

On two different occasions during the war the government attempted to obtain the use of East India Company ships on a short-term basis to transport troops and stores to America. On 5 February 1776 the Admiralty asked the Company for permission to hire several East Indiamen. The Company had no plans to employ these vessels until 1777, and the Admiralty promised to return them to England within 'six months'. This proposal, however, came to nothing because of a legal technicality in the Company's bylaws. In February 1782 the Board again attempted to secure the use of several unemployed East Indiamen. The Board found, however, that it could not gain complete operational control of the vessels because the Company insisted that the ships 'be discharged from the King's Service as the Company's Service may render it necessary'. The Board was apparently unwilling to accept this condition; in any event the plan was never put into effect.[1]

The Admiralty and the Board, although unable to procure Company shipping for service in America, succeeded in the first years of the war in obtaining cargo space on outward-bound East Indiamen to transport naval stores to the East Indies. In the late summer and early fall of each year the Company informed the Admiralty of the number of ships to be dispatched to the East Indies in the ensuing year with the destination and times of departure of each ship, and requested that the Admiralty inform the Company of the amount and destination of naval stores intended to be sent to India.[2] The Admiralty

[1] CRL, Miscellaneous, 60, p. 23, 70, p. 41; Miscellanies, 21, pp. 372, 374, 25, p. 541.
[2] CRL, Miscellanies, 22, pp. 26, 455, 23, p. 249, 24, pp. 182–3, 25, p. 16.

thereupon ordered the Board to supply this information to the Company.[1] The Board then proceeded to determine the tonnage of stores to be sent in the ensuing year. After this information had been transmitted to the East India Company, its Committee for Shipping informed the Board of the amount of naval stores each ship in the Company's service would take on board and ordered the masters of the East Indiamen to receive the King's stores. On receipt of the Company's shipping orders, the Board directed the officers of the appropriate King's Dockyards to load them on board the Company's ships, taking receipts from the ships' masters and transmitting them to the Board. The Board then sent an account of the naval stores dispatched to India to the senior navy officer in Indian waters.[2]

These arrangements worked very well until the opening months of 1781. But on 21 March 1781 the Company informed the Board that it could not transport 450 tons of naval stores to India because of a lack of shipping; and on 19 April 1781 the Company reported to the Board that its ships could not carry forty tons of sheet copper because of a 'scarcity of tonnage'. By June 1781 the Company's shipping shortage had become so acute that it was forced to leave some 2000 tons of goods in England for want of transport. On 16 June 1781 the Company had to inform the Board 'that it will be impossible for the Company to receive any naval, victualling, or other stores for His Majesty's Service on their shipping which shall proceed to India in the ensuing season'.[3] The Company's shipping shortage arose from the need to transport large numbers of the King's troops to India. As a consequence the Board had no alternative but to employ its own shipping to support military operations in India.

The first troops in the King's service to be sent to India during the American War consisted of 1169 men of the 73rd Regiment who departed from Britain in December 1778. The

[1] CRL, Miscellaneous, 60, p. 112, 61, p. 185, 63, p. 43, 65, p. 86, 67, p. 105.
[2] PRO, ADM/106/2593, Sept. 15, Oct. 2, Nov. 10, 1775; ADM/106/2594, Nov. 7, Dec. 6, 18, 1776; ADM/106/2595, Jan. 18, 1777; ADM/106/2598, Nov. 5, 9, 18, 1778; ADM/106/2599, April 1, 6, 7, 8, 17, 1779; CRL, Miscellanies, 24, pp. 282–3.
[3] CRL, Miscellanies, 25, pp. 186–7, 202, 287–8; PRO, ADM/1/3913, June 16, 1781.

73rd Regiment was transported to India on board seven East Indiamen at the expense of the East India Company. Officials of the Company supervised the embarkation of the troops, and the Company provided everything required by the troops for their passage to India, even paying the masters of the ships 'table money' for the regiment's officers. The only item supplied by the government was bedding.[1] All other troops in the King's service subsequently sent to India during the war on East Indiamen were provided for in a similar manner. Thus it seemed at the beginning of the fighting in India that the transport of King's troops to India would not place any demands on the shipping resources of the Board. But this was not to be the case, for the military situation in India soon called for the dispatch of more troops and stores than the East India Company could carry.

The next King's troops to sail for India were 245 recruits of the 73rd Regiment who were embarked on four East Indiamen in the summer of 1780.[2] In 1781, however, large detachments of the King's troops were sent to India, and the Company's shipping resources were not capable of transporting them as well as meeting all the demands placed on it for the transport of its own stores and troops. In January 1781 the second battalion of the 42nd Regiment, the 98th Regiment, and the 100th Regiment were dispatched to the Cape of Good Hope, but ended up proceeding to India instead. Some of the troops in this force were embarked on East Indiamen, but the bulk of them were carried on board eleven Navy Board transports.[3]

In the summer of 1781 the 78th Regiment and 200 recruits for the 73rd Regiment were sent to India. These troops were to embark on board six East Indiamen at Portsmouth in May 1781, but the number was limited to 1168 because of lack of space on the Company's ships. Consequently, a number of troops and some stores which had to be left behind were

[1] CRL, Miscellanies, 23, pp. 367–9, 396–7, 462–3; PRO, ADM/1/4137, f. 80; ADM/106/2598, Dec. 24, 1778; NMM, ADM/N/248, Dec. 19, 1778.
[2] CRL, Miscellanies, 24, pp. 402, 421; NMM, ADM/N/249, June 22, 1780.
[3] G. Rutherford, 'Sidelights on Commodore Johnstone's Expedition to the Cape', *Mariner's Mirror* (July, 1942), xxviii, 204; PRO, ADM/1/4144, f. 20; NMM, ADM/N/250, Jan. 16, 1781; CRL, Miscellanies, 25, pp. 122–3; Mackesy, op. cit., 389–90.

subsequently transported to India on board two naval storeships.[1]

On 26 July 1781 the government decided to send to India the 101st Regiment, the 102nd Regiment, and the 23rd Light Dragoons provided 'that the East India Company will have the vessels necessary for transporting the above force'. Shortly after this decision had been made, the Secretary at War, Charles Jenkinson, expressed doubts whether 'the Company will have it in their power to convey at once so large a body to the East Indies'.[2] By December 1781, however, the Company had managed to assemble eighteen ships at Portsmouth on which were embarked the three regiments of King's troops and a battalion of Hanoverian troops in the Company's service.[3] But the Company managed to bring this concentration of shipping about only with a great effort, and the Board was forced to employ 1000 tons of transports to carry the battalion of Hanoverian troops from Germany to Portsmouth. In 1782 the Board also had to supply transports to carry a second battalion of Hanoverian troops in the Company's service from Germany to England.[4] Although this second battalion of Hanoverians, which sailed from England for India in the summer of 1782, was the last large body of troops to be sent to India during the conflict, the Company's shipping shortage persisted almost until the end of the war; for 220 tons of clothing for the King's troops in India could not be shipped with the second battalion of Hanoverians for lack of room on the Company's ships. By the fall of 1782, however, the Company had assembled eighteen ships 'to carry out the Company's Goods, and His Majesty's Naval and Military stores', and it had also bought a ship, the *Prime*, to be fitted to carry masts to the ships of the Royal Navy serving in India. The war ended, however, before these measures could affect the military situation in India.[5]

[1] PRO, ADM/1/4144, f. 121; ADM/1/4145, f. 34; ADM/1/4146, f. 14; NMM, ADM/N/250, Sept. 19, 1781; CRL, Miscellaneous, 68, pp. 181, 241; Miscellanies, 25, pp. 234–6, 243–4.

[2] G, no. 3379; NMM, SAN/T/7, July 26, 1781; Add. MSS., 38308, f. 163.

[3] CRL, Miscellanies, 25, pp. 467–9, 471–2.

[4] PRO, ADM/1/4145, f. 139; ADM/1/4147, f. 57.

[5] CRL, Miscellanies, 26, pp. 65, 366; PRO, ADM/1/3914, Oct. 10, 1782, Jan. 2, 1783.

The procurement of passages on East India Company ships for the vast majority of King's troops which were sent to India during the American War represented a great saving of transport tonnage. If vessels of the transport service had been required to carry all the King's troops which were sent to India, thousands of tons of transports would have had to be employed in this task.

The procurement of shipping on a short-term basis by the Navy Board during the American War was of great importance to the British conduct of the war but it was not the decisive element in the transport service. It was rather a stopgap measure that was employed in emergencies or an opportunistic one to be used when there was space available on board merchant ships proceeding to places where the Board wanted to transport troops and stores. If it added flexibility to the transport service and increased its carrying capacity, the ships of the service itself had still to carry the vast majority of troops and the great bulk of stores.

CHAPTER V

Long-term Procurement of Tonnage

THE SUCCESS of the British war effort depended to a considerable degree on the ability of the Navy Board to charter sufficient shipping on a long-term basis. If the Board failed to procure enough tonnage to enable the transport service to meet the logistical requirements of the war, the British forces abroad faced almost certain destruction.

The Board's ability to charter ships on a long-term basis was in a large part determined by the economics of the British shipping industry in wartime. During the American War the transport service obtained most of its ships from the British merchant marine. It has been estimated that in 1775 approximately 6000 British vessels amounting to some 600,000 tons were engaged in overseas trade.[1] At the outbreak of the war, however, the amount of merchant shipping under the British flag was reduced by the withdrawal from British jurisdiction of American-owned ships,[2] and during the war the ranks of the British merchant service were further depleted by enemy action. According to one authority, 3386 British merchant vessels were captured, 495 recaptured, 507 ransomed, and 2384 remained in possession of the enemy. Thus, a large percentage of the total tonnage of the British merchant marine was lost through enemy action during the American War.[3]

---

[1] Charles Wright and C. Ernest Fayle, *A History of Lloyd's* (London, 1928), 156–7; Ralph Davis, *The Rise of the English Shipping Industry in the Seventeenth and Eighteenth Centuries* (London, 1962), 27.

[2] It has been estimated that at the beginning of the American War at least one out of every four ships in the British merchant marine was American built. See Davis, ibid., 68. However, these figures are misleading for many American built vessels were British owned. The number of ocean going merchant ships under American control at the beginning of the war is not known.

[3] Wright and Fayle, op. cit., 156.

The demands of trade also restricted the number of ships available for employment in the transport service. Wartime shipping profits could be large, and there was little except the fear of capture to prevent a shipowner from employing his vessel in trade rather than in the transport service. Thus, in order to procure shipping the Navy Board was compelled to enter the open market and offer freight rates which could compete with those in the civilian carrying trade. The Board did not have at its command any of the economic, legal, or administrative devices employed by the British and American shipping authorities during the Second World War to gain control over merchant shipping.

The problems faced by the Navy Board in procuring shipping were increased by the fact that it had to compete for tonnage not only with the civilian carrying trade, but also with other government departments which hired shipping. Until 1779, when the Navy Board assumed responsibility for the transport of army provisions, agents of the Treasury hired shipping, and throughout the war the Ordnance and Victualling Boards chartered shipping in direct competition with the Navy Board. Because there was very little cooperation between these departments and almost no coordination of their activities, endless confusion resulted.

Despite numerous obstacles, the Navy Board in its efforts to charter shipping enjoyed certain advantages. War disrupts trade. It closes markets and forces large numbers of ships' owners to find alternative employment for their vessels. At the beginning of the war, British merchant ships were denied access to American ports, and the British carrying trade with the American mainland ceased. In addition, the outbreak of hostilities in the Straits of Gibraltar consequent upon Spain's entry into the war in 1779 all but destroyed Britain's Mediterranean trade. Both events forced large numbers of British merchant ships out of their regular trades and left a number of vessels available for employment in the transport service.

The Navy Board's ability to obtain shipping was influenced, as has been said, by the fact that wartime commerce gave shipowners willing to hazard their vessels the opportunity for making enormous profits. A merchant whose ship sailed without the

protection of a convoy could earn a large return on his investment if the ship was fortunate enough to return to England with
a commodity such as sugar when prices were inflated by wartime shortages. But the same merchant also ran the risk of
losing both his cargo and ship to the enemy, and the ranks of
eighteenth-century merchants abound with examples of men who
went bankrupt by investing in ships that were captured while
sailing without convoy. On the other hand, the alternative of
sailing with a convoy also had economic disadvantages. Convoys were subject to long delays resulting in heavy expenses for
the merchant whose ship lay idle while waiting for the other
ships of a convoy and their naval escort to assemble. Furthermore, the convoy system imposed on the British commodity
markets recurrent cycles of shortages and gluts with their
accompanying price fluctuations. The price of sugar in London,
for example, would be artificially high before the arrival of a
West India convoy, but a few hours after such a convoy had
docked in the Thames with a whole year's crop on board, the
price of sugar would plummet to absurdly low levels. These
cycles of rising and falling prices cut deeply into the profits to
be made in the carrying trade. Thus, the merchant and shipowner were faced with a cruel dilemma. To sail without convoy
presented a chance for making a large profit, but it also involved
running great risks. To sail with convoy greatly mitigated the
risk of capture but reduced, or in some cases completely
destroyed, the profits of a ship engaged in the carrying trade.[1]

One solution open to a shipowner who wished to minimize
wartime risks was to charter his ship to the government. By
turning his ship over to the transport service he gained two
major advantages. The profits made by a ship in the transport
service, although small when compared to those in trade, were
steady because the Navy Board paid monthly freight according
to the ship's measured burden. And the shipowner ran only a
small risk of losing his investment through capture by the
enemy, since ships of the transport service were usually employed only under heavy naval escort. In addition, the Board

[1] For an account of the economic problems caused by convoys, see Richard Pares,
War and Trade in the West Indies, 1739–1763 (London, 1936), 497–8.

compensated the owners of ships in its service which were taken or destroyed by the enemy.[1]

Most shipping hired on a long-term basis by the Navy Board was supplied by the ship brokers, underwriters, and merchants of London. These men tendered for employment hundreds of ships which hailed from both London and the Out-Ports. The London ship broker, John Wilkinson, was the largest single supplier of ships to the Board during the American War. In the last week of 1775 Wilkinson tendered to the Board fifty-five vessels; on 16 December 1776 he tendered another twenty-six ships; and on 15 January 1777 he offered for charter another twenty-seven ships.[2] Among the other large suppliers of ships for the transport service were Cope and Bignell; J. J. Angerstein; Mure, Son, and Atkinson; Drake and Long; and Ord and Richardson.[3] These brokers and merchants were agents for ships from the Out-Ports as well as from London.[4]

The Navy Board also employed London brokers and merchants to transmit information to shipowners outside London and to gather intelligence about shipping. On 9 February 1780 the Board requested that Wilkinson inform his correspondents in the Out-Ports that fourteen days' freight would be allowed such ships 'as sail [for Deptford] from the ports they are now in on or before the 1st of March next'.[5] On 31 October 1780 the Board requested that Cope and May and Wilkinson make inquiries concerning the possibility of procuring shipping for the transport service in Holland and Germany.[6] Scarcely a day passed during the war when at least one London broker or merchant did not attend the Navy Board on business relating to the transport service. For these services the London ship brokers and merchants apparently exacted their commissions from the shipowners rather than from the Board. On 16 March

[1] For a detailed description of the eighteenth-century British shipping industry during wartime, see Davis, op. cit., 315–37.

[2] PRO, ADM/106/2593, Dec. 23, 26, 1775; ADM/106/2594, Dec. 16, 1776; ADM/106/2595, Jan. 15, 1777.

[3] PRO, ADM/106/2593–2610, passim.

[4] E.g., PRO, ADM/106/2601, Nov. 16, 1779; ADM/106/2602, Jan. 27, 1780.

[5] PRO, ADM/106/2602, Feb. 9, 1780.

[6] PRO, ADM/106/2604, Oct. 31, 1780.

1778 the Board informed the Admiralty that it had never hired shipping on commission with the exception of five ships which were chartered in Hamburg in the spring of 1776. The owners of these ships refused to have their freight paid to them in England, and the Board arranged that it be paid in Germany through a merchant in Hamburg who received a commission of 2 percent.[1]

In an effort to procure additional shipping the Board on occasion sent agents to the Out-Ports and overseas. As early as October 1775 John Robinson, Secretary to the Treasury, suggested to the Board that agents be sent to ports on the west coast of Britain to charter shipping.[2] This proposal was not acted on until 1776.[3] In February 1776 the search for shipping was extended when British diplomatic representatives were ordered to make inquiries in German ports about the possibility of hiring vessels there.[4] At the same time the Board sent George Marsh, the Clerk of the Acts, to Hamburg and William Butts, Clerk of the Survey of Deptford Dockyard, to Amsterdam to charter ships. In 1778 the Board dispatched the Second Assistant to the Surveyor of the Navy to Glasgow to hire transports.[5] The Board also made use of various officials in the naval service permanently stationed in ports outside of London.[6] Overseers supervising the construction of the King's ships in private yards at various ports were also employed.[7]

The Navy Board advertised extensively as part of its efforts to persuade shipowners to charter their vessels to the transport service. When the Board desired to hire a large amount of tonnage, it would conduct a comprehensive advertising campaign in such London newspapers as the *Daily Advertiser, Morning Chronicle and London Advertiser, Public Advertiser, London Gazette,*

[1] NMM, ADM/B/196, March 16, 1778.
[2] PRO, ADM/1/4130, f. 118.
[3] G, no. 1809; PRO, ADM/106/3318, f. 22.
[4] NMM, SAN/T/1, Feb. 20, 1776; G, no. 1824.
[5] NMM, ADM/B/191, Feb. 24, 1776; ADM/N/245, Feb. 19, 1776; PRO, ADM/106/2597, Jan. 23, 1778.
[6] E.g., PRO, ADM/106/2596, Sept. 3, 1777; ADM/106/2603, May 24, 1780.
[7] E.g., PRO, ADM/106/2604, Sept. 9, 13, Nov. 20, 1780; ADM/108/1B, Nov. 11, 1781.

and *St James Chronicle*.[1] On 17 December 1778 the Board ordered that 'Publication be made to treat for Transports for foreign service on Monday the 4th of January next',[2] and on 19 December 1778 the following advertisement appeared in the *Daily Advertiser*:

The principal Officers and Commissioners of his Majesty's Navy do hereby give Notice, that they shall be ready to treat, on Monday the 4th of next Month, at Noon, for the Hire of TRANSPORTS for foreign service.

This advertisement was repeated in every issue of the *Daily Advertiser* until 4 January 1779. Similar advertisements were published in every issue of the *Public Advertiser* from 19 December 1778 to 4 January 1779, and in ten issues, between 21 December 1778 and 4 January 1779, of the *Morning Chronicle and London Advertiser*.[3] Such advertising campaigns made it difficult for a small group of ship brokers and merchants to monopolize the business of chartering ships to the transport service. At the same time the Board adhered to a policy of chartering any proper ship tendered without regard to political or personal patronage. It could not be otherwise, for the transport service employed so much shipping that no single ship broker or group of brokers could possibly supply the number of ships required.[4]

Newspaper advertisements, while of great assistance to the Board in its endeavours to obtain shipping, were not decisive, for in the end it was the prospect of financial reward which induced men to charter ships to the transport service. One feature of the transport service which made it financially attractive to shipowners was the fact that vessels under charter to the Board after entering pay sailed '*at the Risque of Government from the*

---

[1] Examples of the Navy Board's newspaper advertisements can be found in British Museum, Burney Collection of Newspapers, 662.b.–728.b. The Board never gave directions for advertisements to be placed in provincial newspapers, but this may occasionally have been done by local officials.

[2] PRO, ADM/106/2598, Dec. 17, 1778.

[3] *Daily Advertiser*, Dec. 19, 1778–Jan. 4, 1779; *Public Advertiser*, Dec. 19, 1778–Jan. 4, 1779; *Morning Chronicle and London Advertiser*, Dec. 21, 1778–Jan. 4, 1779.

[4] Cf. the disregard of patronage considerations in awarding contracts for military supplies during the Seven Years War; see Sir Lewis Namier, *The Structure of Politics at the Accession of George III* (London, 1957), 45–58.

Enemy'.[1] In other words, the Board compensated the owners of ships under charter to it for any damage which their vessels sustained by hostile action. When the transport *Hawke* arrived in the River Thames, the Deptford officers 'survey'd the Damage the master has sworn to have received in the hull, masts, sails & rigging in an action with a Rebel privateer on the 15th August last'. On the basis of the report of the survey made by the dock-yard officers, the Board on 17 October 1777 awarded the owners of the *Hawke* £18 6s 5d for repairs.[2] Most of the compensation, however, paid by the Board to shipowners because of enemy action was for the loss of ships rather than for damage. Pay-ments, which were made in navy bills, were based on the valua-tions of the ships made at the time they entered the pay of the transport service. The Board deducted from the valuation of all ships taken or destroyed by the enemy a sum to cover the 'wear & tear' which a ship had received from the day it was appraised to the day it was lost.[3]

The Navy Board did not award compensation for ships lost through enemy action until inquiries had been made to deter-mine the cause of the loss, for the Board was not bound to pay for any vessel which had been taken or destroyed by the enemy through the negligence of the ship's master, owner, or crew. From time to time agents for transports were ordered to investigate the causes of the loss of a ship under charter to the transport service.[4]

If the owners of a ship which had been destroyed or taken by the enemy did not accept the Navy Board's decision concerning compensation, the Board had the right 'by the Charter Party ... in all cases of capture to defer payment for ships till the masters and ships companies are acquited by a Court Martial'.[5]

When the reasons for the capture or destruction of a ship were obvious and there was no question of negligence, the Board paid promptly for the ship which had been lost. For

[1] *London Gazette*, Oct. 14, 1780.
[2] PRO, ADM/106/2596, Oct. 17, 1777; ADM/106/3318, f. 115.
[3] PRO, ADM/49/135, f. 65; ADM/106/2594, Oct. 30, 1776; ADM/106/2604, Oct. 7, 1780.
[4] E.g., PRO, ADM/106/2598, Dec. 19, 1778.
[5] SP, 151, Navy Board to Admiralty, Aug. 30, 1782; NRS, *Barrington Papers*, ii, 195; PRO, ADM/106/2606, Nov. 5, 1781.

instance, in the case of the unarmed transport *Favourite*, which was known to have been forced by bad weather to part from her convoy and was subsequently captured, the Board on 11 April 1777 resolved:

The Board think it . . . unnecessary to put the owners to the trouble & expence of procuring any further proof by a court martial or otherwise, and do direct the Bills be made out for her freight to the day she was taken, and for the value of her according to what is stipulated in the charterparty, after a proper abatement shall be made for her wear & tear during the time she was in the service, and a bill of sale of her shall be made to his Majesty to enable the Board to property in her in case she should be retaken.[1]

Occasionally, although it was known that the cause of the loss of a vessel in the transport service was not due to negligence, the Commissioners of the Navy were unable to compensate the owner immediately because the ship's accounts had not been audited and approved. In such cases the Board would pay the owners in advance most of the money due to them and hold back six months' freight until the ship's accounts had been certified. This was the procedure followed in the case of thirty-two victuallers and transports which were lost when the British forces surrendered at Yorktown.[2]

Upon payment by the Board of compensation for a ship which had been captured, all future rights to that ship were signed over by her owners to the Crown, thus giving the Board the right to claim the vessel as property of the Crown if she were recaptured. On the night of 15 June 1776 the transport *Annabella* was captured by the Americans at the entrance of Boston Harbour, and on 15 November 1776 the Board compensated her owners for their loss by paying them £1593 18s in navy bills.[3] The *Annabella* was renamed *Rising States* by the Americans, converted into a privateer, and dispatched on a cruise to

---

[1] PRO, ADM/106/2595, April 11, 1777.

[2] French Ensor Chadwick, ed., *The Graves Papers* (New York, 1916), 149; PRO, ADM/106/2607, Jan. 8, Feb. 18, 1782; SP, 151, Navy Board to Admiralty, Aug. 20, 1782.

[3] PRO, ADM/106/2594, Nov. 15, 1776; HCA/32/437, June 17, 1777. For an account of the capture of the *Annabella*, see William Bell Clark, *George Washington's Navy* (Baton Rouge, La, 1960), 160–5.

European waters in February 1777. She was captured off Belle Isle on 15 April 1777 by H.M.S. *Terrible* and brought into Portsmouth as a prize.[1] This news reached the Board on 29 May 1777, and on 4 June it ordered Samuel Seddon, its attorney, to 'lay in a claim for her on the part of his Majesty'.[2] On 17 June 1777, the case of 'Our Sov. Lord the King agt. the . . . [*Rising States*] & the Arms Stores Ammunition and other goods laden therein' commenced in the High Court of Admiralty as a routine condemnation of a prize, but quickly changed in character when Samuel Seddon, on behalf of the Navy Board, presented proof that the *Rising States* was in fact the former transport *Annabella* and therefore the property of the Crown. On 21 June 1777 the court ruled that all goods, furniture, arms, ammunition, stores, and tackle placed on board the *Rising States* by the Americans were a legitimate prize of war, and they were therefore awarded to the captors. But the court also ruled that 'said Ship and so much of her Tackle Apparel and Furniture as was belonging to her at her Capture by the American Rebels [are] to be awarded to Samuel Seddon Esq. the Claimant on behalf of the Principal Officers and Commissioners of the Navy on the part of his Majesty on paying 1/8 for salvage of sd. ship & such part of her tackle apparel and furniture as was belonging to her at [the time of] her capture by the American Rebels.'[3]

The Navy Board not only paid compensation for ships which had been taken or destroyed by the enemy, but also for ships or their equipment which had been requisitioned for the King's service by various military authorities. On 12 November 1777 the Board paid John Wilkinson £38 17s 2d for a ship's boat 'supplied from the Lord North transport for the King's service on Lake Champlain'.[4] In December 1781 the Board had to pay for the transport *Margery*, which had been requisitioned by Admiral Marriot Arbuthnot. But because Arbuthnot did not immediately inform the Board that he had taken the *Margery* into the King's service, her owners in addition to compensation

---

[1] For the story of the voyage and capture of the *Rising States*, see William Richard Cutter, ed., 'A Yankee Privateersman in Prison in England, 1777–1779', *The New England Historical and Genealogical Register* (April, 1876), xxx, 175–7.

[2] PRO, ADM/106/2595, June 4, 1777.

[3] PRO, HCA/8/1, pp. 79, 81–2; HCA/32/437, June 17, 1777.

[4] PRO, ADM/106/2596, Nov. 12, 1777.

were paid 'an Allowance for the interest of their property, from the time she ceased to be theirs until the claim is settled'.[1] The payments made by the Board as compensation for ships which had been requisitioned were negligible when compared to those which were paid as compensation for loss or damage due to enemy action.

The compensation paid by the Navy Board for vessels captured or destroyed by the enemy or requisitioned protected only a shipowner's investment; he did not make a profit. The prospect of making money was the greatest inducement to shipowners to tender their vessels for employment in the transport service. The success or failure of the Board's efforts to procure shipping, therefore, depended upon its ability to offer freight rates which compared favourably with those that could be made in comparable employment.

The freight of ships in the transport service was paid by the Board at a set rate per measured ton of a ship's burden per month of her employment. While ships were in the service, their owners received two months' freight for every four months that their ships were under charter. When a ship was discharged from the service and her accounts passed by the Board, her owners then received the balance of the freight which had been withheld.[2] The Board withheld this two months' freight in every four as security for the good conduct of the ship's owner, master, and crew.[3]

The freight withheld was also used as security to insure that shipowners paid for any misuse of the King's stores on board their ships. The Board occasionally supplied ships in the transport service with naval stores or a piece of equipment, such as an anchor, which under the terms of the ships' charter parties the owners were bound to provide. In such cases, the Board demanded that a shipowner pay for the naval stores or equipment supplied to his ship and charged him interest at the rate of 20 percent.[4]

Another category of King's stores issued to the ships of the

---

[1] NMM, ADM/N/250, Dec. 29, 1781.
[2] SP, 151, Navy Board to Admiralty, Aug. 30, 1782; Add. MSS., 38343, ff.7–8.
[3] See above, pp. 37–8.
[4] E.g., PRO, ADM/108/1A, June 4, 1780.

transport service included the bedding, provisions, and flat-bottomed boats to be used by the troops. The owners were not required by charter party to supply these stores, but before receiving all their freight they were obliged to account for them. On 22 November 1779 the Board directed one of its agents for transports 'to acquaint the masters of the transports that in case of the expenditure of any of the King's stores they are to produce certificates thereof from the Agent or person whose orders they are under, otherwise they will not be allowed the same on passing their accounts'.[1] On 24 October 1777 David Mayes, master of the transport *Northampton*, avoided having the cost of thirty-two beds abated from the freight of the ship, when he produced a sworn statement from Captain Commandant William Dalrymple stating that the beds were contaminated by an infectious disease and had been thrown overboard on his orders. The owners of the transport *Royal Britain* were not so fortunate, for £7 6s was deducted from the freight of their ship for eight pairs of stockings which were lost from case No. 4396 while it was on board.[2]

The Navy Board paid the freight of ships under charter to it in navy bills which were 'payable in course' rather than in cash. These bills, which were negotiable instruments signed by three Commissioners of the Navy, could be converted into cash six months after the date of issue, provided the Treasurer of the Navy was solvent. If the Treasurer did not have the cash to redeem the bills, they drew 'interest at the rate of four pounds per cent per annum' from six months after the date of issue until they were redeemed. These bills were readily saleable and were usually sold by their recipients at a discount to a broker who speculated in government bonds, the rate of the discount depending upon the state of the Royal Navy's credit. At times during the American War the discount stood as high as 22 percent.[3] This system of payment was the source of numerous

---

[1] PRO, ADM/106/2601, Nov. 22, 1779.

[2] PRO, ADM/49/125, Oct. 24, 1777; ADM/106/3529, Nov. 18, 1781.

[3] For a description of the workings of the system of payment by navy bills, see J. E. D. Binney, *British Public Finance and Administration, 1774–92* (Oxford, 1958), 140–2; Parliamentary Papers, *The Fifth Report of the Commissioners on Fees, &c. of Public Offices* (n.p., 1806), 206–7.

complaints by shipowners, who maintained that because of the discount they were not receiving the full value of the freight that their ships earned. They also complained that they were being discriminated against because the Treasury paid the freight of its shipping in cash, while the Ordnance Board paid half the freight of ships under charter to it in ordnance bills and the remainder in cash.[1] Despite such complaints, the Board rarely varied its method of payment. Navy bills were an important means of borrowing money to pay for the American War.[2]

During the American War the Navy Board was faced with the necessity of procuring huge amounts of shipping in competition with other government departments, such as the Victualling and Ordnance Boards, which in most cases were able to offer higher rates than those paid by the transport service. In addition, throughout the war the freight rates were driven higher and higher by increases in the operating expenses of ships as a result of the steady rise in seamen's wages and the prices of naval stores. With its limited financial means the Board was thus caught between the requirements of the British war effort which, as the war progressed, called for an ever-increasing number of ships, and the demands of the British shipping market for higher freight rates. Always present throughout the war was the possibility that the Board, in its efforts to meet the military requirements for shipping, would bring down the financial structure of the Navy and perhaps even that of the government by an over-extension of the Navy's credit.

The freight rates fixed by the Navy Board for ships in the transport service were governed, among other things, by the overall cost of the service. The expense of the transport service was tremendous by eighteenth-century standards. Between 1 January 1776 and 31 December 1778 the Board spent the following sums on the operation of the transport service:

1776	£783,651	17s	3d
1777	£534,777	10s	2d
1778	£437,025	6s	3d

[1] Add. MSS., 38343, ff. 7–8.
[2] For a detailed account of naval finance and the importance of navy bills, see Binney, op. cit., 139–50.

When the Board assumed the responsibility for the transport of the army's provisions, the yearly expense of the transport service was doubled, costing the Board the following amounts between 1 January 1779 and 31 December 1783:

1779	Transports	£499,193	17s	1d
	Victuallers	£131,387	8s	7d
	Total	£630,581	5s	8d
1780	Transports	£548,745	4s	1d
	Victuallers	£257,233	0s	10d
	Total	£805,978	4s	11d
1781	Transports	£433,650	12s	10d
	Victuallers	£478,913	5s	2d
	Total	£912,563	18s	0d
1782	Transports	£408,629	10s	$\frac{1}{4}$d
	Victuallers	£480,514	19s	5d
	Total	£889,144	9s	$5\frac{1}{4}$d
1783	Transports	£405,147	12s	10d
	Victuallers	£323,963	11s	4d
	Total	£729,111	4s	2d [1]

Some idea of the size and importance of this expenditure can be seen by the fact that the Navy Board paid for virtually all goods and services required by the Royal Navy, except provisions, ordnance, and wages, with navy bills and on 1 February 1780 navy bills to the value of £4,051,268 12s 7d were in circulation, and from this sum £950,571 16s 11d was spent on the transport service. Approximately 23 percent of the navy bills in circulation on 1 February 1780 represented expenditures on the transport service, and it can therefore be concluded that the cost of the transport service comprised one of the Royal Navy's greatest financial burdens.[2]

The greatest expense of the transport service was freight. The cost of the transport service in 1776 breaks down as follows:

[1] PRO, ADM/106/3525–3526.
[2] NMM, ADM/BP/1, Feb. 25, 1780; Binney, op. cit., 139–50.

Freight	£703,148	18s	1d
Stores	21,020	12s	10d
Cabins	14,745	0s	8d
Forage	7,649	6s	2d
Bedding	18,935	19s	3d
Agents, surveyors, and other officials	8,957	2s	1d
Contingency for boat hire	1,645	7s	1d
Superintendent and steward	722	10s	11d
Pilotage	902	0s	2d
Guns	5,925	0s	0d
Total	£783,651	17s	3d[1]

The cost of freight for ships in the transport service was so large that the Board had to calculate what effect an increase of freight would have on the credit of the Navy before increasing its freight rate. If the freight rate of ships in the transport service was increased too much, the number of navy bills in circulation would rise steeply. There would then be a corresponding increase in the rate of discount, and the credit of the Navy would as a result be jeopardized. Thus, the Board could not go into the open market when it needed shipping and offer any freight rate necessary to procure the tonnage required. It therefore adopted the policy of increasing its freight rate only under great pressure and then just enough to remain competitive. At the same time it was forced to seek methods of procuring shipping which did not require a general increase in its freight rate.

The first shipping crisis of the war occurred in the winter and spring of 1776. At this time the British government was preparing a massive reinforcement for the armies in North America. They wished this force to arrive early in the spring. Shipping was urgently required to transport it.[2] In 1775, before the news of Lexington and Concord had reached England, the Navy Board was hiring ships for the peacetime operations of the transport

---

[1] PRO, ADM/106/3525, Jan. 1–Dec. 31, 1776. This account does not include payments made for ships taken or destroyed by the enemy. In 1777 the Navy Board paid £23,604 3s 10d to owners of ships lost through enemy action. PRO, T/1/541, An account of Navy Bills issued between Jan. 5, 1777 to Dec. 2, 1777.

[2] G, no. 1699.

service at 9s per ton. In November 1775 the Board was forced to increase its freight rate to 10s per ton in order to procure 1800 tons of shipping needed to transport Hanoverian troops from Germany to Gibraltar and Minorca.[1] When the decision was made to dispatch large reinforcements to America, the Board was given the task of providing the shipping required to transport at least 27,000 infantry, a regiment of cavalry, and approximately 950 horses to North America. The Board accordingly took 'every adviseable method to invite [ships] to come to Deptford from the Ports of Bristol, Liverpool, Whitehaven, Hull, Whitby, and other places'. The freight rate was increased from 10s to 11s per ton per month, and agents were sent to the Out-Ports in an effort to obtain the required tonnage.[2] Sufficient ships, however, were not forthcoming, and it was reported to the Board that only two ships could be hired at Liverpool because the transport service's freight rate was not high enough to compete with the profits to be made in the Greenland fishery and in the slave trade. There is also some evidence that freight rates may have been driven up by 'combinations' of London ship brokers and merchants who were playing the Navy Board off against the Treasury.[3] The government met this situation by ordering the different departments of the government which hired shipping to work out a coordinated freight rate policy, and by directing the Navy Board to seek ships in Germany and Holland.

In February 1776 the government informed the Treasury, Board of Ordnance, and the Victualling Board that in the future their freight rates could not exceed those of the Navy Board.[4] At the outset this plan to establish some kind of national policy for freight rates was almost destroyed when one of the Treasury's contractors continued to give 12s per ton for shipping while the Board offered 11s. He was eventually restrained by the

[1] NMM, ADM/B/194, Jan. 3, 1777; Add. MSS., 38343, f. 7.
[2] NMM, ADM/B/191, Jan. 18, 1776; ADM/B/194, Jan. 3, 1777; G, no. 1809; PRO, ADM/106/3318, f. 22; Encouragements given to the owners of transports & victuallers in the employ of the Navy Board from 1776 to 1782, [undated], Barham MSS. at Exton Park.
[3] NMM, ADM/B/191, Jan. 31, 1776; NRS, Sandwich Papers, i, 88.
[4] Edward E. Curtis, The Organization of the British Army in the American Revolution (New Haven, 1926), 180–1; NRS, Sandwich Papers, i, 88; Add. MSS., 38343, f. 2.

Treasury after it had received a strong protest from Maurice Suckling, Comptroller of the Navy.[1] By the last week in April, the Board had been able to hire 33,806 tons of shipping in Britain at 11s per ton.[2] Transport for a large number of horses, however, was still required. The freight rate of the transport service, therefore, was increased to 12s 6d per ton at the end of April, while the other government departments held their freight rates down to 11s per ton. By this means the Board was able to hire an additional 7010 tons of shipping.[3] But after April the Treasury was able to charter only nine ships at 11s, yet this department had by some means to provide shipping to carry the army's provisions to America. On 12 June 1776, therefore, it raised its freight rate to 12s 6d per ton, while the Navy Board, having provided most of the shipping for the transport of troops and horses, dropped its rate to 11s. This manœuvre enabled the Treasury to hire more than seventy ships during the next seven weeks. Despite the less attractive rate offered by the Navy Board, the transport service managed to charter an additional 2769 tons between 12 June and the end of August.[4]

While the different departments were manipulating freight rates in order to force British shipowners to charter their vessels to the agency most in need of the tonnage, the Navy Board was attempting to solve the shipping shortage by a totally different method. In February 1776 the Board began to hire shipping in Germany and the Netherlands. There were two reasons why it should extend the quest for shipping overseas. The obvious one was the simple need for tonnage, but the government had not overlooked the possibilities of using the threat of foreign competition as a means of keeping British freight rates within reason and as a way of increasing the number of British ships which would enter the transport service.[5] In order to forestall any legal complications that might arise out of the employment of foreign transports to carry troops to America, the Admiralty

[1] NMM, SAN/T/1, Feb. 23, 1776.
[2] NMM, ADM/B/194, Jan. 3, 1777.
[3] Add. MSS., 38343, f. 3; SP, 145, Prices & Tonnage of Transports hired by the Navy Board between 1st Nov. 1775 & 4 Nov. 1776 as sent to the Treasury [on] the 3d January 1777.
[4] Add. MSS., 38343, f. 3; NMM, ADM/B/194, Jan. 3, 1777.
[5] NMM, SAN/T/1, Feb. 20, 1776; G, no. 1824.

consulted the King's law officers who were of the opinion that the Acts of Trade and Navigation 'are all prohibitory only in Cases of Ships employed in Trade, and do not extend to ships employed as Transports in His Majesty's Service'.[1] Thus safeguarded the Navy Board dispatched agents to Hamburg and Holland.[2] Approximately 21,000 tons were hired for the Board in the Netherlands as well as four ships for the Treasury.[3]

Without the large number of Dutch ships hired in 1776 to assist in carrying reinforcements to North America, the Navy Board probably would not have been able to procure the necessary tonnage. However, the use of them raised various problems. Payment was not according to their measured tonnage, but rather at the rate of 22s per last. At the time of hiring this was thought to work out to about 11s per ton, but it later proved to be equal to 15s 4d per ton.[4] As well as being obliged to pay a high rate of freight, the Board had to place a British petty officer or midshipman on board each vessel to supervise the masters. Despite such precautions, the Dutch masters were highly uncooperative. They were suspected of having so much private cargo on board that Germain issued orders that they must be unloaded under guard and searched when they reached New York. They were then to be escorted away from the American coast by warships and informed 'that if they are afterwards met with nearer shore they will be made a prize of'.[5]

By July 1776 the Navy Board had the 'unprecedented' number of 416 ships amounting to 128,427 tons in the transport service—more transports than had ever been assembled at any one time during the Seven Years War. In the words of one official, 'The country [is] drained of ships for transport purposes'.[6]

After the campaign of 1776, the tonnage requirements of the

[1] PRO, ADM/7/299, f. 301.
[2] NMM, ADM/B/191, April 12, 1776.
[3] NMM, ADM/B/194, Jan. 3, 1777; Add. MSS., 38343, f. 3.
[4] Add. MSS., 38343, f. 3; PRO, ADM/106/2596, Dec. 2, 1777.
[5] PRO, ADM/1/4132, f. 19; ADM/1/4133, f. 10; ADM/106/2594, Oct. 4, Dec. 30, 1776; NMM, ADM/B/191, April 17, 1776; ADM/N/247, June 4, 19, 1776.
[6] SP, 145, Transports hired at different periods by the Navy Board, [1777]; HMC, *American Manuscripts*, i, 37.

transport service declined until 1779. In 1777 and 1778 ships of the transport service were employed primarily in amphibious operations in America and were not deeply involved in the logistical support of the British troops overseas. In 1777 the Treasury's shipping, in addition to transporting all the army's provisions, carried a great part of its stores and replacements to North America. At the end of 1776 and the beginning of 1777 the Navy Board discharged from the service 149 vessels amounting to 50,000 tons, and by June 1777 only 264 ships amounting to 78,472 tons remained in the service.

The relative lack of demand for tonnage during 1777 is reflected in the Navy Board's procurement policy. While the Ordnance Board was chartering shipping at rates which varied between 12s and 14s per ton and the Treasury was paying 12s 6d, the Navy Board was offering only 11s. Although it maintained a lower rate of freight than other government departments, from September 1776 to May 1777 the Board was able to charter seventy-six ships with a total tonnage of 21,549 tons.[1] In 1778, however, the Board assumed greater responsibility for the transport of army equipment to North America, and on 10 March 1778 its freight rate was increased from 11s to 12s per ton. The additional shilling placed upon the freight rate of the transport service was not due to an increase in the demands for tonnage, but was rather a reflection of the British defeat at Saratoga, the impending entry of France into the war, and wartime increases in seamen's wages and the cost of naval stores. The Board maintained the freight rate of 12s per ton throughout 1778, and on 4 January 1779 it even lowered it to 11s 6d. On 28 January 1779 the transport service's freight rate was again increased to 12s per ton when it was found 'that a sufficient number of transports could not be procured at 11s 6d ℔ ton ℔ month'.[2] The beginning of 1779, however, marked the end of the period of the war in which few demands were placed on the transport service. From 1779 to well after the end

---

[1] SP, 145, Transports hired at different periods by the Navy Board, [1777]; Add. MSS., 38343, ff. 5–7; Curtis, op. cit., 181; NMM, ADM/B/194, June 20, 1777.

[2] PRO, ADM/106/2597, March 10, 1778; ADM/106/2599, Jan. 4, 28, 1779; SP, 145, Relative to Transports, Feb. 10, 1778.

of hostilities, the Navy Board was faced with ever-increasing demands for shipping.

The tonnage requirements of the Navy Board were greatly increased in 1779 when it took over from the Treasury the responsibility for the transport of the army's provisions. Between 31 December 1778 and 31 December 1779 the strength of the transport service increased from 201 ships with a total tonnage of 57,107 tons to 318 ships totalling 94,017 tons.[1] The demands placed upon the transport service were further increased by the entry of France and Spain into the war for, in addition to supporting the British forces in North America, it had to move men and material to the East and West Indies and to other widely scattered British possessions. While the burden increased, the difficulties faced by the Board in procuring additional tonnage and maintaining the ships it already had under charter were also intensified. After 1778 the operating costs of ships in the transport service rose precipitously. The French and Spanish challenge to British sea power was met by a total mobilization of the Royal Navy which resulted in a fierce three-cornered contest for the limited supply of seamen and naval stores among the ships engaged in trade, the ships of the transport service, and the ships of the Royal Navy. As profits decreased for ships in the transport service, the owners of ships under charter to the Navy Board sometimes refused to cooperate with the government. At the same time the Board found it impossible to increase the tonnage of the transport service, for the shipping resources of Britain were stretched to the breaking point.

In 1779 the Navy Board managed to charter a further 37,910 tons of shipping at 12s per ton which was enough to meet all its requirements.[2] In January and February 1779, however, the Board had a foretaste of the problems which were to plague it until the end of the war. In February 1779 the Board received a number of requests from the owners of ships for increases in their rate of freight. It was the Board's policy at this time to keep vessels at the freight rates at which they had been

---

[1] An account of the number of ships and their tonnage which appear to have been in service at the end of each year during the present war, [undated], Barham MSS. at Exton Park.

[2] Ibid., Barham MSS. at Exton Park.

hired. If a vessel had been originally hired at 11s per ton, her rate of freight stayed at that level even if the Board increased the amount of freight it was offering to vessels just entering the service.[1] About the same time requests of a different kind, but equally as embarrassing, began to be made. On 22 January 1779 John Garret, owner of the transports *Mary* and *Sally*, petitioned the Board requesting that he be paid four months' freight instead of the usual two months in every four because his ships had just returned from overseas and he had been 'obliged to pay the wages to all the seamen & at a very considerable Expence get others in their room . . . whereby I have been obliged to advance £700 or £800 more than if the ship[s] had been continued in the service abroad'.[2] And on 26 February 1779 a firm of London ship brokers requested that all withheld freight be paid to ships which had been in the transport service for more than three years.[3] Both these requests reflected the shipowners' need for cash in order to meet the mounting costs of seamen's wages and shipbuilding materials. The increased expenses of the shipowners resulted mainly from the changing pattern of the operations of the transport service. Before 1779 one of the major advantages which the Navy Board had over other government departments in its competition for shipping was the fact that vessels in the transport service were generally employed in amphibious operations in America. As a result, such ships received relatively little wear and tear, for they spent long periods between operations lying idle in American ports. Even more important was the fact that by not returning to England great savings were made in seamen's wages. Under law when a ship returned to Britain her owners were required to pay all the wages of her seamen. Therefore, if a ship in the transport service shuttled back and forth between American and British ports, as did victuallers, every time she returned to Britain her owners were forced to pay off the entire crew and hire a new one usually at higher wages. On the other hand, if a ship remained in America, her seamen continued to receive the same wages as they did when they first signed on. In addition, a

[1] PRO, ADM/106/279, Feb. 19, 1779.
[2] PRO, ADM/106/280, Jan. 22, 1779; ADM/106/2599, Jan. 29, 1779.
[3] PRO, ADM/106/2599, Feb. 26, 1779.

shipowner's wage bill was usually lowered by a long stay over-seas owing to the high rate of desertion among the crews of the transports in America, for under law any seaman who deserted forfeited his wages.[1] Thus, as more and more transport service tonnage was devoted to carrying army provisions, a task which involved numerous round trips between the British Isles and America, the owners of shipping under charter to the Navy Board were faced with the problem of spending more money for seamen's wages.

In 1780 the effects of the extension of the war and the Navy Board's assumption of the responsibility for the transport of the army's provisions came to a head to form the single great problem of how to find enough shipping to carry on the war. The Board tried to solve this problem in three different ways. It attempted to induce more British ships to enter the transport service by offering financial rewards, it tried to hire ships overseas, and it did not allow any ships to leave the service.

The Board opened its campaign to entice shipowners with financial rewards on 24 May 1780, when it resolved to lower the number of seamen that owners were bound to supply from seven to six men per 100 tons of a ship's burden. At the same time the Board reduced from four to three the number of cables each of 120 fathoms in length with which the owners, by the terms of their charter parties, were required to equip their ships. These concessions were devised to raise the value of its freight rate without actually increasing it. The savings in seamen's wages and provisions alone were calculated to give shipowners a benefit equal in value to an increase of 1s per ton in the freight rate.[2] But only limited concessions of this kind could be made without jeopardizing the operational capabilities of the trans-port service. As it was, when the news of the Board's reduction in the size of ship's crews reached the Principal Agent for Trans-ports in America, he reported that any decrease would greatly weaken the combat effectiveness of the British forces in America.[3]

The Navy Board originally intended the reduction in the size

---

[1] Add. MSS., 38343, ff. 7–8.
[2] PRO, ADM/106/2603, May 24, 1780; SP, 151, Navy Board to Admiralty, Aug. 30, 1782.
[3] PRO, ADM/49/2, f. 229

of crews to apply only to those ships which entered the transport service after 24 May 1780. However, it was forced to extend this concession to virtually the entire service when the shipowners, led by the London ship brokers, refused to man those of their ships which had entered the service before 24 May at the rate of seven men per 100 tons. On 29 May, under pressure from owners and brokers, it directed that all ships then in the Thames could be manned at six men per 100 tons regardless of the date when such ships had entered the service. On 28 June the Board received a report from Cork that the masters of transports and victuallers in that port, on orders from their owners, were manning their ships at the rate of six men per 100 tons. At first the Board resolved that all such ships should be mulcted, but the next day it gave in to the pressure of the owners and directed that all ships then in Britain or which in the future returned from overseas might be manned at the rate of only six men per 100 tons.[1]

On 31 August 1780 the Navy Board proposed to the Admiralty that in the light of 'the present scarcity of shipping' the government buy seven ships with a total tonnage of approximately 6000 tons to serve as naval storeships in place of vessels in the transport service. These ships were to be part of the Royal Navy and manned by naval personnel. The Admiralty approved this plan, and it was put into effect.[2] The Navy Board made a similar proposal to the Admiralty on 1 August 1782 when it suggested that the government purchase 6000 to 8000 tons of shipping to serve as transports and 'to be commanded by lieutenants and manned by government'.[3] Both suggestions were put forward by the Board as a means of relieving some of the pressure on the transport service, but in reality they were very little help. It could not be hoped that approximately 14,000 extra tons of shipping would fulfil the tonnage requirements of the transport service. In addition, having the government man and equip these vessels placed the burden of finding the necessary naval stores and seamen on the Royal Navy instead of on private shipowners.

[1] PRO, ADM/106/2603, May 25, 29, June 28, 29, 1780.
[2] NMM, ADM/BP/1, Aug. 31, 1780.
[3] PRO, ADM/106/2609, Aug. 1, 1782.

In the autumn of 1780 the Navy Board was forced to make further financial concessions to the shipowners. On 5 October it decided that the owners of all ships entering the service after that date would be compensated if their vessels were taken or destroyed by the enemy in such a way that a financial loss would not be incurred because of the discount on navy bills.[1] Despite this concession, the Board was not able to procure additional tonnage, and the owners of ships already under charter complained that 'the present freight do not afford any benefit'. On 6 November 1780 it yielded and reluctantly increased its rate of freight from 12s per ton to 12s 9d per ton for all ships which entered the service after that date, as well as for all ships which returned to the British Isles in the future. On 3 May 1782, after receiving numerous complaints from the owners of ships not included in this advance, the Board raised the freight rate of all ships in the transport service to 12s 9d per ton. This increase of 9d, as well as the provision which permitted ships to be manned at the rate of only six men per 100 tons of the ship's burden, amounted to an overall rate of 13s 9d per ton, which was 'the highest *general* price ever given by [the] Board'.[2]

The search for neutral ships for hire began in the fall of 1780. On 10 October 1780 the Board, having received a tender for a Dutch ship from Robert Hambleton, a British merchant resident in Amsterdam, asked him to inform the Dutch ship brokers that it was in the market to charter Dutch bottoms. At the end of October it requested a number of London ship brokers to make inquiries about the possibilities of hiring Dutch and German ships. As a result of this effort, the Board received tenders for five or six Dutch vessels, but it had great difficulty in coming to terms with the owners. Moreover, the outbreak of war between England and the Dutch Republic at the end of the year not only cut short negotiations but also increased the difficulties of

[1] PRO, ADM/106/2604, Oct. 5, 1780; SP, 151, Navy Board to Admiralty, Aug. 30, 1782.

[2] PRO, ADM/106/2604, Oct. 28, 31, Nov. 6, 1780; ADM/106/2608, May 3, 1782; SP, 151, Navy Board to Admiralty, Aug. 30, 1782; Encouragements given to the owners of transports & victuallers in the employ of the Navy Board from 1776 to 1782, [undated], Barham MSS. at Exton Park.

obtaining British ships; for at the outbreak of hostilities, the Royal Navy put Holland under blockade and proceeded to destroy the Dutch carrying trade, thereby giving British merchants the opportunity of making 'extraordinary profits' by employing their ships in trades which the Navy had forced the Dutch to vacate.[1]

The attempts made by the Navy Board in 1780 to increase the number of ships in the transport service failed. On 31 December 1779 there were 318 ships totalling 94,017 tons under charter to the Board. By 31 December 1780 the Board had managed only to charter a further 10,730 tons of shipping. The situation did not markedly improve. On 31 December 1781 the transport service numbered 369 ships with a total tonnage of 113,140 tons. In the two years between 31 December 1779 and 31 December 1781 the strength of the transport service increased only by fifty-one ships amounting to 19,123 tons.[2]

During 1781 and 1782 the Navy Board did not change the terms under which it chartered shipping. The transport service's rate of freight stood at 12s 9d during these years simply because the Board did not think that an appreciable amount of tonnage could be obtained by an increase in the freight rate.[3] Sir Charles Middleton told Lord Keppel in March 1782 that the only methods by which he thought a large number of ships could be produced would be a general embargo which 'will naturally throw a great number of ships into naval service', or for another department of the government, such as the Board of Ordnance, to hire shipping at an advanced rate of freight and then lend the ships to the Navy Board.[4] A general embargo, even if politically practicable, would have been a very crude method of procuring shipping. An embargo would prevent all merchant ships from leaving British ports, and although it would force ships into the transport service, it would also hurt the British

---

[1] NMM, ADM/N/249, Oct. 20, 1780; ADM/BP/1, Oct. 31, 1780; PRO, ADM/106/2604, Oct. 10, 31, Nov. 9, 13, 28, Dec. 4, 15, 20, 25, 1780; SP, 151, Navy Board to Admiralty, Aug. 30, 1782.

[2] An account of the number of ships . . . in service . . . during the present war, [undated], Barham MSS. at Exton Park.

[3] PRO, ADM/106/2609, Aug. 1, 1782.

[4] NRS, *Barham Papers*, ii, 50.

war effort by hampering such vital trades as the Baltic timber trade. It was, therefore, resolved that the Board of Ordnance should charter shipping for the transport service at an advanced rate of freight.

This decision was a hollow victory for Middleton, who had been campaigning for months for a rationalization of the government's shipping procurement policy. When the Rockingham-Shelburne ministry came to power in March 1782, Middleton deluged Lord Shelburne with papers and memoranda urging that the Navy Board assume control over the Victualling and Ordnance Boards' shipping. Middleton based his argument for centralization on the grounds that the competition for shipping between the Victualling, Ordnance, and Navy Boards artificially drove the freight rates up, and that the transport service, which required the greatest amount of tonnage, could never procure enough ships until the Victualling and Ordnance Boards stopped hiring ships. Although there had been a degree of cooperation between the various departments of the government in obtaining shipping in 1776, this cooperation had broken down in the course of the war. The Victualling and Ordnance Boards required only a fraction of the tonnage needed by the transport service; the Board of Ordnance, for example, never had more than 9800 tons of shipping under charter to it at any one time during the war. When these two departments required a ship, however, they would enter the market and offer a rate of freight well above that which the transport service was giving, a practice which led to shipowners refusing to let ships to the transport service at a lower rate. This produced a situation in which, according to Middleton, 'no increase of price on the part of the Navy Board would procure shipping while the present competition exists. The only consequence of such a measure would be a higher demand on the part of the owners from the other Boards & a general increase of freight throughout the Kingdom.'[1]

In the spring of 1782 the Navy Board attempted to bring

[1] SP, 151, Middleton to Shelburne, June 28, 1782; Navy Board to Admiralty, Aug. 30, 1782; Middleton to Shelburne, Sept. 9, 1782; NRS, *Barham Papers*, ii, 81, 170; Curtis, op. cit., 180.

8—S.A.W.

about some cooperation between the Boards which hired shipping. In March it obtained the momentary agreement of the
Victualling Board to a proposal to hire ships on the same terms
as the transport service. But this arrangement failed in June
1782 when the Victualling Board, finding itself unable to charter
shipping on this basis, advanced its freight rate without informing the Navy Board.[1]

While it was attempting to persuade the Victualling Board
to coordinate its freight rates with those of the transport service,
the Navy Board obtained authorization to hire 20,000 tons of
shipping at an advanced rate of freight through the Ordnance
Board. That is, the Ordnance Board was to hire the ships and
then lend them to the transport service. Several thousand tons
were procured by this means.[2] No attempt was made to take up
the full 20,000 tons, because it became clear that no economy
would result: the Board might as well put up its own rates.[3] It
was evident to the Navy Board by the summer of 1782 that the
policy of hiring ships through the Ordnance Board at an
advanced rate of freight was at best a temporary expedient
capable of producing only a few thousand tons of shipping. It
was also apparent that unless there was a large increase in the
freight rate for the service, with all the inherent financial
dangers which that step implied, the Navy Board would be faced
in 1783 with the impossible task of conducting the transport
service with a disastrously decreasing amount of shipping.

Because of its inability to charter all the shipping it needed,
the Navy Board during the last years of the war was forced to
retain in service every ship that it possibly could. Most of its
ships were hired for six or twelve months 'certain'. That is, by
the terms of a ship's charter party the Board was required to
keep a ship in the service for at least six or twelve months. But
after the expiration of the guaranteed period of employment a
shipowner could not withdraw his vessel without the consent of
the Board. In 1780, when the Navy Board became aware of the

---

[1] PRO, ADM/106/2607, March 20, 26, 1782; ADM/106/2608, June 11, 1782;
ADM/108/1B, March 25, 1782; NMM, ADM/BP/3, March 26, June 26, 1782.
[2] SP, 151, memorandum, July 30, 1782; PRO, ADM/1/4147, f. 130;
ADM/106/2607, March 25, 1782.
[3] NMM, ADM/BP/3, June 26, 1782.

difficulty of procuring additional tonnage, it began to refuse to discharge ships and insist that upon a ship's return to England, its owner repair and refit it for further service.[1]

The owners of ships which were detained complained to the Board that they were being forced into an economic trap by this policy. Some even threatened to break their charter parties and withdraw their ships without the Board's consent. The Board in turn threatened to sue them for breach of contract because 'Their claim generally to be discharged is not founded in fact. By their contract we are at liberty to retain them while the public demands them.'[2] Throughout the last three years of the war, despite the threats, complaints, and protests of the shipowners, the Board stuck to its policy of retaining every vessel in service that was fit for employment.

This policy undoubtedly hindered the chartering of additional vessels, for it appears that ships kept in the transport service in the last years of the war were losing rather than earning money. The word must have spread quickly that to charter a vessel to the transport service was tantamount to entering economic bondage. The Board certainly realized the difficulty it was creating, but the military situation forced it to keep control over every ship possible.

The last three years of the war were not profitable ones for the owners of ships detained by the Navy Board. These ships earned a fixed rate of freight, while the costs of naval stores and seamen's wages were rapidly increasing. As a consequence, the owners were forced in many cases to invest large amounts of money in the maintenance of their ships, while the profits which these ships made shrank and in some cases disappeared. On 2 August, 1782, for example, Ralph Elliot, an owner of the transport *Polly*, requested that the Board increase the freight of his ship. Elliot stated that in thirty-three months of employment the *Polly* had earned £4198 16s 4d in freight while it had cost him £5583 5s 3d to maintain her, with the result that his net loss was £1384 8s 11d.[3] From 1780 to 1783 many other owners

---

[1] SP, 151, Navy Board to Admiralty, Aug. 30, 1782.

[2] PRO, ADM/106/2608, May 3, 1782; Undated memorandum, Barham MSS. at Exton Park.

[3] PRO, ADM/108/1C, Aug. 2, 1782.

of ships in the transport service faced similar problems. On 24 July 1781 twelve shipowners wrote to the Navy Board stating that they were

the owners of transports lately arrived from abroad, and ordered by your Honors to be again reffitted for service; [we] beg leave to represent to your Hon. Board, that the present freight of twelve shillings & nine pence ℔ ton ℔ month is by no means adequite to the heavy expense we are at in fitting out our ships, occasioned by the enormous price of all kinds of naval stores and provisions, which within these twelve months have advanced, in sundry articles near 20 ℔ cent, and which added to the high discount on Navy Bills, and the premium on bills abroad seldom less than 15 ℔ cent, renders it impossible to us to continue our ships in the service at the present freight; We therefore most earnestly request your Honors will take this matter into consideration, and add at least, one shilling ℔ ton to the present freight of twelve shillings and nine pence; under which we are truly sensible no ship can afford a living profit to her owners.

After considering this petition the Navy Board informed them, 'that we cannot comply with their requests'.[1]

Although the Navy Board adhered to its policy of not increasing freight rates, it did manage to give some relief to the owners. On 6 November 1780 it resolved that ships returning from overseas which had been ordered to be refitted for further service be granted two weeks' freight for the time which they spent being refitted if they had been abroad for a year, three weeks' freight for a year and a half, and one month's freight for more than two years' service abroad.[2] The Board attempted as well to supply those owners whose ships had been ordered to be refitted with some money to finance the refits. On 4 May 1782 it resolved to pay the owners of vessels which were refitted for further employment all freight which had been withheld during the prior period.[3] These minor concessions, however, did little to ease the plight of the owners, and from 1780 until the end of the war the Board was deluged with communications demand-

[1] PRO, ADM/108/1B, July 24, 1781.
[2] PRO, ADM/106/2604, Nov. 6, 1780.
[3] PRO, ADM/106/2608, May 4, 1782.

ing that their vessels either be paid more or discharged from the service.[1]

Without chartering any appreciable amount of new shipping and by retaining in the service the vessels already under charter, the Navy Board was able to maintain barely enough ships in operation during the years from 1780 to 1782 to meet the demands which the war placed on the transport service. But this policy had obvious disadvantages during a period when more and more ships were being worn out by continuous use or required longer and longer periods in dockyards to be refitted and repaired.[2]

By the end of 1782 the transport service had run out of resources. There was no apparent end in sight to the military commitments which it had to fulfil, yet it was unable to procure any additional tonnage, and the number of ships it did have under charter was slowly being reduced by the enemy, the elements, or continuous employment. Between 31 December 1781 and 31 December 1782 the number of vessels in service had dropped from 369 ships to 318 ships which amounted to a decrease of 17,969 tons.[3] The end of the war in the beginning of 1783 prevented a catastrophe. In 1782 enough tonnage could have been procured to enable the British to continue the war into 1783 without disaster only if the government had employed economic measures similar to those used during the Second World War to limit or prevent tonnage from being absorbed by non-essential civilian commerce. A government-controlled war economy was, however, beyond the comprehension of the eighteenth-century mind, and the idea of a general embargo was the only suggestion of this nature that was brought forward as a means of solving the shipping problem during the American War. Thus, at the end of 1782 lack of shipping had brought the transport service to the edge of an abyss from which only peace could save it.

[1] E.g., PRO, ADM/106/2602, March 2, April 24, 1780; ADM/106/2604, Oct. 3, 18, 1780; ADM/106/2605, May 19, July 26, Aug. 6, 1781; ADM/106/2607, Jan. 17, 1782; ADM/106/2608, May 13, 1782; ADM/108/1C, April 6, July 10, 1782.

[2] E.g., PRO, ADM/106/3529, Jan. 15, 1781.

[3] An account of the number of ships ... in service ... during the present war, [undated], Barham MSS. at Exton Park.

CHAPTER VI

The Measurement, Inspection, and Fitting-Out of Ships entering the Transport Service

BECAUSE the exigencies of global war compelled the transport service to rely heavily on chartered vessels as transports, victuallers, and storeships, some system had to be devised for making certain that all such ships were suitable for government service. The Navy Board's solution to this problem was to require that whenever possible all ships entering the transport service be inspected, measured, and fitted-out at a Royal Dockyard. The use of Royal Dockyard personnel to perform these duties gave the Navy Board a decided advantage in its dealings with shipowners, for unlike other departments of the government which also hired shipping, the transport service had at its command the resources to ascertain whether or not a ship met certain minimum standards. In addition, the Board's reliance on Royal Dockyards to certify vessels for the transport service provided a relatively objective method for determining how much freight a ship should earn and the amount each ship's owner should be compensated if his ship were taken or destroyed by the enemy.

The Navy Board never negotiated with shipowners over the freight rate or the terms of the charter party. The conditions under which a ship entered the transport service were the same for every ship, and when the Board changed the terms of its charter parties, these changes applied to every ship entering the pay of the transport service after the date on which the Board's resolve took effect. The Board always put forward the terms under which it would be willing to charter a vessel on an unconditional basis. Shipowners who demanded a higher rate of freight than that offered by the Board were invariably informed that their ships were not wanted at that price.[1] If an owner tendering a ship for charter to the transport service accepted the terms offered by the Board, he was directed to have his ship proceed to a place where she could be inspected, measured, and appraised by officials of the Board. No ship was taken into the service until it had been inspected and certified as fit.

Most of the ships employed in the transport service were measured, surveyed, appraised, and fitted-out by Deptford Dockyard, but a number of vessels were made ready for service at Portsmouth and Plymouth Dockyards. In addition, some vessels were taken into the service overseas or at British ports which were not the seat of a Royal Dockyard. The Board generally insisted that such ships first be measured and appraised by such officials as agents for transports, and then be remeasured and reappraised at the first King's Dockyard they reached. On 13 October 1780 the Board placed an advertisement in the London newspapers stating that it desired to hire transports at Bristol and Liverpool and that the vessels 'will be surveyed, measured, and valued by Overseers of the King's ships building at those ports . . . subject to a resurvey, measurement, and valuation at the first King's port they arrive at'.[2] The Navy Board, however, preferred whenever possible to have ships enter the transport service at one of its dockyards, preferably Deptford.

The Board undoubtedly lost the use of a number of ships because of its insistence that all vessels had to be inspected at a Royal Dockyard before entering its service. Patrick Lockie, agent for the owners of the *Lady Hope*, informed the Board on 20 May 1779 that the ship was then at Glasgow and 'it would be utterly impracticable to get her around to either of the ports [Deptford, Plymouth, and Portsmouth] mentioned'.[3] Occasionally, however, the Board offered the owners of ships monetary

[1] E.g., PRO, ADM/106/2594, Aug. 23, 1776; ADM/106/2599, Feb. 8, 9, 1779; ADM/106/2606, Nov. 13, 1781.

[2] *Morning Chronicle and London Advertiser*, Oct. 13, 1780. See also PRO, ADM/106/2595, Jan. 14, 1777; ADM/106/2606, Dec. 24, 1781.

[3] PRO, ADM/106/280, May 20, 1779.

inducements to send their ships to Royal Dockyards. On 19 April 1780 the Board resolved:

in consideration of the great want of transports, & the small no. offered. Agreed to allow the owners of such ships as may be tendered, the following days pay for such as shall arrive at any of the King's Yards before the 1st of June.

From Liverpool	one month
Bristol	three weeks
Any port in the Channel from the Downes to the Lands End	eight days
Any Port on this side of Flamborough Head .	fourteen days
The otherside of Flamborough Head . . .	three weeks

Acquaint the Regulating Captains at Whitehaven & Pool and the Overseers at Liverpool & Bristol herewith.

The following day the Board resolved to allow ships from Leith and Greenock one month's pay for proceeding to a Royal Dockyard.[1] If a vessel did not arrive at a dockyard in the time specified by the Board, it did not receive an allowance for the time spent on its passage, and in some cases it was not even chartered.[2] Only when it was in great need of shipping did the Navy Board make allowances to shipowners for the time their ships spent reaching a Royal Dockyard, and in most cases it did not grant any compensation.[3]

When a ship tendered for employment in the transport service arrived at Deptford it was 'surveyed by the master attendant, master shipwright and clerk of the survey at Deptford yard, and . . . hired and freighted on their report'.[4] The first step which they took to ascertain whether a ship was fit for employment was to make a thorough inspection of the ship's timbers, planking, masts, yards, and rigging. The ship was usually grounded out or put upon ways for this inspection, and the dockyard officials determined the condition of the hull by drilling holes in her timbers and planking or by seeing how easily a sharp instrument could be inserted into various parts of the vessel. This is still the classic method of testing the soundness of the hull of a wooden ship. On 8 August 1775 the Deptford

[1] PRO, ADM/106/2602, April 19, 20, 1780.
[2] E.g., PRO, ADM/106/2606, Oct. 24, 1781; ADM/106/2607, Jan. 7, 1782.
[3] E.g., PRO, ADM/106/2605, July 10, 1781.
[4] NRS, *Barham Papers*, ii, 248.

officers reported that they had examined the *Liberty* 'by cutting out several pieces, in the lower frame, between the Hooks, and find several successive Timbers, on the Starb[oard] side, very much decayed, and the ship in general, in those parts damp and defective; We therefore cannot take upon us to recommend her, to be employed as a transport on foreign service'. On 30 November 1775 the Deptford officers informed the Board 'that when we survey'd the Unity transport . . . on Mr. Fletchers ways [on] the 26th August, we were very particular, as we always are in Cases of this kind in examining the Bottom, trying the Seams, Butts & hidden Ends in several places, and after seeing such Works perform's as appear'd to be necessary and the Bottom grav'd, we judged her in every respect fit for His Majesty's Service'.[1]

The rigging of a ship was usually inspected at the same time as the hull and on 31 May 1776 the officers at Deptford reported that 'Whenever a Survey is taken onboard a transport the Rigging is constantly attended to'.[2] In August of that same year, however, the Board told the Deptford officers: 'we have been informed [that] the mizon mast of the [transport] Richmond is found defective and we are very much surprised that so little care is taken in surveying the Masts & Yards of the ships taken into His Maj. Service, and that they [the officers] must be answerable for the consequences if the ship is not in readiness to sail [on] the next tide'.[3] Such oversights, however, were rare. The inspections carried out by the Deptford officers were usually thorough, and a large number of vessels were rejected for charter to the transport service because of structural defects. On 3 February 1779 the Deptford officers reported that the *Fortitude* was 'very Old, defective, & not fit for the Transport Service', and on 26 May 1779 the *Cleveland* was reported as 'old, too small & not fit for the Service'. On 5 November 1779 the *Friendship* was said to be 'defective in boring & not trust worthy'. On the same day the *John* (1) was also declared 'very old, defective and not fit for the service', and the *John* (2) was

---

[1] PRO, ADM/106/3318, f. 15; ADM/106/3402, p. 310.
[2] PRO, ADM/106/3403, p. 33.
[3] PRO, ADM/106/2594, Aug. 31, 1776.

reported as 'defective in boring & not fit for the Service'.[1] It was the policy of the Board not to hire any British ships which had been built in the Netherlands, although in 1776 a number of Dutch ships were chartered by the Board in Holland, and the officials rejected a number of vessels on this ground.[2]

After the Deptford officers had found that a ship was structurally sound and had not been built in the Netherlands, they then proceeded to measure her. The Board did not wish to hire any ship which was less than four feet ten inches high between decks. There appears to have been a misunderstanding, however, between the Board and the officers of Deptford Dockyard, because before 19 February 1779, the dockyard officers were, on the basis of a warrant of 3 October 1754, accepting ships which were only four feet eight inches between decks.[3] A large number of ships were refused employment in the transport service because they were not of sufficient height between decks.[4] The height between the decks of a vessel was of great importance to the comfort and health of any troops embarked.

Of far greater importance, however, to both the Navy Board and the shipowners was the amount of the ship's measured tonnage. As a general rule, the transport service did not hire any ships that measured less than 200 tons burden. The Board often abandoned this policy when it was in great need of shipping and would employ smaller vessels as victuallers under charter parties that ran for only 'six months certain'.[5]

The tonnage of a ship in the transport service was of great importance to both the Navy Board and the shipowners since the freight of a ship was paid on this basis. But as one authority noted, 'There are few subjects which require more investigation than the tonnage of ships; for at present the mode of finding the tonnage of a ship is so replete with error, that a new method is required'.[6] The tonnage of a ship is nothing more than its

[1] PRO, ADM/106/3404, pp. 84, 184, 292–3.
[2] E.g., PRO, ADM/106/2600, May 10, 1779; ADM/106/3403, p. 1; ADM/106/3404, p. 169.
[3] PRO, ADM/106/3404, p. 97.
[4] E.g., PRO, ADM/106/3403, pp. 22, 184, 402.
[5] PRO, ADM/106/2604, Nov. 29, 1780; ADM/106/2607, Feb. 11, 1782.
[6] William Burney, ed., *A New Universal Dictionary of the Marine; Being, A Copious Explanation of the Technical Terms and Phrases usually employed in the Construction,*

volume expressed in tons instead of cubic feet, but the difficulty arises from the fact that it is of necessity calculated by an arbitrary method. On 20 January 1776 the Navy Board ordered the officers of the Royal Dockyards to determine the tonnage of ships being tendered for charter to the transport service by the following method:

to take the length from the Back of the Main Post at the Rabbet of the Keel to a Perpendicular from the Upper Part of the Stem. The Breadth from the broadest Part from out to out of the Plank either above or below the Wale, which shall be found to be the greatest; then subtract 3/5 of the Breadth so found, from the Length thus taken, and the remainder will be the Length of the keel for Tonnage; This Length multiply by the Breadth, and the Product again by half the Breadth, and divide by Ninety four, the Quotient is the tonnage. When there happens to be an After False Post or Posts, it is to be excluded.[1]

The Board modified slightly its method of finding the width of a ship on 16 February 1781, when it ordered that 'the Plank or Thickstuff above or below the Wale where taken all that it exceeds the thickness of the Plank of the Bottom' should be subtracted from the breadth of the ship.[2] Therefore, if L equals the length and W equals the width, the officials of the Royal Dockyards employed the following formula to ascertain the tonnage of a ship:

$$\frac{(L - 3/5W) \times W \times W/2}{94} = \text{tonnage.}$$

However, the formula by which most 'merchants and ship-owners' of the time appear to have calculated the tonnage was to:

Multiply the length of the keel by the breadth of beam, and that product by half the breadth of the beam and divide the last product

Equipment, Machinery, Movements, and Military, as well as Naval, Operations of Ships (London, 1815), 569.
[1] PRO, ADM/95/95, pp. 163–4; ADM/49/134, f. 113.
[2] PRO, ADM/49/135, f. 82.

by 94; and the quotient will be the tonnage. Example, Suppose the ship's keel 72 feet, breadth of beam 24 feet, then

$$\frac{72 \times 24 \times 12}{94} = 220 \cdot 6 \text{ [tons]}.^1$$

The formula employed by the dockyard officers was the tonnage formula in common use modified by defining the length of a vessel as the ship's measured length minus three-fifths of its width. Therefore, the tonnage of a ship calculated by the dockyard officers differed greatly from the amount of tonnage arrived at by the common formula. For example, a vessel with a keel of seventy-two feet and a width of twenty feet will, according to the formula used by the dockyard officers, be 128 tons; but if the formula in common use is employed, the tonnage of the same vessel will be 154 tons. A ship eighty feet long and thirty feet wide will be 297 tons as calculated by the dockyard officers, while the same ship will be 384 tons if the common formula is employed. A ship ninety feet long and thirty-five feet wide will be 586 tons if calculated by the formula in common use, but only 450 tons according to the Navy Board formula. The difference between the two formulae is even greater than it appears at first sight, because for a ship of a given length, the wider the ship the greater the discrepancy. For example, a ship seventy feet long and twenty feet wide, if calculated by the dockyard officers' formula, will be 124 tons, while the tonnage of the same ship will be 149 tons according to the formula in common use—a difference of twenty-five tons. If, however, the ship is seventy feet long and twenty-four feet wide, the difference between the tonnage calculated by the two formulae will be forty-four tons. The dockyard formula gives a figure for a ship's tonnage which is approximately 81 percent of the amount arrived at by the common formula. Because the freight of ships in the transport service was paid according to the measured tonnage of a ship as determined by the dockyard officers, the Board, by modifying the formula in common use, reduced by approximately one-fifth the amount of freight it was obliged to pay for each vessel.

---

[1] Burney, op. cit., 568–9.

The adoption of this special formula, while saving the government money, led to endless confusion and the necessity of having to measure a number of ships at least twice. Understandably, the Deptford officers 'seldom find the Tonnage by measurement equal to what transports are tender'd for'.[1] Even greater confusion resulted from the fact that the Board's order of 20 January 1776, stipulating the method to be used to find the tonnage of ships tendered for charter to the transport service, was transmitted only to the dockyards and not to the agents for transports or any other persons who measured ships for the Board. More surprising is the fact that the Board, once it had become aware that its officials were employing two different methods to calculate tonnage, did little to correct the discrepancy. Lieutenant Stephen Harris, Agent for Transports at Cork, was certainly finding the tonnage of victuallers by the common formula, and it appears that other agents for transports were also employing this method.[2] Instead of rectifying this situation in the obvious way by issuing the correct formula to agents for transports and all others concerned, the Board on 26 September 1781 resolved:

having found upon measurement of ships that have been hired into His Maj. Service abroad and at the Out Ports, a great difference in the tonnage as so measured and what they measured when surveyed by the Officers of any of His Majestys Yards. Give directions to Captain Tonken and Lieut Harris in case of their having occasion to hire any ships that cannot be measured at a King's Yard at the time of hiring to insert a clause in the Charter Party subjecting the owners to a remeasurement by the Officers of one of His Majesty's Yards when opportunity offers & to abide by such remeasurement. Capt. Tonken to circulate it to the other Agents in America. And to add it in future as a clause to the Agents Instructions.[3]

After they had determined the tonnage of a ship tendered to the transport service, the dockyard officers transmitted to the Board a return of the tonnage and a description of the ship. On 27 October 1775, for example, the officers at Deptford Dockyard sent the following return to the Board:

[1] PRO, ADM/106/3404, p. 106.
[2] PRO, ADM/49/125, Oct. 24, 1780.
[3] PRO, ADM/106/2606, Sept. 26, 1781.

In Obedience to your directions of the 20th Ins. we have surveyed and measured the ships undermention'd and find them fit for the Transport Service, and having computed their tonnage, we send you an account thereof with their ages &c. as follows;

Ships Name	Masters Name	Tonnage	Age	Height between Decks			Sort	Form of Bottom
				fore	mid	aft		
Earl of Orford	Jam. Johnson	231	4 years	5' 9"	5' 7"	6' 2"	ship	full
Union	W. Willis	343	6 months	6' 1"	5' 6"	5' 4"	bark	full

Earl of Orford—Built in America, bottom, sheath'd flush fore & aft, is roomly and has good accommodations with a proper lower deck, she is getting ready and will come down as soon as possible.

Union—Built at Whitby, bottom single, has rise to her quarter deck & forecastle is roomly, and has good accommodations . . . she is getting ready and will come down as soon as possible.[1]

When the dockyard officers sent a return of a ship's tonnage to the Board, they would issue directions to the owners to begin fitting their ships for sea.[2]

After a vessel had been measured and inspected by the officers of the dockyards, it then had to be manned, stored, and fitted-out in accordance with the terms of its charter party before it began to earn freight. This task was usually completed fairly quickly because, as the Deptford officers noted, 'it is the owners interest to get down & in Pay as early as possible [and] we presume there is not unnecessary delay'.[3] The shipowners were obliged to supply their ships with all the equipment, such as sails, blocks, and anchors, necessary to make them seaworthy. They were also required to supply provisions for the ships' crews, but not those to be consumed by any troops which might be embarked. Owners were compelled to man their vessels at the rate of seven men per 100 tons of the ship's measured burden and to supply four cables of 120 fathoms each. On 24 May 1780,

---

[1] PRO, ADM/106/3318, f. 10.
[2] PRO, ADM/106/3404, p. 106.
[3] PRO, ADM/106/3404, p. 134.

however, the Navy Board reduced the required number of men to six per 100 tons and the number of cables from four to three.[1]

Owners also had to arm their ships with 'at least six Carriage Guns of six pounders, or less bore as the Board shall think proper according to the size of the ship', and had to provide twenty rounds of ammunition per gun.[2] On 29 November 1779 the Board partially modified this requirement when it resolved 'to permit the owners of the transports to fit them with carronades instead of common guns, taking care they are not less than 12 pounders'.[3] After 26 January 1776 the Board paid the owners of ships an allowance, called 'gun money', of £5 per gun in an effort to prevail upon shipowners to equip their ships with more than six guns.[4]

Before the introduction of payments of gun money, the Board had difficulty inducing shipowners to arm their vessels, and several ships were dispatched unarmed to America during 1775 and 1776 because their owners refused to sign charter parties containing a clause that required their ships to be armed.[5] This was a minor problem, however, when compared to the obstructions that the Commissioners of the Customs placed in the way of arming vessels of the transport service. In 1774 the government had an Order in Council issued 'prohibiting the Exporting out of this Kingdom or carrying coastwise gunpowder or any sort of arms or ammunition'. This prohibition was designed to prevent the Americans from procuring munitions in Britain.[6] The Customs Service applied this ban on the shipment of arms and ammunition to ships proceeding from the Out-Ports to Deptford to be fitted as transports. As a result most of the ships chartered by the transport service in 1775 and the beginning of 1776 arrived at Deptford without guns, and the Board either had to send ships to the ports from which the unarmed transports hailed to pick up their guns, or to obtain

---

[1] PRO, ADM/106/2603, May 24, 1780; SP, 151, Navy Board to Admiralty, Aug. 30, 1780. See above, pp. 97-8.
[2] PRO, ADM/106/2596, July 4, Oct. 3, 1777; ADM/106/3402, p. 315.
[3] PRO, ADM/106/2601, Nov. 29, 1779.
[4] E.g., PRO, ADM/106/279, Sept. 10, 1778; ADM/106/2597, Jan. 30, 1778; ADM/106/2600, July 19, 1779.
[5] NMM, ADM/B/191, Jan. 22, 1776.
[6] PRO, ADM/1/5168, Oct. 19, 1774.

an Order in Council permitting the ship to carry arms before it left its home port for Deptford. Orders in Council were also needed to permit the Board's armed transports to sail from Deptford after being fitted-out. It was not until 9 February 1776 that an Order in Council was issued giving blanket permission for ships tendered to the transport service to carry guns on coastal voyages.[1] The literal application of these regulations by the Customs Service caused many delays in fitting the transports intended to carry reinforcements to North America in the spring of 1776.

After a vessel in the transport service had been manned, fitted, and armed, the owner's only remaining responsibility was to procure the licence required by the Prohibitory Act which would permit his ship to proceed to America. These licences were issued by the agents for transports to the masters of the vessels in the transport service upon payment of a fee of two guineas to the Admiralty.[2]

On the day that a vessel in the transport service had completed its equipment and was fully manned in accordance with the terms of its charter party, it entered the pay of the Navy Board. When a ship was ready to enter into pay, her master or owner signified the fact to the dockyard officers who then reinspected the ship to see if she was complete and everything was in order. A return was then sent to the Navy Board stating that

we have Surveyed the Ship undermentioned hired for the Transport Service, and find her completed, fitted, & victualled, and stored so far as relates to the owners and the masters parts ℔ return, and having all her men on board, was ready to enter into pay the day against her name expressed.

Ships name	Masters name	Burthen	When ready to[3] enter into pay
John & Jane	William Dawson	377	16 April 1777

[1] NMM, SAN/T/1, Jan. 2, 1776; ADM/N/245, Feb. 7, 1776; ADM/B/190, Aug. 21, 1775; ADM/B/191, Jan. 15, Feb. 3, 6, 1776; PRO, ADM/1/5168, March 2, Aug. 5, 1775, Feb. 5, 9, 1776; ADM/106/2593, Aug. 14, 21, 1775.
[2] NMM, ADM/N/246, March 8, 1776.
[3] PRO, ADM/106/3318, f. 90.

Only on rare occasions did vessels under charter to the transport service enter into pay before they had been completely fitted-out and manned by their owners. The Plymouth Dock-yard officers, for example, entered some ships into pay before they were completely ready in February 1776.[1] But this action was contrary to the Board's general policy not to do so until they were 'in every respect complete with stores & provisions on the owners part and ready to sail tomorrow if required'.[2]

Procedures similar to those used to insure that vessels entering the transport service were fit for employment were utilized to make certain that ships were properly repaired and refitted by their owners. Most of the vessels of the transport service returning to Britain from overseas were badly in need of repair and refitting.[3] When a vessel returned from overseas, the Board would order her to be inspected to determine whether or not she was fit for further service. These inspections were usually conducted by dockyard officers, but Lieutenant Stephen Harris, Agent for Transports at Cork, often inspected and supervised the refitting of victuallers.[4] After a vessel had been inspected and found fit for further employment, her owners were ordered to repair and refit her.[5] The owners of ships in need of refitting were required by the ship's charter party to carry out the requisite repairs and to provide the stores and equipment necessary to bring the ship up to a state of seaworthiness approximating that required of ships just entering the service. While a ship was being refitted, it did not continue to earn freight.[6] It was, therefore, in the interest of the owners to complete the refitting as quickly as possible. When this had been done, she was inspected for a second time by the dockyard officers, and, if found properly refitted, was reported ready to begin to earn freight again. For example, on 3 April 1776 the Deptford officers sent the Navy Board the following return:

---

[1] PRO, ADM/108/1A, Feb. 27, 1776.
[2] PRO, ADM/106/2593, Nov. 4, 1775; ADM/106/2594, Sept. 2, 1776; ADM/106/2599, April 12, 1779.
[3] E.g., PRO, ADM/49/2, f. 197.
[4] E.g., PRO, ADM/106/2599, Feb. 12, 1779; ADM/108/1C, June 1, 1782.
[5] E.g., PRO, ADM/106/2601, Dec. 13, 1779.
[6] PRO, ADM/106/3529–30.

We pray leave to acquaint you we have survey'd the ship under-mentioned, returned from America and continued in the Service, and found her completed, fitted and stored so far as relates to the Owners and Masters parts to perform, and all her men on board the day against her expressed.

Ships name	Masters name	Measured burthen	When ready to[1] enter into pay
Jane	Matthew Moran	221 tons	1 April 1776

The officers of the Royal Dockyards appraised all vessels entering the transport service while they were being made ready to enter pay. These appraisals were used by the Navy Board as the basis upon which it calculated the amount of compensation to be paid to shipowners whose vessels were taken or destroyed by the enemy. The hull of a ship was valued by the dockyard officers at a flat rate ' ℔ ton for the tonnage which she is paid freight for'.[2] Also the dockyard officers made a complete inventory of the ship's masts, yards, rigging, stores, equipment, and furniture. Every conceivable object to be found on a ship was assigned a value. All anchors, for example, were valued at 28s per hundredweight and all new copper kettles at 14d for every gallon of their capacity; used kettles were valued at 1s per gallon of capacity. Thus, after taking their inventory, the dockyard officers had merely to affix their assigned value to each item in the inventory and add up the total. This total, when added to the value of the hull, became the appraised value assigned to the ship.[3] These appraisals were then passed on to the Navy Board. For instance, on 8 May 1777 the Deptford officers forwarded the following return:

We pray leave to send you the Valuation of the Ship undermentioned taken into His Majesty's Service (Transp.) in the course of last month.

[1] PRO, ADM/106/3403, p. 7.
[2] PRO, ADM/106/2605, May 5, 1781; ADM/49/125, Oct. 24, 1780.
[3] PRO, ADM/106/3402, pp. 416–17; ADM/49/125, Oct. 24, 1780.

Ships name	Masters name	Burthen	Value of the		Total[1]
			hull, masts & yards	furniture & stores	
John & Jane	W. Dawson	377	£2455.2.0.	£876.18.0.	£3332.0.0.

The dockyard officers were under orders to transmit such returns within fourteen days of the ship entering pay.[2]

When one considers the arbitrary methods employed by the dockyard officers, it is not surprising that many shipowners objected to the appraisals made of their ships. Occasionally, at the request of an owner, the Board would order a second valuation. In 1782 the transport *Royal Club* was appraised twice by the Portsmouth Dockyard officers, but when the owner requested that a third valuation be made by the Deptford Dockyard officers, the Board resolved that 'We cannot depart from the 2nd valuation'. The owner then informed the Board that he 'refuse[d] to submit to the valuation put on her by the officers of Portsmouth yard', to which the Commissioners of the Navy replied that they were 'determined to abide by it' and that as far as they were concerned the matter was closed.[3] In most cases the requests for revaluation received short shrift from the Board.[4] If an owner did manage to induce the Board to order the dockyard officers to revalue his ship, it was unlikely that the original appraisal would be changed.

On 16 November 1781 the Board, at the request of the owners, directed the Deptford officers to reappraise the transport *Free Britain*. The Deptford officers informed the Board on 19 November that they did not see any reason to change their opinion of the value of the *Free Britain*, and the owners of the ship were told by the Board that 'no alteration can be made' in the appraisal.[5] The refusal of dockyard officers to change a valuation of a ship is understandable. It was they who had made the first appraisal and any departure from it would be an

---

[1] PRO, ADM/106/3318, f. 93. The dockyard officers' reports of inspections, measurements, and valuations of vessels tendered to the transport service may be found in PRO, ADM/106/3318, 3402–4.

[2] PRO, ADM/106/2595, Feb. 7, 1777.

[3] PRO, ADM/108/1B, Feb. 26, 1782; ADM/106/2607, March 18, 1782.

[4] E.g., PRO, ADM/106/280, Oct. 16, 1779; ADM/106/2601, Oct. 16, 1779.

[5] PRO, ADM/106/2606, Nov. 16, 19, 1781.

admission that they had made a mistake. However, the ship-owners' wish to have their vessels appraised at the highest possible value is equally understandable, for these appraisals served as the basis upon which the Board calculated the amount of compensation to be paid for ships lost through enemy action.

The measurements and appraisals made by the dockyard officers of vessels entering the transport service were of great importance to the Navy Board, for they supplied it with the information required to settle the ship's freight and the amount of compensation to be paid for vessels which were lost. Despite the fact that the methods employed to determine the tonnage of a ship and its value were somewhat arbitrary, it is clear that without the reports of the dockyard officers it would have been virtually impossible to formulate a rational policy for the payment of freight or compensation. Of far greater importance to the conduct of the transport service, however, was the Board's requirement that every ship which was tendered for employment had to be inspected by the officers of the Royal Dockyards before it could enter the service. There were, especially in the last years of the war, scores of vessels in the service which were in a bad state of repair or whose seaworthiness was doubtful; but most of these vessels had been seaworthy and in good repair when they entered the service and had deteriorated during years of continuous employment. The inspections made by the officers of the dockyards ensured that only ships which were structurally sound, completely fitted and manned, and of the proper dimensions were chartered. During the American War hundreds of ships were rejected by the dockyard officers for employment in the transport service because they were rotten, too old, too low between decks, not properly outfitted, or simply unseaworthy.

CHAPTER VII

The Growth of the Provision Problem, 1775-79

URING the American War of Independence the British
armies were unable to obtain an adequate supply of provisions in North America. As a consequence, thousands
of tons of shipping, scores of warships, and countless troops had
to be diverted to the task of procuring the provisions required to
maintain the British forces in North America. The principal
burden of this task fell on the Treasury, which was in charge of
the transport of army provisions to America from the outbreak
of the war until 1779, when this responsibility was transferred to
the Navy Board. The inability of the British to live off the land
during the American War had important military implications;
it affected the strategies of both the British and American
armies and was undoubtedly one of the major factors in the
ultimate American victory.

Immediately after Lexington and Concord the Americans
invested Boston and 'cut off all supplies of provisions from the
country'.[1] On 19 May 1775 General Thomas Gage, requested
that provisions be sent 'immediately' from Europe, to the army
in Boston because 'All the Ports, from whence our Supplies
usually come, have refused suffering any Provisions or Neces-
sarys whatever, to be Shiped for the Kings Use . . . and all
Avenues for procuring Provisions in this Country [are] shut up'.[2]

---

[1] G. D. Scull, ed., *Memoir and Letters of Captain W. Glenville Evelyn of the 4th Regiment* ('*King's Own*,') *from North America, 1774–1776* (Oxford, 1879), 55. See also PRO, CO/5/92, f. 145; *Diary of Frederick Mackenzie: Giving a Daily Narrative of His Military Service as an Officer of the Regiment of Royal Welch Fusiliers during the years 1775–1781 in Massachusetts, Rhode Island and New York* (Cambridge, Mass., 1930), i, 29.

[2] Clarence Edwin Carter, ed., *The Correspondence of General Thomas Gage* (New Haven, 1933), ii, 679.

The Treasury in the late summer and early fall of 1775 dispatched more than thirty shiploads of provisions for use of the army, but only eight of these vessels reached Boston; those ships which were not captured were driven by the weather to the West Indies. Despite the best efforts of the Treasury, an army officer at Boston as late as 10 March 1776 exclaimed 'Provisions is our want'. Throughout their stay at Boston the British were 'obliged . . . to have recourse to every means and artifice to procure provisions, money, forage, and fuel'.[1]

Although a limited amount of provisions for the army at Boston was obtained from the supplies remaining on board troop transports which had just arrived from Europe, the British soon found it necessary to search for supplies. Transports were sent to Quebec for flour and oats, to Georgia for rice, to St Eustatius for salt provisions. While the coasts of New England were scoured in search of cattle, transports and troops went to Nova Scotia to cut hay and firewood; at one point during 1775 thirty-eight transports were in the Bay of Fundy seeking forage and fuel.[2] Thus, throughout the winter of 1775–76, the British army at Boston supported itself on a hand-to-mouth basis.

While the British forces were passing an ineffectual winter at Boston, the government resolved to dispatch a large army to America to crush the revolt. This decision appears to have been predicated on the assumption that the British forces in the campaign of 1776 would be able to subdue and hold an area in America from which they could draw supplies. The only dissenting voice within the government to the policy of committing British forces to major operations on the North American mainland was that of the Secretary at War, Lord Barrington, who maintained that the employment of large armies against the Americans was a course filled with dangers. He argued that the Americans should be forced to submit by having their sea-borne

---

[1] Eric Robson, *The American Revolution* (London, 1955), 103; Add. MSS., 21680, ff. 77, 93; Add. MSS., 38343, f. 1; PRO, CO/5/92, f. 166.

[2] Troyer Steele Anderson, *The Command of the Howe Brothers during the American Revolution* (New York, 1936), 94; Edward E. Curtis, *The Organization of the British Army in the American Revolution* (New Haven, 1926), 114, 116, 118, 119; NYHSC, *Kemble Papers*, i, 55; Add. MSS., 21680, f. 42; PRO, CO/5/92, ff. 68, 145, 184, 296; CO/5/93, ff. 23–4.

trade destroyed by the Royal Navy.[1] But Barrington's was a lone dissent, for Lord Sandwich undoubtedly reflected the prevailing British opinion of American military capabilities when he told the House of Lords on 16 March 1775: 'Suppose the colonies do abound in men, what does that signify? They are raw, undisciplined, cowardly men. I wish instead of 40 or 50,000 of these brave fellows, they would produce in the field at least 200,000, the more the better, the easier would be the conquest; if they did not run away, they would starve themselves into compliance'.[2] In this state of mind the British resolved to commit the bulk of their army to operations on the North American mainland in the summer of 1776.

On 22 August 1776 the British army landed on Long Island. Victory followed victory throughout the summer and fall of 1776. The Americans were defeated in every major encounter, and by the end of the campaign British forces occupied Newport, Rhode Island, as well as Long Island, the Bronx, New York City, and all of eastern New Jersey. One of the major objectives of the campaign had been fulfilled; by occupying eastern New Jersey the British had gained control of a region from which they could obtain some of the supplies necessary to support the army in America. As early as 1 October 1775 Gage had advocated invading New York because 'it appears to me most necessary for the prosecution of the war to be in possession of some Province . . . from whence you can draw supplies of provisions and forage. And that New York seems to be the most proper to answer those purposes.' Lord George Germain on 21 June 1776 wrote to General Howe that the government hoped 'you have now got a footing in New York, and that you will be able to draw some Part of the supplies for your Army from that Province'. On 30 November 1776 Howe informed Germain that he was occupying eastern New Jersey and 'propose[d] to quarter a large body of troops in that district, without which we should be under much difficulty to find covering forage, and supplies of fresh provisions for the army'.[3] Thus,

[1] Shute Barrington, *The Political Life of William Wildman, Viscount Barrington* (London, 1814), 140–50.
[2] Quoted in Bernard Donoughue, *British Politics and the American Revolution: The Path to War, 1773–75* (London, 1964), 253.
[3] PRO, CO/5/92, f. 291; CO/5/93, ff. 192, 304.

it is understandable that when the King heard that Howe's 'post will extend from the River Delawarr to Rhode Island', His Majesty thought that the army in America was 'in possession of so extensive a Country that he [Howe] will not require to be entirely provided from Europe'. Basically Germain agreed with the King, for he stated that the conquest of eastern New Jersey provided the army with 'extensive and good winter cantonments'. According to Howe, the main purpose of the campaign in New Jersey was 'to get and keep Possession of East Jersey' as an area from which to draw provisions; and by Christmas Day 1776, with the King's troops holding a string of posts along the Delaware River, it appeared to British officials on both sides of the Atlantic that this objective had been attained.[1]

The British occupation of New Jersey, however, was of short duration, for on 25 December 1776 the Continental Army under the command of General George Washington crossed the Delaware River and in a surprise attack annihilated the Hessian brigade garrisoning Trenton. On 2 January 1777 the British launched a strong counter-attack against the Americans at Trenton; but on the night of 2–3 January the Americans slipped around the left flank of the British force advancing on Trenton, and on 3 January attacked and mauled the British 4th Brigade at Princeton. The victory at Princeton jeopardized the British position in eastern New Jersey and opened the way for the Americans to attack New Brunswick. Although the taking of New Brunswick would have cut off the British forces on the Delaware River from their main base at New York, because of the exhaustion of the Continental Army after a week of continuous marching and fighting, Washington decided to break off the engagement. On 7 January 1777 the American forces went into winter quarters at Morristown, New Jersey, a position of great natural strength which enabled Washington to threaten all of eastern New Jersey. In consequence the British were forced to evacuate all of New Jersey except a small bridgehead around Perth Amboy.[2]

The American winter campaign of 1776–77 had far-reaching

[1] G, no. 1950; PRO, CO/5/94, ff. 2, 15.
[2] For an account of the winter campaign of 1776–77, see William S. Stryker, *The Battles of Trenton and Princeton* (Cambridge, Mass., 1898).

effects on the conduct of the war. As one British officer put it, 'Throughout this whole Expedition [the occupation of New Jersey] we certainly allways erred in imprudently separating our Small army of 6,000 men by far too much and must hope it will serve as a lesson in future'.[1] The strategy and tactics adopted by Washington after Trenton and until the end of the war prevented the British from spreading out and occupying large tracts of country from which they could draw supplies to support their forces in America. Washington's strategy, although never formulated, was basically one of keeping the Continental Army intact as a force and stationed in key positions of great natural strength far enough away from the main British force to make the launching of a British surprise attack on his position very difficult, but close enough to threaten large-scale surprise assaults on isolated British detachments. The positions occupied by the Continental Army, such as Morristown, Valley Forge, Middlebrook, and the Hudson Highlands, were picked by Washington because they fulfilled these strategic requirements.

This strategy was facilitated by the irregular nature of warfare in America. For long periods of time the main American and British armies were not in direct contact with each other, and the distance between the two forces was often as much as twenty miles. American bushwhackers, bodies of militia, light troops, and men who were little better than banditti roamed the no-man's-land between the two armies. During the periods between major battles, this no-man's-land was the scene of savage small-unit actions, raids, counter-raids, and countless ambushes. The letters, diaries, and dispatches of British officers serving in America contain hundreds of accounts of these incidents.[2] This American irregular warfare, which from the military point of view is war by flea bites, had a greater effect on the British conduct of the war than is at first apparent. It tied down large numbers of British troops on guard duty, denied the British freedom of movement, and made every excursion from

[1] Harry Miller Lydenberg, ed., *Archibald Robertson, Lieutenant-General Royal Engineers, His Diaries and Sketches in America, 1762–1780* (New York, 1930), 120–1.
[2] E.g., PRO, CO/5/94, f. 31; Lydenberg, op. cit., 124; Eric Robson, ed., *Letters from America, 1773–1780* (Manchester, 1951), 38; *Diary of Frederick Mackenzie*, ii, 661.

the British lines a potential major military operation. Then, lurking in the background behind the bushwhackers, militia, and light troops was a force—the Continental Army—capable of launching a surprise attack and destroying, as it did at Stony Point, any large force which became isolated from the main British army.

Owing to the presence of large numbers of American irregulars and light troops, backed up by the Continental Army, foraging could not be conducted at will by the British because of the fear of ambush. When foraging parties were sent out, they had to be protected by large forces. In effect, most foraging expeditions became large-scale military operations. In the winter of 1777–78 approximately 3000 troops had to be deployed in order to protect British wagon trains along the fifteen-mile road between Chester and Philadelphia. In December 1777 General Howe, in order to procure 1000 tons of hay at Darby, a town approximately seven miles from Philadelphia, was forced to dispatch 5000 troops to protect the foraging parties; but even in the presence of this force there were 'small parties [of Americans] sculking, as is their custom, to seize upon straggling soldiers'. In March 1778 a foraging expedition went down the Delaware River from Philadelphia to Salem, New Jersey, to obtain hay and livestock. It was necessary to guard the foragers with H.M.S. *Camilla* and the 17th, 27th, 46th Regiments, the Queens Rangers, 100 Loyalist Pennsylvania Militia, four cannon, and two howitzers. It was not only in the Philadelphia area that the British had to employ large forces to conduct foraging operations, for in May 1782 it took a naval force of two frigates and some thirty transports to seize a number of cattle on Martha's Vineyard.[1]

The failure of the British forces to obtain adequate supplies of firewood illustrates the nature of the problem confronting them. Timber was the most plentiful commodity in all America, but throughout the war the British forces faced one firewood shortage after another. In New York City the need for firewood

---

[1] Robson, *American Revolution*, 161–2; PRO, CO/5/95, f. 86; Lydenberg, op. cit., 161; Bernhard A. Uhlendorf, trans. and ed., *Revolution in America: Confidential Letters and Journals, 1776–1784, of the Adjutant General Major Baurmeister of the Hessian Forces* (New Brunswick, N. J., 1957), 155–6, 509.

became so great during the winter of 1779-80 that after every tree in the city was cut down the troops broke up ships and houses for firewood; but still there was not enough fuel, and in March 1780 the army ate its rations uncooked.[1] One of the principal reasons for the firewood shortage was the fact that the British forces during the war were concentrated mainly in urban areas, such as Boston, Newport, New York, Philadelphia, and Charleston, where in peacetime most of the fuel consumed by the inhabitants was imported by water. In 1761 Cadwallader Colden estimated that New York City consumed annually more than 20,000 cords of firewood brought by water from New Jersey or Long Island.[2] Thus, during the American War the British for the most part occupied areas which consumed firewood, while the Americans controlled the regions which produced it.

Throughout the war the British made great exertions to procure fuel in America. For example, the coal mines at Spanish River in Cape Breton were worked, and throughout the war numerous transports and warships were used to carry coal from Cape Breton to America.[3] But despite the best of efforts, Cape Breton coal never came near to meeting British fuel requirements, and the British were obliged to resort to foraging. In the first year of their occupation of Newport they denuded of firewood all of Aquidnek, Prudence, and Cononicut Islands, and the shores of lower Narragansett Bay. The British garrison at Newport, after exhausting all the nearby supplies of firewood, in January 1778 began regularly to procure wood on Long Island. Frederick Mackenzie, who exhibited an almost pathological interest in firewood during his stay at Newport, noted in his diary that these woodcutting expeditions to Long Island usually consisted of 100 troops, four or five transports, and a frigate to protect the force from the Americans who were waging a maritime guerrilla war against the British in Long Island Sound.

---

[1] Uhlendorf, ibid., 341; Violet Biddulph, ed., 'Letters of Robert Biddulph, 1779-1783', *American Historical Review* (Oct., 1923), xxix, 92; Oscar Theodore Barck, *New York City during the War of Independence* (New York, 1931), 111-18.

[2] Carl Bridenbaugh, *Cities in Revolt, Urban Life in America, 1743-1776* (New York, 1955), 25-7, 232-5.

[3] E.g., HMC, *American Manuscripts*, i, 200, 251, 280.

This force, which was usually gone for about a month, would return to Newport with approximately 400 cords of wood. The consumption of the garrison, however, was three hundred cords a week. As a result, the troops at Newport existed for long periods with only a two-thirds allowance of firewood, and by the time the British left Newport large numbers of wharfs, houses, and all the town's fences had been converted into firewood. There is no doubt that Mackenzie was correct when he observed, 'It would be less expensive to send coals from England'.[1]

The failure to capture and hold a region of North America from which to draw supplies created a logistical nightmare for the British. As long as the King's forces in America remained penned up on narrow bridgeheads, the great bulk of the provisions, forage, and fuel required to maintain them in America had to be supplied from the British Isles. As one historian has noted, 'the main channels of communication ran straight from Great Britain to the battle lines'. After the debacle of the winter campaign of 1776-77 in New Jersey, General Howe and his Commissary General, Daniel Wier, informed the Treasury 'that all supplies must continue to be sent from hence [Britain], & no certain dependence had of obtaining them in America'.[2]

The continuing dependence of the army in America on British sources of provisions surprised Charles Jenkinson and John Robinson, and both were greatly worried by the expense and difficulties inherent in the task of provisioning an army of 30,000 men operating at a distance of 3000 miles from the source of supply. Despite considerable evidence to the effect that provisions could not be obtained in America, the hope of this died hard in London. In 1778 the King told Robinson that he was 'hurt to find much must depend on chance as to keeping the army well supplied'.[3] In the summer of 1778 Germain put forward the idea that one of the advantages to be derived from an

---

[1] Bridenbaugh, op. cit., 233; *Diary of Frederick Mackenzie*, i, 169-70, 185, 222, 237-8, 302.
[2] G. S. Graham, 'Considerations on the War of American Independence', *Bulletin of the Institute of Historical Research* (May, 1949), xxii, 22; PRO, CO/5/258, f. 34.
[3] Add. MSS., 38209, f. 163; Add. MSS., 37834, f. 1.

invasion of the American South would be that 'from thence Our Islands in the West Indies might draw supplies of Provisions and Lumber for want of which they are now greatly distressed'.[1] When the British invaded the South, however, hopes of obtaining significant quantities of provisions and timber there were dashed by the rise of American guerrilla warfare. British officials both in America and London had to face the fact that the army in America only rarely had control of more territory than the ground upon which the King's troops stood and that there was no escape from the necessity of provisioning the British forces in America from Europe.

The Treasury was the department of the British government responsible for procuring provisions for the army. In the summer of 1775, when it became necessary to succour the army at Boston, the Treasury arranged for the conveyance of provisions to America. A contract was entered into with the firm of Mure, Son, and Atkinson to transport the provisions to Boston 'at the Rate of Freight current in time of Peace, and the Treasury had no concern with the Ships'. The Treasury found, however, that shipping provisions by freight was not satisfactory because a large number of ships went astray. When it became apparent in the first weeks of 1776 that a year's supply of provisions for the army had to be dispatched to America, the Treasury did not welcome the responsibility of providing the shipping required for the task. Unlike the Navy Board, the Treasury did not have any specialized knowledge of maritime affairs; also it lacked personnel with the technical skills necessary to manage shipping, and it had no facilities, such as dockyards, at its command. Thus, at the beginning of 1776, the Treasury suggested to the Admiralty that it take over the responsibility for transporting the army's provisions. The Admiralty, however, rejected this proposal and informed the Treasury that the conveyance of army provisions was 'no part of the Duty of that Office [the Admiralty] and that they could not under take the Service'. The Treasury, therefore, in the winter of 1776 had no choice but to begin to hire shipping to transport army provisions to America.[2]

[1] PRO, CO/5/96, f. 25.
[2] Robson, *American Revolution*, 102–3; Add. MSS., 38343, f. 1.

On 22 February 1776 the Treasury contracted with the firm of Mure, Son, and Atkinson to hire enough shipping to carry the army's provisions to North America. For conducting this business the firm received a commission of $2\frac{1}{2}$ percent. Subsequently, however, the Treasury thought this commission too high. At a meeting on 27 June 1777, for the purpose of reconsidering it, Richard Atkinson, attending on the behalf of the contractors, stated, that although $2\frac{1}{2}$ percent was the usual commission charged by merchants, his firm was willing to act as the Treasury's shipping agent for any commission that the Lords of the Treasury thought proper. As a consequence, on 10 July 1777 the Treasury lowered the commission to $1\frac{1}{2}$ percent.[1]

There is considerable evidence that the Treasury's relations with Mure, Son, and Atkinson were far from satisfactory. According to reports at the Navy Office, Mure, Son, and Atkinson were chartering vessels which had been rejected by the transport service as unfit and Treasury victuallers were sailing for America without any government cargo 'between-decks'. Furthermore, Richard Atkinson was deeply involved in a rum-contract scandal. On 4 February 1778 Charles Cornwall, a Lord of the Treasury, posed the question which must have been on the minds of the entire Treasury Board when he asked Charles Jenkinson 'Whose eye . . . will constantly inspect or control such an agent as Atkinson, or any other, who may be employed?'[2] But the Treasury, unless it could prevail upon some other government department, such as the Navy Board, to take over the responsibility for the transport of army provisions, had no choice but to do business with Mure, Son, and Atkinson, for this firm was highly successful at moving the army's provisions across the Atlantic.

The ships chartered by Mure, Son, and Atkinson to carry army provisions to North America were usually large, heavily armed, well-manned, and for the most part sailed independently or in small groups without naval escort. In order to strengthen the defensive capabilities of these vessels, the Treasury usually

[1] Add. MSS., 38342, f. 314; PRO, T/29/45, f. 27; T/29/46, ff. 97, 115; Curtis, op. cit., 120, 121n.

[2] Add. MSS., 38209, f. 277; SP, 145, Gregson to Shelburne, March 17, 1778; NRS, *Barham Papers*, i, 51.

embarked between twenty to fifty army recruits on board each outward-bound victualler. If there were no army recruits available, extra seamen were employed to help defend the ships. This policy of heavily arming the victuallers and having them sail without escort was very successful, and only a few vessels were captured. This success, however, owed much to luck. If the Treasury had continued to dispatch victuallers without convoy after the entry of the European powers into the war, its rate of loss most likely would have been very much higher.[1]

The Treasury's shipping conveyed enormous amounts of provisions to America. By the beginning of 1778 the Treasury had a fleet of victuallers consisting of 115 ships with a total tonnage of 30,052 tons. From 1776 through 1778 these ships managed to transport all the provisions required to maintain the British army in North America. The only major provision crisis in America during the period when the Treasury was responsible for the transport of the army's provisions occurred at New York in the winter of 1778-79 when the army was reduced to eating oaten bread. This shortage, however, was not due to a failure of transport, but rather to the fact that the officials in America had neglected to inform the Treasury of the increased consumption of provisions brought about by the need to feed Loyalist refugees from Philadelphia. This crisis was successfully surmounted by the timely arrival at New York in

---

[1] It is an axiom of naval warfare that ships sailing without convoy suffer heavy losses from enemy action. Although this doctrine has been rejected at times by ship-masters and naval authorities, usually with disastrous results, it has always been adhered to by underwriters. For example, Major Baurmeister recorded in his journal that in 1778 'English goods arrive from Europe [at New York] insured at 11 per cent with convoy, and 22 per cent without convoy'. Uhlendorf, op. cit., 241-2. And 'In 1782, the premium on a voyage from London to Jamaica was 12 per cent with convoy, or 20 per cent without'. Charles Wright and C. Ernest Fayle, *A History of Lloyd's* (London, 1928), 158. Ships sailing with convoy during conflicts other than the American War in the eighteenth century also paid lower insurance rates than vessels sailing without convoy. In 1739-40 the insurance 'Rates between Genoa and London were ... [in] August [1739] 5 guineas (2 guineas abated if with convoy), October 1739 to March 1740, 8 guineas per cent (3 guineas abated if with convoy)'. A. H. John, 'The London Assurance Company and the Marine Insurance Market of the Eighteenth Century', *Economica* (May, 1958), xxv, 137-8. Similar figures can be amassed for other wars and different trade routes which all point to the conclusion that it is safer to sail with convoy than without it.

January 1779 of a number of victuallers from Cork. The success of the Treasury's fleet of victuallers in transporting the army's provisions to America during the years 1776–78 was a great logistical and administrative achievement.[1]

While it was justifiably proud of its triumphs in the field of ocean transport, the Treasury desperately wanted to be relieved of this responsibility. On 3 June 1777 the Treasury held a meeting to study 'the present state of shipping employed in transporting provisions and stores to America and how far it may be practicable to reduce the price per ton'. At this meeting it was resolved to direct Mure, Son, and Atkinson to inform the owners of ships under charter to the Treasury 'that as many of them will be discharged, a preference of continuing in the Service will be given to those who will take 11/s [per] ton M'. At the same time it was decided to seek the advice of the Navy Board on freight rates.[2] George Marsh, Clerk of the Acts, attended the Treasury on 17 June 1777 and explained the Navy Board's ship chartering policy. In the following month the Board supplied the Treasury with further information on its transport service. The central fact which emerged was that the Navy Board was able to hire shipping at 11s per ton, while the Treasury was paying 12s 6d. The Treasury accordingly attempted to lower its freight rate to 11s per ton, but found that it was impossible to go below 12s.[3] After effecting this reduction, the Treasury took no further action until 25 November 1777, when it resolved to

Write to the Commissioners of the Navy . . . and desire they will attend My Lords Friday next, and inform them whether, as it may be a saving to the Public, on the Discharge of the present [Treasury] Victuallers, in Case of Exigencies of state should require this Service to be carried on to the present extent requiring about 26,773 tons of shipping or lesser Tonnage, the Navy Board can undertake to carry it on at the Rate of 11s ℔ Ton ℔ Month, by ships of sufficient force so as to secure the effectual supply of the army. The provisions to be

---

[1] Add. MSS., 38343, ff. 1–8; Add. MSS., 38375, ff. 45–8; NYHSC, *Kemble Papers*, i, 167, 170, 172; Piers Mackesy, *The War for America, 1775–1783* (London, 1964), 65–9, 222–4.

[2] Add. MSS., 38342, f. 315; PRO, T/29/46, ff. 73–4.

[3] Add. MSS., 38342, ff.315–16; PRO, T/29/46, f. 93.

prepared under Order of their Lordships, and put on Board ships provided by them at Cork.[1]

No account has survived of the negotiation at the end of 1777 between the Treasury and the Navy Board, but on 20 December 1777 the Treasury directed Mure, Son, and Atkinson to discharge every victualler in its employment which would not serve for 11s per ton.[2] The negotiations, however, broke down, and on 16 January 1778 the Navy Board informed the Treasury that it could not take over the task of transporting army provisions because

we find that the great increase of the navy, and equipment of the fleet, which there is in appearance will be further extended, together with the having the heavy load of the transport service upon this office, there being now near 78,000 tons of shipping under our directions, renders it impossible for us to undertake the management of a business of such variety and uncertainty in addition to it, without prejudice to His Majesty's affairs, and subjecting them to disappointments and inconveniences more especially in our peculiar department as commissioners of the navy which no consideration can lead us to hazard.

The Treasury had no choice but to countermand the order given to Mure, Son, and Atkinson to discharge all ships that would not serve for 11s and to continue to employ the shipping already under charter to it at 12s.[3]

After the Navy Board refused to undertake the responsibility for the transport of army provisions, the Treasury in February 1778 examined a plan put forward by Charles Cornwall to reorganize the whole machinery for procuring and transporting army provisions. Cornwall's scheme called for the creation of a board which would be 'under the directions of the Treasury' and 'instructed to purchase, either by public advertisement or otherwise, the provisions, and to engage for the freight necessary'. The new board was to consist of three men. It was proposed that Charles Jenkinson be the chairman of the board and

[1] PRO, T/29/46, f. 181.
[2] Add. MSS., 38342, ff. 316–17; PRO, T/29/46, f. 204.
[3] PRO, T/29/46, f. 224; T/29/47, f. 23; NMM, ADM/B/195, Jan. 16, 1778; SP, 145, Gregson to Shelburne, March 16, 1778.

10—S.A.W.

represent the Treasury, while the other two members were to be a Commissioner of the Navy and a Commissioner of the Victualling. Cornwall thought the inclusion of a commissioner from both the Navy and Victualling Boards was vital to his plan because these men would bring with them a specialized knowledge of shipping and provisions. In order to effect this, Cornwall was prepared not only to let the two commissioners keep their respective seats on the Navy and Victualling Boards, but also to pay them £500 a year in addition to their regular salaries. If this was not enough, Cornwall was prepared to 'go a great way even in enlarging the salary stated in the plan to procure their assistance', for he felt that 'The knowledge & practice these two Com. will bring with them will make the business not a difficult one'. Cornwall's plan, however, appears to have been rejected by the Treasury because of 'difficulties, as to the choice of men & various other circumstances'. The Treasury therefore resolved that its 'freight service must be continued this year, as it has been carried on the last two years —And that it must be left in the very same hands'.[1]

The Treasury did not consider any other proposals until the first months of 1779, when it again entered into negotiations with the Navy Board for that department to assume responsibility for providing the shipping required to transport the army's provisions. These negotiations and their ultimate success were made possible only because there had been a major change in the personnel of the Navy Board. In August 1778 Charles Middleton had become Comptroller. Middleton, unlike his predecessor in the office, Maurice Suckling, was an advocate of administrative rationalization and a bureaucratic imperialist.[2] It is probable that the Treasury entered into the negotiations knowing that Middleton would ultimately accept the responsibility for the transport of army provisions if satisfactory terms for the transfer were arranged.

On 26 January 1779 the Treasury studied once more the problem of transporting army provisions to America and resolved to 'Write the Commissioners of the Navy directing them

[1] Add. MSS., 38209, ff. 277-80, 330-1.
[2] NRS, *Barham Papers*, i–iii, passim.

to attend this Board on Tuesday next the 2d of February'.[1] The entire problem was explained to the Comptroller and several Commissioners of the Navy on 2 February, and at the same time it was proposed by the Treasury that 'the Navy Board should take the same under their Direction and management'. Middleton replied that he would put the Treasury's proposal before the Board, but that before a decision could be reached he required more information about the Treasury's victuallers. He was then invited to put additional questions in writing.[2]

On 4 February the Navy Board discussed the proposal that it assume responsibility for the transport of army provisions and resolved to inform the Treasury that it must have still more information before reaching a decision. At the Navy Board's request Richard Atkinson, on behalf of Mure, Son, and Atkinson, attended one of its meetings to furnish further particulars.[3] Thereupon, on 11 February, the Commissioners of the Navy informed the Treasury that 'We are of the opinion, [that] it will prove not only a Benefit to His Majesty's Service, but a very great saving to the Public, if the management of these Transports [now in the employment of the Treasury] can be made a part of the Duty of this Board'. The Navy Board then went on to outline a number of conditions which would have to be complied with if it undertook the responsibility for the transport of army provisions. It insisted that the victuallers proceed with convoy under naval escort on the ground that while sailing independently might have been suitable 'in the Infancy of the War', now that European powers were belligerents, convoys were required. It also demanded that all the ships chartered by Mure, Son, and Atkinson be replaced by vessels chartered by the Board in order 'to prevent any dispute that may otherwise arise, between us & the Owners'. The letter ended with a long statement to the effect that the Commissioners of the Navy expected a large financial reward from the Treasury in return for relieving it of the responsibility of managing the victuallers.[4] At the same time it was also made clear through unofficial channels

---

[1] PRO, T/29/48, f. 43.   [2] PRO, T/29/48, f. 49.
[3] NMM, ADM/B/198, Feb. 5, 1779; PRO, ADM/106/2599, Feb. 4, 5, 1779; T/29/48, f. 52.
[4] PRO, T/64/200, pp. 2-3.

that the Navy Board was to have complete control over the appointment of all the officials needed to administer the shipping engaged in the conveyance of army provisions.[1] The Treasury considered the Board's terms for undertaking the management of the victuallers on 16 and 23 February and resolved to accept its conditions. It was further decided that the transport service should begin conveying army provisions in May. Only details, such as the size of the monetary reward to be given to the Navy Board, remained to be settled before the transfer of responsibility was complete.[2]

The final terms under which the Treasury would transfer the responsibility for the transport of provisions to the Navy Board were agreed upon in March 1779. After some preliminary negotiations, the Board on 12 March met with the Treasury which agreed to pay

during the Continuance of this service £300 a year to the Comptroller, and each of the other eight Commissioners of the Navy resident in London, and £150 a year to the Secretary of that Board. Also an allowance of £400 to be distributed by them among their Clerks as a reward for their trouble & pains in the execution of this service.[3]

On the same day directions were issued to discharge from service every Treasury victualler upon its return to Europe. On 23 March the Treasury informed the Commissioners of the Navy that 'This Board now depends entirely upon the exertions of the Navy Board, for carrying on the service for victualling the troops serving abroad'.[4]

While the Treasury and the Navy Board believed the transfer of responsibility for the transport of army provisions from the Treasury to the transport service to be an administrative reform which would improve the conduct of the war, the clerks in the Navy Office made no effort to conceal their opposition to the new arrangement. Their principal complaint was that the money granted to them by the Treasury was not an adequate return for the work required to manage the victuallers. There were frequent reports of insubordination among the clerks, and

[1] NRS, *Barham Papers*, ii, 153.   [2] PRO, T/29/48, ff. 56, 60–61.
[3] PRO, T/29/48, ff. 65, 71, 74–5; T/64/200, p. 7; T/64/201, p. 10.
[4] PRO, T/29/48, ff. 75, 85.

on one occasion they went so far as to submit a protest to the Board. But their complaints were rejected by Middleton who informed them that they all 'ought to be discharged' and that if they continued in their refusal to submit to the new arrangement, he would 'enter a new sett of Clerks'. This marked the end of the incipient rebellion, for as one of the clerks explained, they 'sunk under the grand hand of power'.[1]

Of far greater importance than the protest of the Board's clerks was the opposition to the new arrangement by Lord George Germain. On 1 March 1779, after learning of the negotiations between the Board and the Treasury over the management of the army victuallers, Germain had William Knox write to the Treasury requesting a statement of its plans concerning the transport of the provisions. On 9 March the Treasury informed Knox that they 'have it now under their Consideration with the Navy Board, for that Boards undertaking to provide in future Transports to carry out the further supplies for the troops at their respective stations under proper Convoys of His Majesty's Ships of War to be from time to time appointed by the Board of Admiralty'.[2] A week later Germain wrote to the Treasury 'expressing in the strongest terms, his anxiety lest the important service of victualling the Armies abroad should suffer under the Plan now adopted for that purpose'. The Treasury did not answer Germain's letter until 23 March when it sent him all the correspondence, memoranda, and minutes relating to the negotiations with the Board, at the same time informing him 'that the Navy Board having offered to undertake this service . . . [the Treasury] thought it their duty to put it into that Channel'. Germain did not approve of placing control of the army victuallers in the hands of the Navy Board because he had a deep distrust of all naval authorities in general and of Lord Sandwich, the First Lord of the Admiralty, in particular. Germain thought that on numerous occasions in the past the Admiralty and the Navy Board, by not producing warships and transports promptly, had impeded his plans for the conduct of the war in America, and he believed that placing

---

[1] SP, 146, Gregson to Shelburne, [undated].
[2] PRO, T/29/48, ff. 71–2.

army victuallers under the control of the Navy and requiring naval escort would subject them to the same kind of delay and frustration that had characterized his past dealings with the Royal Navy. But Germain's protest proved unavailing, for the Treasury was determined to be rid of the task of managing the victuallers.[1]

The transfer in the spring of 1779 of the responsibility for the transport of army provisions from the Treasury to the Navy Board was a necessary step for the better conduct of the war. When the need for regularly transporting army provisions arose in 1776, the British army was engaged in putting down a revolt in America, and the only naval opposition faced by the King's forces was that of American armed vessels. The entry of France into the conflict changed the war from one fought mainly in America into a world war in which Britain had to face major naval powers while provisioning from the British Isles large numbers of troops not only in North America, but in the West Indies and the Mediterranean as well. In short, the logistical problem confronting the British in 1779 had changed greatly from the one which had faced them in 1776, and the only means of coping with this situation was the centralization and rationalization of the administration of the shipping employed in support of the King's forces abroad. The transfer from the Treasury to the Navy Board of the task of conveying army provisions to troops overseas put into the hands of the Board control of the vast bulk of shipping under charter to the government. The Navy Board was the only department of the British government which had the means and the skill needed to manage the shipping required to maintain the British forces overseas, and there is no question that its assumption of the responsibility for army victuallers greatly mitigated the danger of a disaster arising from mismanagement of the shipping under charter to the government.

[1] PRO, T/29/48, ff. 85-6; CO/5/258, ff. 73-4. For Germain's misgivings about the naval authorities, see Mackesy, op. cit., 53-4, 118-19.

CHAPTER VIII

The Navy Board's Victuallers

WHEN THE Commissioners of the Navy in 1779 assumed responsibility for transporting army provisions, they faced one of the most formidable logistical problems in history. The Navy Board had to transport enough provisions to feed a force overseas which at the end of 1779 numbered more than 63,000 effectives, not counting provincial troops, Loyalist refugees, Indians, and auxiliaries. The task was made even more difficult by the fact that during the American War the British army was not concentrated but deployed in such widely separated places as Minorca and Mackinac. According to Charles Jenkinson, in December 1779, 38,203 effectives (including men under the Convention of Saratoga but exclusive of provincial troops) were in America, 7059 in Canada, 10,510 en route to or in the West Indies, 369 in West Africa, 4930 at Gibraltar, and 2134 at Minorca.[1] In addition to transporting the provisions required to sustain these troops, the Board had to convey enough extra provisions to build up reserve supplies in such places as New York to enable the army to subsist if maritime communications with Britain were cut by enemy naval forces.

Upon assuming control of the transport of army provisions, the Navy Board decided that the victuallers should 'sail from Corke under convoy of H.M. ships of war [which were] to be regularly appointed to that service'.[2] In order to keep to a minimum the number of naval vessels required as escorts, the Board planned to ship vast quantities of provisions in each convoy and, whenever possible, to dispatch the victuallers with the regular trade convoys. It was decided, therefore, that provisions

[1] Add. MSS., 38212, ff. 309–10.
[2] HMC, *American Manuscripts*, i, 398.

for the troops in the Floridas, Georgia, New York, and Rhode Island should be dispatched each year in one or two large convoys to New York, where those bound for the Floridas, Georgia, and Rhode Island would be transhipped. 'The West India supplies if contracted for in England can accompany the usual Fleets & the Quebec ones [can] be put under the protection of the Newfoundland spring ships, & such others as may sail in the course of the year for the River St. Lawrence.'[1]

The success of this plan depended upon the ability of the Admiralty, Navy Board, and Treasury to coordinate their activities. The Treasury had to ensure that the correct amount and type of provisions would be available for loading and shipping at the proper time and place; the Navy Board had to be able to produce the required victualler tonnage at the right place and time; while the Admiralty had to see that warships appeared at the proper place and time to escort the victuallers. If either the provisions, victuallers, or naval escort failed to appear at the right place and time a major mix-up would occur.

Within weeks of taking over the transport of army provisions, the Navy Board found that it was also necessary for it to enforce the Treasury's provision contracts. The Board discovered that it was almost impossible to assemble convoys of victuallers without having control of the machinery for inspecting and receiving provisions into the King's stores. On 3 April 1779 Lieutenant Stephen Harris, Agent for Transports, was ordered by the Board to proceed to Cork, the Treasury's main provision depot in the British Isles, and take charge of the victuallers there.[2] When Harris was sent to Cork, it was thought by both the Navy Board and the Treasury that he would manage only the shipping, and that Robert Gordon, the Treasury's Commissary at Cork, would continue to inspect and receive the provisions from the contractors.[3] Harris and Gordon found, however, that it was

[1] PRO, T/64/200, p. 6. No plan was formulated by the Navy Board in 1779 for the regular supplying of Gibraltar and Minorca as it was recognized that Spanish belligerency presented naval problems in provisioning these places which would ultimately have to be solved by the Admiralty.

[2] PRO, ADM/106/2599, April 3, 1779; T/64/200, p. 13.

[3] PRO, T/64/200, p. 8; T/64/201, p. 16. For a brief account of Robert Gordon's activities at Cork, see Edward E. Curtis, *The Organization of the British Army in the American Revolution* (New Haven, 1926), 83.

impossible to coordinate their activities. Dispute between them apparently arose over disagreements about the best way to load victuallers, but it soon became clear to the Board that the entire organization for processing provisions at Cork would have to be reorganized. On 23 June Harris wrote to the Board:

I am sorry to observe that the Progress made in loading the Transports is so very slow that they will not be ready in less than 10 or 12 days. I have frequently mentioned it to Mr. Gordon, who assures me that . . . the contractors, who ship provisions at the expense of the Crown, have it not in their power to procure a greater number of lighters, or make greater dispatch, how far this may be true I cannot pretend to say from my own knowledge . . . [but everyone at Cork] agree[s] that there are fifty two Lighters employed in the Port & the greatest number that we have had any day since we began to load has been eleven, but oftener six.

Harris went on to say that he had spoken to Gordon concerning

the loss of stowage in the transports in not having a proportion of Half Barrels in every ship, his answer was that he had represented it to the Treasury, who had in some of their contracts provided a few, but in others had not; and I find even in those that they had not confin'd them to any proportion in shipping. . . [and the contractors] sent all their contract in half barrels in one Fleet & the whole [barrels] in another, by which means the Intention of having them was entirely frustrated & the loss of stowage much greater.[1]

On 2 July the Board transmitted copies of Harris's letters to the Treasury and recommended that the loading and stowage of provisions on victuallers be put completely under the control of Harris 'whose judgement and activity we have the best opinion', and on 7 July the Treasury directed Gordon to turn over this task to Harris.[2] The matter, however, did not end there for on 16 July Harris informed the Board:

I am sorry to acquaint you that without your interposition it will not be possible for me to carry on the service here. Mr. Gordon who has long been accustomed to direct the shipping as well as other matters under Government in this Port, still wants to retain that power, & has used every means in his power to continue in it.

[1] PRO, T/64/200, pp. 20–2.
[2] PRO, T/29/48, f. 168; T/64/201, p. 23.

Harris then stated that he and Gordon had had violent disagreements over the best location for transferring provisions from lighters to victuallers. On the same day that Harris wrote to the Navy Board, Gordon sent a letter to the Treasury complaining of the activities of Harris. After considering all the letters from Cork, the Treasury ordered Gordon on 22 July to turn over the management of loading the victuallers at Cork to Harris.[1] Although he complied with this order, Gordon's days at Cork were numbered, for the Navy Board had resolved to reform the entire system of receiving, inspecting, loading, and dispatching army provisions.

During the summer of 1779 it became clear to the Navy Board that the dispute between Harris and Gordon played only a small part in delaying the dispatch of provisions overseas. On 17 May 1779 Gordon reported to the Treasury that the contractors sent English flour to Cork for shipment to America in casks 'so ill coopered that when they come to be pressed and worked in ship, a great quantity of flour works out, and for want of lining hoops in the Heads, the heads sometimes work in, by which means whole barrels are lost . . . [and that] the Pease casks are so very thin & made of such brittle stuff . . . and being [also] made of green wood pease all work out through the joints'.[2] Almost all barrels and casks of English provisions arriving at Cork for dispatch to America were

not fit to be reshipped until they are cooper'd—the greater part of these provisions are received by one House, which has the direction of coopering, and reshipping of them. This House in order to keep as much of the business in it as possible has not employed any extra coopers to give greater dispatch, but have gone on in the old mode of loading, which has been to make the ships wait until they were ready; and it has been carried to such lengths, that ten or twelve sail have been from seven to eight weeks taking in their cargoes.[3]

The Navy Board thought that the loading and dispatch of army provisions could in the future be expedited if a proportion of the provisions were shipped overseas from an English port.

[1] PRO, T/29/48, f. 190; T/64/200, p. 28; T/64/201, p. 24.
[2] PRO, T/1/555, Robert Gordon to John Robinson, May 17, 1779.
[3] Stephen Harris to Charles Middleton, July 20, 1779, Barham MSS. at Exton Park.

This plan would reduce the congestion at Cork and enable the Board to take advantage of trade convoys. Meanwhile, the Board had concluded that it would have to set up machinery to enforce the terms of the provision contracts to insure that contractors would supply fit provisions on time and in containers which could be properly stowed on board ships. On 15 June 1779 the Treasury, which was about to draw up the provision contracts for 1780, asked the Board for any changes and alterations which it wished to have made in the terms of these contracts.[1] A month later, on 15 July, the Board submitted its plan to the Treasury for the conduct of the army provision service in 1780. The Board wanted only the provisions for East Florida and New York and its environs dispatched from Cork, while the provisions for West Florida, the West Indies, and Canada were to be shipped from the River Thames. Thus, instead of shipping English dry provisions to Cork and combining them with Irish wet provisions before shipment overseas, the Board intended to have contractors deliver at Cork only enough English dry provisions to fulfil the requirements of the troops on the east coast of America. At the same time, enough Irish wet provisions were to be delivered at Rotherhithe to be combined with English dry provisions before shipment to fulfil the requirements of the forces in the West Indies, West Florida, and Canada. The Board also requested that the contractors deliver their provisions packed in '200 half Barrels to every 300 Tons of Provisions . . . for the convenience of stowage, as a want of attention to this article in the present contract has been the means of losing much tonnage'.[2] On 23 July the Treasury accepted these recommendations. At the same time the Treasury resolved that all provisions were to be delivered in future 'upon the requisitions of this Board & according to any Orders which the contractors may receive from the Commissioners of His Majesty's Navy'.[3]

In August 1779 the Navy Board began to set up the bureaucracy necessary to carry out its plan to conduct the army provisioning. On 3 August the Board informed the Treasury

[1] PRO, T/64/201, p. 22.   [2] PRO, T/64/200, pp. 25–6.
[3] PRO, T/29/48, f. 193.

that it had appointed George Cherry as its Agent Victualler in the River Thames. This appointment was approved by the Treasury the next day. Cherry, who had formerly been Agent Victualler to Lord Howe's fleet in North America, was to receive a salary of £400 a year 'without Deduction'. On 20 March 1781 his salary was increased to £500 a year. Under the direction of the Navy Board, Cherry was charged with the task of receiving into the King's stores all provisions delivered at Rotherhithe and of making the provisions contractors abide by the terms of their contracts.[1]

After installing Cherry at Rotherhithe as its Agent Victualler in England, the Board next turned its attention to Cork. On 1 September 1779 the Board told Harris that it was 'satisfyed with his conduct notwithstanding the representations of Mr Gordon', and on 23 October Gordon was dismissed from office by the Treasury at the request of the Navy Board.[2] Harris was then empowered to take over Gordon's work until the arrival of the Board's Agent Victualler at Cork. On 28 October 1779 the Board appointed John Marsh to this position.[3] The Treasury approved this appointment on 4 November, and on 8 December 1779 Marsh began to act as Agent Victualler at Cork with the same salary, duties, and powers given to George Cherry.[4] By the end of 1779 the Navy Board had gained almost total control over the machinery for administering and regulating the delivery of army provisions into the King's stores by the contractors.

With the cooperation and support of the Treasury, the Navy Board next launched a sustained campaign to simplify and rationalize the procedures for inspecting, loading, and dispatching provisions. One of the first steps taken by the Board to speed up the loading of victuallers was to move its English provision depot from Rotherhithe on the Thames to Cowes on the Isle of Wight in the summer of 1780. The loading of victuallers in the Thames was a long and laborious task due to the shortage of

[1] PRO, T/29/48, f. 211; T/29/50, f. 38; T/64/200, pp. 32–3, 36.
[2] PRO, ADM/106/2601, Sept. 1, 1779; T/29/48, f. 269.
[3] Nothing is known of John Marsh's career before his appointment as Agent Victualler at Cork. He was an expert on provisions and most likely had served as some kind of official, such as an agent victualler, in the navy's victualling service.
[4] PRO, T/29/48, f. 269; T/29/49, ff. 3, 30, 55; T/64/200, pp. 43–4; T/64/201, pp. 45, 47.

docks and wharfs from which vessels could be loaded at any tide. Thus, most vessels had to be loaded while lying at anchor in the river from lighters which were in short supply. It was also found that the area occupied by the victualling depot was too small to permit the proper inspection of large quantities of provisions. The Board thus welcomed the offer put forward by a Mr Mackenzie to rent to it a large provision depot at Cowes. Cowes had a major advantage over Rotherhithe in being adjacent to the great anchorage at Spithead, where most convoys proceeding overseas were formed. Outward-bound victuallers, therefore, would not have to proceed from the Thames to Spithead before joining their convoys, and the ships carrying Irish provisions to England for transhipment would have their voyage shortened considerably. After receiving a report from Cherry stating the advantages of Cowes as a location for the provision depot, the Board accepted Mackenzie's proposal on 24 March 1780 and secured the approval of the Treasury by the end of the month. The victualling depot which was moved to Cowes in the summer of 1780 remained there until the end of the war.[1]

In order to speed the dispatch of victuallers, the Navy Board prevailed upon the Treasury to eliminate or simplify many of the customs procedures required for the victuallers. On 30 November 1779 the Board requested that the Treasury authorize John Marsh to sign 'Lighter Bills' as Robert Gordon had been empowered to do. The Treasury said that it did not know the meaning of the term 'Lighter Bill', but if it meant giving Marsh the power to clear vessels through customs the Treasury could not do this, for although Gordon had had the authority to sign customs clearances and discharges, he had been not only the Treasury's Commissary at Cork, but also a surveyor general in the Irish Customs Service. The Board, however, would not be put off and on 29 January 1780 it wrote to the Treasury complaining that the customs officers in England would not allow Irish provisions to be transhipped in English ports until after they had been landed and gone through customs—a great nuisance which wasted time and cost large amounts of money in labour, breakage, and lighter rent. The Board requested,

[1] PRO, T/29/49, ff. 72, 121; T/64/200, pp. 79–83; T/64/201, p. 55.

therefore, that it be permitted to tranship Irish provisions in English ports without having to go through customs. On 4 February 1780 the Treasury complied with the Board's request and issued orders accordingly to the Customs Service. On 17 February 1780 the Treasury, also at the request of the Board, issued directions to the Irish customs officials to permit the transhipment of English provisions at Cork without having to pass them through customs.[1]

On 6 November 1780 the Navy Board put forward another suggestion that resulted in a reduction of the time spent by victuallers in passing through customs. The Navy Board thought:

As allowing Bounty to the Contractors on the Exportation of flour, subjects the business of shipping Provisions to the Custom House and in many instances occasions delays from Holidays &c . . . it is submitted whether allowing the Contractors a Price adequate, and not permitting them to draw the Bounty, will not be more for the Good of the Service.

At the same time the Board stated that since contractors shipping army provisions from Ireland had to pay an export duty for which they were later reimbursed by the Treasury, 'it is proposed to save that trouble by leaving the Contractor liable thereto, making compensation by an adequate advance in the Price [of provisions]'.[2] These suggestions were apparently accepted by the Treasury, for in the spring of 1781, at the request of the Navy Board, it cut the customs procedures which the victuallers were required to pass through to the barest minimum without totally removing these vessels from the jurisdiction of the Commissioners of the Customs. On 12 April 1781 the Treasury ordered that all customs officials were 'to consider Victualling Transports in every respect as Navy Transports and to act accordingly'.[3]

---

[1] PRO, ADM/106/2602, Jan. 29, 1780; T/29/49, ff. 16, 44, 55; T/64/200, pp. 64-5, 67-8.

[2] PRO, T/1/560, Navy Board to Treasury, Nov. 6, 1780, enclosing Memorandums having reference to the Treasury Contracts for Army Provisions for the Year 1781; Improvements suggested in the mode of making new contracts for the army in America, [undated], Barham MSS. at Exton Park.

[3] PRO, T/29/50, ff. 46, 65.

The Navy Board also succeeded in effecting a major reform in the handling of provisions shipped to and from Ireland. Most wet provisions consumed by the army were procured in Ireland, while the bulk of the dry provisions was produced in England. In the contracts of 1779 and 1780, the contractors were required to deliver at Cork all English dry provisions destined for the forces on the American east coast. At the same time they had to deliver to Rotherhithe or Cowes all Irish wet provisions consumed by the troops in Canada, the West Indies, and West Florida. The fault in this system lay in the fact that provisions requiring transhipment had to be loaded and unloaded at least four times. For example, a cask of English flour bound for New York had to be loaded at Cowes, unloaded at Cork, then put on another ship bound for America, and finally unloaded a second time upon reaching New York. In many cases, moreover, not enough time for conducting a proper inspection of the provisions and their containers was allowed before they were taken into the King's store. Also, if there was a long delay in unloading the provisions from the contractors' ships, the government was liable for demurrage.[1]

In 1781 the Treasury eliminated the worst features of the system of transhipment employed during the preceding two years. At the request of the Navy Board the Treasury changed the terms of the provision contracts to require that all Irish wet provisions be delivered to Cork and that all English dry provisions be delivered at Cowes, thus reducing from four to two the number of times that transhipped provisions had to be put on and taken off ships.[2] After the introduction of the provisioning contracts of 1781, the only transhipped provisions which had to be unloaded and then reloaded at either Cork or Cowes were those destined for garrisons, such as Goree, which were not large enough to require an entire shipload of either wet or dry provisions at one time.

[1] PRO, T/1/560, Navy Board to Treasury, Nov. 6, 1780, enclosing Memorandums having reference to Treasury Contracts for Army Provisions for the Year 1781; T/64/200, p. 58.
[2] Improvements suggested in the mode of making new contracts for the army in America, [undated], Barham MSS. at Exton Park; PRO, T/1/560, Navy Board to Treasury, Nov. 6, 1780, enclosing Memorandums having reference to Treasury Contracts for Army Provisions for the Year 1781.

The Navy Board also attempted to strengthen the enforcement of the provision contracts, a step vital to its success in conveying army provisions abroad. One of the most difficult and frustrating problems faced by the Board was the failure of the contractors to deliver provisions into the King's stores at the times specified by their contracts. As early as 23 November 1779, the Board had complained of the ill effects of late deliveries and suggested that penalty clauses be inserted in all provision contracts as a means of preventing non-compliance with the terms of these agreements.[1] In 1780 the provisions for the troops in the West Indies and Canada failed to appear at Rotherhithe in time to be shipped with the spring convoys. This failure was considered by the Navy Board on 8 May 1780, and it was resolved to 'take notice of the disappointments & dangers that may attend the army abroad if the contracts are not more punctually complied with'.[2] On the same day the Board sent the Treasury an account of the amount of provisions which had been delivered at Rotherhithe and warned that it would be difficult to supply the army in Canada and the West Indies unless the contractors punctually delivered the provisions.[3] Upon receipt of this report, the Treasury warned the contractors that if they did not abide by the terms of the contracts and deliver the provisions at the correct times the Treasury would sue them for breach of contract. Despite the best efforts of the Treasury, it was too late in the season to repair the damage done by the late deliveries made by the contractors. When the last Quebec convoy of the 1780 season was assembled in the middle of August, George Cherry reported to the Navy Board that contractors had failed to deliver 54,920 pounds of beef and 229,767 pounds of butter in time to be shipped to Canada.[4]

On 4 August 1780 the Board stated to the Treasury that it thought the best way to make army provision contractors abide by the terms of their contracts was to include in the Treasury

[1] PRO, ADM/106/2601, Nov. 23, 1779; T/64/200, pp. 49–50.
[2] PRO, ADM/106/2602, March 27, 1780; ADM/106/2603, May 8, 1780; T/64/200, pp. 69–70.
[3] PRO, T/64/200, pp. 86–7.
[4] PRO, T/29/49, ff. 99–100; T/64/200, pp. 106–7.

contracts penalty clauses similar to those used on the Navy's Victualling Board contracts.

In the Contracts for supplying his Majestys *Ships* abroad with provisions, the Contractor is obliged by the conditions of his Contract, to have always ready, whatever Quantity may be demanded of him, and in case of failure either as to time, quantity, or quality, the Commanding Officer has a power to purchase what may be wanted, let the price be what it will, and the difference is charged on the Contractor . . .

We must beg leave to represent to their Lordships that unless the Contractors for supplying the Army abroad with Provisions are obliged by considerable Penalties to deliver them at stated periods agreeable to the terms of their Contracts, the Service will at all times be considerably retarded, and the consequences may prove fatal to the Troops. This is a circumstance which we think the more necessary to urge to their Lordships at this time, as the want of punctuality in the present year . . . has prevented us from making use of opportunities of convoy which we had provided for.[1]

Despite the protests of the Navy Board, army provisions continued to arrive late at the depots. The victuallers which were intended to convey a year's provisions to the garrison at Halifax, for example, were prevented from sailing in the spring of 1782 because the contractors did not deliver the required wet provisions. The Board, after waiting more than six weeks for these wet provisions, had the Treasury break the contract and issue orders for Halifax to be supplied from the stores in New York.[2]

The Navy Board, however, did have a way of making contractors deliver their provisions on time. Before a contractor could be paid, he had to produce a receipt signed by either George Cherry or John Marsh stating that he had delivered into their hands a certain amount of provisions, and at times Cherry and Marsh refused to accept and sign for provisions which were delivered late. The firm of Henniker and Devaynes complained to the Treasury on 18 May 1781 that unless it was granted an 'Indulgence for some little Extention', the firm

[1] PRO, T/64/200, pp. 104-5.
[2] PRO, T/1/570, Navy Board to Treasury, April 3, 1782; ADM/106/2607, March 11, 22, 26, 1782; ADM/106/2608, April 3, 1782.

11—S.A.W.

would be left holding a large amount of provisions because Cherry had informed it 'that what shall not be tender'd within the said 15 July will not be received at all', and it would not complete the deliveries by that date.[1] Despite this pressure which the Board could exert on the contractors, the Commissioners of the Navy were plagued until the end of the war by the problems caused by the tardy delivery of provisions.

Another source of delay in the dispatch of victuallers was the failure of the contractors to deliver into the King's stores 'provisions [which] are good, sound, and wholesome, and [in] packages sufficient and fit for His Majesty's Service'.[2] Marsh and Cherry rejected and condemned large quantities of provisions delivered by the contractors as being unfit for human consumption or for being packed in substandard containers.[3]

Added to the frustrations and delays caused by the delivery of bad provisions in unfit containers was the uncooperative conduct of the contractors' agents at Cork. On 2 January 1780 Marsh informed the Board that a shortage of space for storage was developing at Cork because the agents for the contractors refused to remove condemned provisions from the warehouses. The matter was referred to the Treasury, which on 17 February 1780 directed the contractors to 'forthwith order their agents to remove their condemned provisions from his Majesty's storehouses at Cork, otherwise they will be put out'.[4]

It appears that the contractors' agents at Cork were trying to cause so much confusion that it would be difficult, if not impossible, to conduct a proper inspection of the provisions being delivered into the King's stores. On 12 February 1780 Marsh reported:

[I] must beg leave to remark that it is with the utmost difficulty I can keep any exact Accounts from the Irregularities of the Agents [of the contractors], and the little Assistance they give, as well as the confusion that is caused by the provisions coming in such bad order

---

[1] PRO, T/1/567, Henniker and Devaynes to Treasury, May 18, 1781.
[2] PRO, T/1/563, receipt issued on April 25, 1780 to Browne and Conner by George Cherry.
[3] E.g., PRO, T/29/50, f. 30; T/64/200, pp. 46, 52–3, 99–100; ADM/106/2602, March 7, 1780; ADM/106/2606, Sept. 3, 1781.
[4] PRO, T/29/49, ff. 99–100; T/64/200, pp. 56–7; T/64/201, pp. 52–3.

principally with respect to the Casks, and the Damages they sustain, which renders the closest Inspection necessary, particularly with regard to wet provisions, which I am obliged to examine very minutely from having discovered Impositions that are attempted, & been under the necessity of rejecting some large supplies of Beef and Butter, finding the former to be for the most part lean Cow Beef, and the Butter of an inferior Quality . . . [which] causes a most extraordinary Delay and trouble from whence the service may suffer if the Agents in future do not comply better with their contracts.[1]

After numerous complaints by the Agent Victuallers of the disorders caused by the contractors' agents, at the beginning of 1781 the Treasury had the contractors supply Cherry and Marsh with the names of all their agents, and on 28 March 1781, at the request of the Navy Board, the contractors were limited to maintaining only one agent each at Cork and Cowes.[2]

In 1780 and 1781, in an attempt to prevent the delivery of unfit provisions in substandard containers, the Navy Board requested that the Treasury insert a number of new clauses in the provision contracts. On 6 November 1780 the Board requested that the provision contracts for 1781 include terms requiring that all peas be properly dried before delivery, that the contractors' warranties be extended from six to twelve months, that the 'strongest injunction' be put in the contracts to prevent the use of unfit containers, and that due to the

Inconvenience arising from the Packages of Beef and Pork not containing equal weights, and the particular Pieces being cut of various sizes, it is further proposed to stipulate that each Barrel of Beef shall contain 30 Pieces of 7 Pounds each, making 210 Pounds, and each Barrel of Pork 52 Pieces of 4 Pounds each, making 208 Pounds, & half Barrels in Proportion. The Pork to be free of Heads & Feet & the Beef from Legs, Shins, & Marrow Bones.[3]

The Treasury accepted these proposals, and by 30 November 1780 the contractors had agreed with the stipulations set forth by the Commissioners of the Navy with the exception of the

[1] PRO, T/64/200, p. 74.
[2] PRO, T/29/49, f. 268; T/29/50, f. 47.
[3] PRO, T/1/560, Navy Board to Treasury, Nov. 6, 1780, enclosing Memorandums having reference to Treasury Contracts for Army Provisions for the Year 1781.

requirement calling for an extension of the warranties from six to twelve months. A compromise, however, was agreed upon whereby a contractor's warranty would continue to run for only six months, although it would begin on the actual date of delivery instead of the day stated in the contracts.[1] The Navy Board, still dissatisfied with the six months' warranty in the 1781 provision contracts, continued to put pressure on the Treasury for an extension of the warranties. On 5 September 1781 the Board convinced the Treasury that it should push for 'insurance of flour by the contractors for twelve months instead of six', and on 8 November 1781 the Treasury and the contractors agreed

That five Barrels of Flour shall be taken promiscuously from each 1,000 Barrels delivered to be kept in proper warehouses under the joint keys of the Commissary & Contractors, which samples shall be examined at the Expiration of 12 months from their Delivery, when, if found good, the Contractor to be no further liable, if otherwise, the Contractor to be answerable for all Damages, which may have arisen in the year from the bad quality of the flour only.[2]

Despite the rejection of large quantities of provisions and a general tightening of the terms of the provision contracts, the Board was never able to overcome the problem of the contractors supplying bad provisions in substandard containers. Almost every report from the armies overseas contained complaints about the state of provisions arriving from Europe. On 11 November 1779, for example, Daniel Wier, Commissary General at New York, complained to the Treasury of the 'insufficiency of [provision] ... Packages', and on 27 June 1780 Wier informed the Treasury that a measurement of the contents of a number of five-bushel pease casks upon arrival from England showed that the contents of these casks averaged only 'four bushells, seven quarts one pint each'. On 16 December 1780 Wier wrote from New York: 'The Provisions, I am happy to acquaint their Lordships are remarkably good, and the packages, much better than sent out before, the flour, not withstand-

<hr>

[1] PRO, T/29/49, f. 227.
[2] PRO, ADM/108/4A, Sept. 5, 1781; T/29/50, f. 227.

ing falls short, from six to ten pounds ℔ barrel, & the butter
. . . is much more deficient.'[1]

Early in 1781 the Navy Board started to put into effect
measures to find out what caused the apparent shrinkage of
provisions in transit. The Board not only wanted to prevent
this shrinkage, but also to determine who was at fault because
'the contractors are only subject to replace provisions when they
do not keep good the time warranted by contract or prove
inferior thereto . . . for any damage which may be otherwise on
the masters part we mulct the ship, but under circumstances of
weather, or loss of ships the public must sustain the loss'.[2] On
27 February 1781 the Treasury, at the request of the Navy
Board, directed the commissary generals overseas 'to examine
one barrel of provisions in ten, in order to ascertain the average
weight . . . & from time to time to make returns to this Board,
and also to the Agent Victualler at each port of any deficiencies'.[3]
The Navy Board on 1 August 1781 supplemented the Treasury's
orders by requesting that the commissary generals dispatch to
the Navy Office lists of all victuallers unloaded under their
direction, 'distinguishing the species & quantity deficient in
each ships cargo and the cause from whence the same may have
arisen whether proceeding from embezzlement, insufficiency of
casks, bad stowage, or what other cause'.[4]

Dissatisfied with the steps taken in 1781 to tighten up the
inspections of provisions arriving in overseas ports, the Navy
Board had the Treasury on 27 July 1782 issue to the commissary
generals a standardized 'Form of a Return . . . [to be employed]
in transmitting Accounts of provisions'. And on 23 September
1782 the Board directed that all agents for transports 'when
they find any cask or provisions defective to be very particular
in the account they give thereof especially as to the ships name
it is in & when & where shipped'.[5] The innovations in the
system of inspecting army provisions introduced by the Navy

[1] PRO, ADM/108/4A, March 13, 1781; T/29/50, ff. 16, 17, 25; T/64/201,
p. 100; T/64/114, p. 218.
[2] PRO, ADM/106/2608, June 14, 1782.
[3] PRO, ADM/108/4A, March 8, 1781; T/29/50, f. 22; T/64/201, p. 97; T/64/104,
p. 24; T/64/119, f. 40.
[4] PRO, ADM/106/2605, Aug. 1, 1781.
[5] PRO, ADM/106/2609, Sept. 23, 1782; T/64/105, p. 40; T/64/107, p. 76.

Board appear to have attained the desired effect, for on 4 August 1783 Nathaniel Day, Commissary General in Canada, reported to the Treasury that 'With respect to the new supply of provisions so far as time [h]as permitted an Examination they appear to be sweet sound & wholesome [and in] every way fit for issuing to His Majesty's Troops, the packages in good condition being the strongest & best that have yet come to this Province'.[1]

The failure of the Admiralty to provide promptly warships required to escort outward-bound convoys of victuallers was yet another of the many problems which confronted the Navy Board in its efforts to transport provisions to the troops overseas. Several times during the years from 1779 to 1780 the Board saw months of preparation and labour wasted by the failure of the naval vessels required to escort the convoy to appear at the appointed time and place. This situation was partly caused by the great shortage of frigates and sloops-of-war in the Royal Navy brought about by a prewar building policy which had concentrated on the construction of ships-of-the-line instead of escorts. For the most part, however, such delays were the fault of the Admiralty, for when it consented to allow the Navy Board to take responsibility for the transport of the army's provisions, it did not fully comprehend the scope, nature, and importance of the task. Thus, it appears that the Admiralty at first underestimated the number of escorts required to convoy the army's provisions and during 1779 and 1780 tended to assign a low priority to the task of escorting army victualling convoys.

The Navy Board had planned that the provisions required by the forces on the east coast of America should be carried each year from Cork in two large convoys. It was intended that the first group of victuallers should depart for America in the late spring or early summer, and that the second convoy should leave Ireland in the late summer. On 17 March 1779 the Board wrote to the Admiralty requesting that naval escorts be supplied for the group of victuallers which were intended to sail from Cork for New York in May or June 1779. At the same time the Board

---

[1] PRO, T/1/580, Nathaniel Day to Treasury, Aug. 4, 1783.

wrote to the Treasury requesting that it 'solicit' the Admiralty to grant a convoy for the victuallers.[1] The Treasury wrote a second time to the Admiralty on 27 March requesting that 'their Lordships [of the Admiralty] . . . give the necessary Orders for stationing and appointing from time to time such convoys as may be adequate to the great importance of this service'. At the same time the Treasury stated that it had

received a letter from Lord George Germain expressing in the strongest terms his anxiety, least the important service of victualling the Armies abroad should suffer under the Plan now offered for that purpose —And, that My Lords think it necessary to repeat to their Lordships [of the Admiralty] their earnest request that the greatest attention be paid to this service; as the Preservation of the Armies in America will depend on the punctuality of the convoys.

On 30 March the Admiralty told the Navy Board that the convoys it requested would be provided.[2] By 27 May 1779 the Board had assembled 8000 tons of victuallers at Cork to carry the first embarkation of provisions to New York and shortly thereafter Sir Andrew Snape Hamond in H.M.S. *Roebuck*, the escort, arrived at Cork. But because of delays in loading the ships, the convoy did not sail until 19 July. Hamond complained to the Admiralty which in turn sent protests to the Navy Board and Treasury.[3] The failure of the first New York-bound convoy of victuallers to leave Cork at the appointed time appears to have been the fault of Harris and Gordon, who did not make the correct arrangements for the loading of the ships.

The departure of the second group of victuallers from Cork was delayed for several months when the naval escort failed to appear. On 5 June 1779 the Board requested escort from Cork to America for the second division of victuallers and was informed by the Admiralty on 8 June that the escort would be provided. On 9 July the Board reminded the Admiralty of the

[1] NMM, ADM/B/198, March 17, 1779; PRO, T/64/200, p. 8.
[2] PRO, ADM/1/4288, March 27, 1779; T/29/48, f. 82; NMM, ADM/N/248, March 30, 1779; HMC, *American Manuscripts*, i, 404–5.
[3] NMM, ADM/N/249, July 5, 1779; T/29/48, f. 208; T/64/200, p. 103.

need for escorts for its victuallers.[1] By 4 September the victuallers at Cork were loaded, and on 6 September the Board wrote to the Admiralty requesting that 'the Ships intended to convoy them may be ordered as soon as possible as the season of the year advances so fast as to make us apprehensive for the security of their passage'. The Admiralty told the Board on 15 September that H.M.S. *Richmond* and H.M.S. *Raleigh* had been ordered to Cork to escort the victuallers to America.[2] In the summer of 1780 the Board stated to the Treasury that the delay in the sailing of the second division of victuallers from Cork in 1779 had resulted 'from the circumstance of the United Fleets being masters of the Channel and Contrary winds'.[3] There appears to have been more to the story than that, however, for on 16 September 1779 the Board wrote to the Admiralty saying that it had 'accidentally heard' that H.M.S. *Richmond* was proceeding to Cork with a convoy under escort and there was also talk in naval circles to the effect that H.M.S. *Richmond* was further delayed because when the Admiralty 'ordered her to be victualled for foreign service they omitted to order her to be stored, so that when she joined the Raleigh at Ply[mouth] it was found that she was only stored for Channel service'. Finally, on 24 December 1779, the second division of victuallers left Cork for America carrying six months' supply of provisions which had been intended for consumption in 1779.[4]

In the early summer of 1779, the Navy Board began to formulate plans for the conduct of the victualling service in 1780. On 28 and 29 June and 5 July 1779 the Board requested that the Admiralty tell it when the trade convoys were to be dispatched to the West Indies, New York, Newfoundland, and Canada, so that victuallers could be sent with these convoys. On 4 September 1779 the Board, on the basis of the information supplied by the Admiralty, submitted its proposals to the Treasury for conducting the victualling service in 1780. The

[1] NMM, ADM/B/199, June 5, 1779; ADM/N/248, June 8, 1779; PRO, ADM/106/2600, July 9, 1779.

[2] NMM, ADM/B/199, Sept. 6, 1779; ADM/N/249, Sept. 15, 1779; PRO, ADM/106/2601, Sept. 6, 1779; T/64/200, p. 103.

[3] PRO, T/64/200, p. 103.

[4] NMM, ADM/B/199, Sept. 16, 1779; PRO, ADM/106/2601, Sept. 16, 1779; T/64/200, p. 103; SP, 146, Gregson to Shelburne, [undated].

Board's plan called for the provisions intended for the army on the east coast of America to be conveyed in two large fleets which were to sail from Cork at the end of May and July. 'By this means we shall hope to get the whole shipped & sent away at a proper season so as to avoid Accidents of weather that must necessarily attend a fleet at a late period on the coast of America.'[1] Thus, the Board intended to follow the same plan for the transport of provisions to Sir Henry Clinton's army as the one attempted in 1779, but again the scheme failed. The ships were delayed at Cork for a variety of reasons, including a delay in loading and the late arrival of the naval escorts, with the result that no provisions of the 1780 contract arrived at New York until November 1780. Clinton, enraged when the army's provisions failed to arrive on time from Britain, dispatched a staff officer to London with a protest to lay before Germain, while Daniel Wier sent an emissary to England to explain the situation to the Treasury. Clinton also deluged the authorities in Britain with a series of complaints and protests about the lack of logistical support he was receiving.[2] The failure during 1779 and 1780 to load and dispatch promptly the victuallers to the army in America, when coupled with similar miscarriages which occurred in the shipment of provisions to Canada, convinced the authorities in London that a change had to be made in the arrangements for the conveyance of the army's provisions.

In the summer of 1780 Germain inaugurated a general review of the conduct of the army victualling service. On 21 July 1780 he wrote to the Treasury concerning the delays in the dispatch of provisions overseas:

besides the danger of Want which the long delay of Convoys may Occasion their infrequency and irregularity must prove extremely prejudicial to the Provisions . . . which ought to be sent out as soon after they are made up as possible, which was the case when they were shipped in Armed Vessels that Sailed without Convoy, but has

[1] Navy Board to Admiralty, June 29, 1779, Barham MSS. at Exton Park; NMM, ADM/B/199, June 28, 29, July 5, 1779; PRO, T/64/200, p. 39.
[2] PRO, ADM/106/2604, Oct. 3, 1780; CO/5/100, ff. 143, 298–9, 309; T/64/110, f. 66; T/64/201, pp. 71–2; William B. Willcox, ed., *The American Rebellion: Sir Henry Clinton's Narrative of His Campaigns, 1775–1782, with an Appendix of Original Documents* (New Haven, 1954), 210, 220, 455–6.

not been so since the Victuallers were . . . obliged to wait for Convoy. On these Accounts and in Compliance with Sir Henry Clinton's Representation and request, it becomes my Duty to State to your Lordships the Inconveniences with which the present mode of sending out the Provisions to the Troops have already been Attended, and to repeat my Apprehensions of the Fatal Consequences which may follow.[1]

On 26 July the Treasury resolved to send a copy of Germain's letter to the Admiralty, at the same time requesting that it 'grant all such convoys for provision transports in future as shall seem by the Commissioners of the Navy to be necessary for the effectually carrying on this service'. An extract of Germain's letter was also dispatched to the Navy Board with a covering note directing the Board to pay the 'utmost Attention' to this 'most essential service'. Germain was told by the Treasury 'that as this service was put under the management of the Commissioners of the Navy after mature Consideration; and as the armed transports are now discharged, & their guns & stores disposed of, it is impossible to revert to that mode of carrying on this service'. The Board received and read the extract of Germain's letter sent to it by the Treasury on 29 July, but did not take any action on the matter for several days. On 4 August, however, the Board sent a long letter to the Treasury which reviewed the entire history of its conduct of the army victualling service and either refuted or denied every one of Germain's complaints. The Board's letter also contained the request that in the future the Treasury 'will not give Ear to the insinuations & representations of disappointed Men, who have been used to advantages that cannot be obtained whilst this business is under our directions'.[2]

On 25 August 1780, in answer to the Navy Board's letter of 4 August, the Treasury stated that it was 'at a loss to judge what is meant by . . . requesting this Board not to give Ear to the Representations of Disappointed men' and reminded the Commissioners of the Navy to 'Continue to exert yourselves in carrying on this very essential service with all possible care, Attention

[1] PRO, T/64/201, pp. 62–3.
[2] PRO, ADM/106/2603, July 29, 1780; CO/5/258, ff. 122–3; T/29/49, f. 158; T/64/200, pp. 102–5; T/64/201, p. 62.

and Dispatch'. No mention was made of the fact that the army's provisions were being dispatched overseas late, although the Treasury believed that these delays were in part due to a 'Want of regular & sufficient Convoys from Europe'.[1] It was, however, determined to speed up the dispatch of provisions to the army overseas. It hoped to do so by prevailing upon the Admiralty and Navy Board to work out a joint plan for the conduct of the victualling convoys. It studied the provision problem on 20 September, and two days later requested that the Navy Board do everything in its power to get the provisions promptly sent overseas. The Treasury also requested that the Admiralty assist the Navy Board as far as possible.[2] On 30 September the Treasury ordered the Navy Board to stop sending an entire year's supply of provisions for Clinton's army in only two convoys and stated:

The Delays, perhaps unavoidable ones, which arise in sending out Such large Embarkations, and the fatal consequences w[hich] may insue from the Misfortune and miscarriage of any of the large Fleets make their Lordships still most anxious to have the supplies sent out in less quantities, and by more frequent Convoys: They direct me to request that you will take this into your most serious & Attentive Consideration & that you will endeavour to form some Plan and arrange and settle some Mode with the Lords of the Admiralty for more effectually sending out such Supplies in future, as may prevent any Disaster happening to the Troops for want of Provisions, and any such similar Inconveniences as are now Represented to have arisen.

The Treasury sent a copy of this letter to the Admiralty, along with a note stating 'in the Strongest manner' that it expected the Admiralty to cooperate with the Navy Board in all matters relating to the shipment of army provisions.[3] The Treasury thus made it clear to both the Admiralty and the Navy Board that it would not in the future tolerate any delays or miscarriages in the shipment of the army's provisions overseas.

On 3 October 1780 the Navy Board submitted a plan for the

---

[1] PRO, T/64/201, pp. 68–9; G, no. 3157.
[2] PRO, ADM/1/4288, Sept. 30, 1780; T/29/49, ff. 190–1; T/64/201, pp. 66–7.
[3] PRO, T/64/201, pp. 70–1.

conduct of the army victualling service in 1781. Instead of dispatching an entire year's supply of provisions to the army in America in two large convoys as had been done in 1779 and 1780, the Board suggested that

as the Lords of the Treasury have proposed supplies to be more frequent and in smaller quantities, we have approved of the measure provided convoys tho' of smaller forces can be allowed for that purpose, we must therefore request their Lordships [of the Admiralty] will inform us whether it will be in their power to furnish us every year with four convoys from Cork to America between the 1st March and 1st Sept.[1]

The Admiralty approved the Commissioners' proposal, and on 7 October 1780 Philip Stephens informed the Treasury:

I am commanded by their Lordships to acquaint you that they have always granted convoys to the army victuallers when the Navy Board have applied for them and tho' their Lordships perceive that the demands for convoys for victualling the army in America are much more extensive than it was originally supposed they would be when the Navy Board first under took this business, yet their Lordships seeing the importance of this service in its utmost extent, will continue to supply convoys when applied for, tho' there is reason to apprehend it will interfere with other very material services.[2]

The Admiralty, under pressure from the Treasury and perhaps also from Germain, had at last to recognize the overriding necessity of supplying naval vessels to escort the outward-bound army victuallers. From 1781 to 1783 very few delays in the dispatch of victuallers from the British Isles were caused by the failure of the Admiralty to provide naval escort.

The securing of convoys for voyages between Cowes and Cork was a recurrent problem which was never satisfactorily solved. In order to make maximum use of the tonnage at its disposal, the Board had to be able to shuttle ships and provisions back and forth between England and Ireland, but the lack of regular convoys restricted the movement of shipping. On 14 April 1781 the Board proposed to the Admiralty that a regular convoy between Cork and Spithead be instituted. H.M.S. *Raleigh* was

---

[1] Navy Board to Admiralty, Oct. 3, 1780, Barham MSS. at Exton Park.
[2] PRO, T/64/201, pp. 74–5.

assigned by the Admiralty to escort regular convoys back and forth between Cork and Spithead. On 18 December 1781, however, the Board requested that the Admiralty issue directions to the naval commanders-in-chief overseas to direct the commanders of all convoys bound for England to put into Cork in order to take under escort any victuallers in that port under orders to proceed to England, for 'This will prevent the requiring a special convoy for that purpose which has occasioned a considerable delay as well as expence on former occasions'. But the problem was not solved by this measure, for on 1 May 1782 the Board wrote to the Admiralty that 'the want of standing convoy between Cork & Spithead has subjected the King's Service to much disappointment and the public to a large expence', and there were now 'Upwards of 1000 tons of transports [which] have been at Cork for three months waiting for convoy while we have been paying demurrage to army contractors for want of these ships [at Cowes] to receive their provisions'.[1] The lack of regular convoys between Cork and Cowes, however, was a relatively minor problem to the Navy Board because there was always a large number of naval vessels in British waters able to escort victuallers between Cork and Cowes on an *ad hoc* basis.

The delays caused by the failure of army provision contractors to fulfil the terms of their contracts and the tardiness of the Admiralty in providing naval escort to outward-bound convoys of victuallers were of minor importance compared with the problems caused by the scarcity of ships. By applying pressure the Navy Board and the Treasury could bring about a slow improvement in the conduct of the Admiralty and the provision contractors, but the shortage of ships was a problem which could not be solved. The tonnage shortage was in part caused by the Board's inability to charter a sufficient number of ships to meet all the needs of the transport service.[2] But the shortage can be attributed to the fact that the British forces from 1779 to 1783 pursued a strategy which demanded larger and larger numbers of victuallers. The problem was apparently insoluble,

---

[1] NMM, ADM/N/250, May 5, 1781; PRO, ADM/106/2606, Dec. 18, 1781; ADM/106/2608, May 1, 1782.

[2] For an account of the Navy Board's efforts to charter shipping, see above pp. 77–103.

but the situation would have been improved if a way had been found to utilize every victualler to the greatest possible extent. The Navy Board, however, found it extremely difficult, if not impossible, to pursue a rational policy of employing its victuallers because military and naval commanders overseas failed to understand the military necessity of quickly unloading and rapidly returning the victuallers to Europe for reemployment. As a result, thousands of tons of desperately needed victuallers were immobilized and needlessly wasted.

The Navy Board had just enough ships at its disposal to fulfil the requirements of the army victualling service. If these vessels were detained overseas for long periods of time, there would not be the tonnage available in Britain to dispatch all the provisions needed by the troops abroad. On 4 December 1779 the Board issued orders to Captain Thomas Tonken, the Principal Agent for Transports in America, 'to avoid by all means the employing victuallers as transports', and on 29 April 1780 Lieutenant Robert Walter, Agent for Transports, was told he must not leave any victuallers in America because 'it is of great importance to the safety of the army that they are regular in their return'.[1] But these orders had no appreciable effect, and it soon became apparent to the Board that a large number of victuallers were being kept overseas. On 27 June 1780 the Commissioners of the Navy wrote to the Treasury:

We must . . . represent in the most serious manner . . . the necessity of directing the Commanding Officer of the Troops at different Stations abroad not to detain upon any account longer than shall be absolutely necessary, the transports employed in carrying the Provisions for the use of the Army, and that like directions may be given to the Naval Commanding Officers to grant a return of convoys to see them to Cork when any number shall be assembled for that purpose . . . We must repeat and desire of having this measure as much enforced as possible.[2]

On 9 July 1780 the Treasury considered the Board's request and directed Clinton to 'pay strictest attention to the speedy dispatch and return of victualling transports'. At the same time the

---

[1] PRO, ADM/106/2601, Dec. 4, 1779; ADM/106/2602, April 29, 1779.
[2] PRO, T/64/200, pp. 95–6.

Treasury wrote to the Admiralty requesting that the 'strictest' orders be issued to the naval commanders overseas to provide promptly escort to empty army victuallers returning to Britain.[1]

The combined orders of the Admiralty, Treasury, and Navy Board were not sufficient to bring about the return of the victuallers from overseas. In the late summer of 1780 the Board informed the Treasury that none of the victuallers which had been dispatched in 1779 to America had returned to Britain and 'although every encouragement by premium & other ways hath been offered for months past to all parts of the Kingdom to induce the Owners of ships to make up the Deficiency occasioned by this Detention, it has not been in their power' to obtain additional tonnage.[2] The situation did not improve during the fall and winter of 1780, for very few ships of the transport service returned from abroad and the resources of the transport service in Britain were nearly exhausted. On 10 October 1780 the Navy Board resolved to

Represent to the Admiralty the necessity of their Lordships inter- fering [with] their authority with the officers commanding abroad not to detain more transports for the use of the army than are absolutely necessary, nor to direct storeships or victuallers to any other purposes than those for which they are sent out, and to furnish convoys with them to Europe as soon as they are cleared, and request their Lordships to procure instructions of a similar nature to be given to the Commanders in Chief of the Army. Send a copy to the Treasury and desire their Lordships assistance in procuring & giving such directions as may be requesite to produce the speedy return of the ships from abroad that we may thereby be furnished with a proper sucession to carry on the service, without which we cannot be answerable for the consequences. Acq[uaint] the several agents [for transports] abroad herewith and direct them to be particularly attentive to apply in time for convoy for transports under orders to return to Europe [and] to keep no more than are absolutely necessary, but to return them by every opportunity.[3]

As a result of the Board's complaints orders were sent to the

---

[1] HMC, *American Manuscripts*, ii, 165; PRO, ADM/1/4288, July 12, 1780; T/29/49, ff. 134-5.

[2] PRO, T/64/200, p. 113.

[3] PRO, ADM/106/2604, Oct. 10, 1780.

naval and military commanders overseas demanding the return of the ships so 'that we may be enabled with greater facility to reinforce you with troops and supply you more regularly with provisions'. However, these orders had little effect for in February 1781 the Board estimated that the detention of victuallers overseas forced it to employ one-third more tonnage than would have been necessary if the ships were promptly returned to Britain.[1]

The problem of victuallers being detained overseas continued to the end of the war. In the fall of 1782 the shortage of victuallers became so acute that the Board did not have the tonnage in the British Isles to meet the logistical requirements of the British army overseas if the war had continued into 1783. The Commissioners of the Navy on 24 September 1782 noted in their minutes 'that we depend upon the return of the army victuallers as it will otherwise be impossible to continue a supply for the army next year', and three days later the Treasury wrote to the commanders overseas that 'the greatest part of the Transport Victuallers are now abroad; and as the certainty of supply of provisions for troops . . . depends on early conveyance which it will be impossible to comply with, but by the speedy return of the transports'.[2] Few victuallers, however, returned to the British Isles, and on 18 December 1782 the Navy Board wrote to Admiral Robert Digby, the naval commander-in-chief in America, that 'supplying the army [during] the ensuing year entirely depends on the return of the shipping from America'. On 31 December 1782 the Treasury wrote to the new commander-in-chief in America, Sir Guy Carleton, that because of the shortage of victualler tonnage in Britain it would be difficult, if not impossible, to supply the army in 1783 and that orders should be issued to 'the Commanding Officers at the different Ports [in America] for assisting each other, as may be necessary to make up any failure that may happen on this side of the water, for want of transports which no means can procure', and that because of 'the present very great difficulty of

[1] PRO, ADM/106/2604, Dec. 4, 1780; ADM/108/4A, Jan. 2, 1781; CO/5/100, ff. 128–9; T/1/569, Navy Board to Treasury, Feb. 27, 1781; T/64/201, p. 89; HMC, *American Manuscripts*, ii, 216, 232.
[2] PRO, ADM/106/2609, Sept. 24, 1782; T/64/107, p. 80.

procuring transports here ... it is of the utmost importance that you should afford every assistance in your power to the commanding officers at other ports in order to make up for any unavoidable failure from hence'.[1] Thus, at the end of 1782, the Navy Board and Treasury both thought that owing to the failure of the victuallers to be promptly returned to Britain, it would probably be impossible to obtain the shipping required to transport the army's provisions in 1783. It is clear that it was only the end of the war early in 1783 that saved the British forces abroad from a major provision crisis.

The problem was further complicated by the fact that customs officers periodically detained victuallers in overseas ports. In 1781, for example, the victualler *Ann*, after unloading part of her cargo at Barbados, was seized by the collector of customs at St Kitts while en route to St Eustatius although James Hill, her master, had a clearance from the collector of customs at Cork stating that the *Ann* was not to be detained by customs officers abroad. The *Ann* was arrested at St Kitts 'on the pretence that she had not what is called a *Register*—which was of manifest prejudice to His Majesty's Service, by delay as well as extraordinary expence incured in hiring other vessels'. The victualler *Jason* was arrested in 1782 by customs officers at Antigua, condemned in the island's Vice Admiralty Court, and sold for not obtaining a clearance from the customs house before unloading her cargo despite the fact that officials of the Commissary General's Department at Antigua maintained that the ship did not need to pass through customs because she was in His Majesty's service.[2] Apart from the questions of law raised by the arrests of the *Ann* and *Jason*, the seizures resulted in the loss of two victuallers.

Occasionally victuallers were lost or detained in ports abroad by mix-ups in the arrangements made for convoys. Brigadier General Archibald Campbell, the army commander at Jamaica, wrote to Admiral Rodney on 20 March 1782 complaining that when the last Jamaica convoy had sailed from St Lucia, a victualler with provisions for the garrison of Jamaica had been

---

[1] PRO, ADM/106/2610, Dec. 18, 1782; T/64/107, pp. 81–2.
[2] PRO, T/1/577, Major General G. Christie to Treasury, Dec. 15, 1781; T/29/53, ff. 32, 58.

12—S.A.W.

left behind and as a result there was 'not a Morsel in Store'. The Navy Board on 20 December 1782 wrote to the Admiralty that three out of ten victuallers dispatched with Lord Howe for the relief of Gibraltar had been lost because for some unknown reason they had to proceed back to Britain independently, resulting, according to the Board, in the loss of three ships which would cost the government 'upwards of £7000'.[1] Although it was galling to have victuallers arrested by customs officials and to have others detained in overseas ports for missing their convoys, or lost because they had been ordered to return to Britain without escort, the total number of ships detained or lost for these reasons was comparatively small.

Impressment as a means of manning the Royal Navy sometimes resulted in victuallers being immobilized in overseas ports when their crews were taken into the Navy. Rodney, while in New York during the fall of 1780, had impressed every seaman who could be found in the city. Then, as his fleet left New York, it encountered off Sandy Hook an inward-bound convoy of victuallers commanded by Lieutenant Robert Carter, Agent for Transports. Rodney impressed a further fifty-six seamen from Carter's victuallers, leaving the ships with just enough men to navigate the vessels from Sandy Hook to Upper New York Bay. The unloading of the victuallers was thus prolonged. Despite attempts to enlist prisoners of war, the departure of the victuallers was further delayed by the inability to procure enough seamen in New York to sail the ships to Cork. A dispatch from Captain Thomas Tonken describing Rodney's actions caused the Board to send letters to both the Admiralty and the Treasury protesting about the impressment of seamen from Carter's victuallers and requesting that the Admiralty issue orders forbidding impressment of seamen from ships of the transport service in overseas ports. The Board's complaint had the desired effect.[2]

The lengthy detention in American and West Indian harbours

[1] NYHSC, *Letter-Books and Order-Book of George, Lord Rodney*, i, 312; PRO, ADM/106/2610, Dec. 20, 1782.
[2] PRO, ADM/49/2, ff. 241, 243–6; T/29/50, f. 11; NMM, ADM/N/250, Feb. 1, 1781; NYHSC, *Letter-Books and Order-Book of George, Lord Rodney*, i, 188. See also pp. 222–3 below.

of large numbers of victuallers due to inadequate port facilities and shortage of warehouse space was a serious cause of delays. The length of time spent overseas by a victualler depended greatly on the facilities for discharging cargo at her destination. Many American and West Indian ports through which the British army was supplied had been damaged in the course of the war or were simply not suitable for handling bulk cargoes from the type of ships employed by the transport service; in consequence, it often took an inordinate amount of time simply to unload a victualler and get the ship ready for sea again. Peter Paumier, the Deputy Commissary General at Savannah, Georgia, found that it took several weeks and much hard work in the summer of 1779 to unload four victuallers, for when fully loaded the ships drew too much water to cross the bar at the entrance of the Savannah River, and three-fourths of their cargo had to be unloaded into small craft off Tybee Island for shipment to Savannah, some twenty miles away.[1]

In addition to the delays of this sort, victuallers were also detained overseas to act as floating warehouses, prisons, and hospitals. The employment of ships for these tasks was in part due to the lack of suitable buildings at such British bases as New York and St Lucia, but it was also the fear of American sabotage which made many British officials prefer to keep large quantities of provisions on ships. Peter Paumier, for example, did not 'think it prudent to have the whole of the provisions on shore for fear of accidents'. Almost 500 buildings in New York had been destroyed by fire in 1776 just after the British forces had entered the city, and in 1778 another fire consumed more than sixty buildings there. Throughout the rest of the British occupation of the city there were numerous small fires, attributed by many British officials to American sabotage; and there was thus a natural desire to keep provisions in the holds of victuallers as long as possible. On 22 September 1780 Captain Walter Young wrote from New York to Charles Middleton stating:

The field to save the public money in this country is great, both in the naval and victualling departments. I am amazed at their not having store-houses to put the provisions in. They would not only

[1] PRO, T/64/120, pp. 4–5.

save the enormous expense of shipping, but the provisions also; for the bread is full of vermin, and the other provisions destroyed by the heat of the hold. There are at present here, in vessels, provisions which have been on board eighteen months, without being looked at.

In St Lucia, as in New York, the shortage of warehouse space resulted in large numbers of victuallers being used as floating warehouses. At the end of 1782 there were 4000 tons of loaded victuallers at St Lucia, but the army commander in the Windward Islands, General Edward Mathew, did not 'conceive it practicable to unload above three or four of them, and from what I understand, the whole of the stores at St Lucia, cannot receive more than the cargoes of two'.[1]

The Navy Board was aware that numerous ships were immobilized in North American and West Indian ports in service as floating warehouses, hospitals, and prisons, and it also realized that this situation arose partly from a shortage of buildings suitable for these purposes. On 2 April 1781 the Board proposed to the Admiralty and Treasury that the problem could possibly be alleviated if agents for transports were authorized to charter ships abroad which were suitable for employment as warehouses, prisons, and hospitals thereby releasing the ships of the transport service for their proper employment. This plan was approved by the Admiralty and the Treasury, and orders were issued to put it into effect.[2] Despite orders from London, a number of victuallers continued until the end of the war to be detained abroad to serve in these capacities.

A number of victuallers were kept abroad to serve as transports. Throughout the war, commanders overseas constantly detained shipping under their jurisdictions in order to obtain additional transport tonnage. By the late fall of 1778, the number of transports at New York had become greatly reduced by the need to supply the tonnage required to carry large bodies of troops from New York to the West Indies and the Floridas, to carry a battalion of marines from Halifax to England, and to transport the inhabitants of St Pierre and Miquelon to Europe.

[1] Oscar Theodore Barck, *New York City during the War of Independence* (New York, 1931), 80–3, NRS, *Barham Papers*, i, 74–5; PRO, CO/318/10, f. 1; T/29/53, ff. 23–24; T/64/120, p. 5.
[2] NMM, ADM/N/250, April 5, 1781; PRO, T/64/107, p. 65.

Admiral James Gambier therefore supplemented the depleted ranks of the transports at New York by detaining and converting into transports a number of army victuallers under charter to Mure, Son, and Atkinson. Victuallers in the service of the Navy Board, as well as those in the employ of the Treasury, were also at times made into transports while in America. On 18 July 1781 General Alexander Leslie reported from Portsmouth, Virginia: 'We fell short of transports, and [were] obliged to fit up three of the victualling vessels.'[1]

On occasion victuallers were also diverted for use on coastwise voyages. In 1782, for example, the Navy Board, in an attempt to obtain masts for the Royal Navy, dispatched the provisions for the troops stationed in Nova Scotia in victuallers which had 'Raft Ports best calculated for taking masts'. The Board intended that these ships after discharging their cargo of provisions at Halifax, would proceed to the Bay of Fundy and there load masts to be carried to Britain. This scheme failed, however, because the army commander at Halifax ordered the empty victuallers to Spanish River in Cape Breton to pick up coal for the garrison of Nova Scotia, which delayed the ships until it was too late in the season to go to the Bay of Fundy.[2]

Many victuallers were detained abroad for long periods while waiting for warships to convoy them to the British Isles, a situation that arose in part from the shortage of escort vessels in the Royal Navy during the American War. The delay in dispatching empty victuallers to Britain from New York, however, appears to have been partly the result of the failure of cooperation between Sir Henry Clinton and Admiral Marriot Arbuthnot, the commanders-in-chief of the army and navy in America. In answer to letters from the Admiralty and Treasury demanding the return to Britain of empty victuallers, Arbuthnot and Clinton would each blame the other for the delays. Clinton maintained that the victuallers were being kept at New York because Arbuthnot would not supply warships to escort them to Britain, while Arbuthnot stated that the victuallers were being detained because the General did not promptly unload them.

[1] PRO, ADM/1/489, f. 119; CO/5/103, f. 38.
[2] PRO, ADM/106/2607, Feb. 13, 1782; ADM/108/1C, Sept. 24, 1782.

On 22 September 1780 Captain Walter Young wrote to Charles Middleton from New York saying, 'I am exceedingly sorry to find such disagreements here between our land and sea officers. The army will be much distressed for provisions by some ridiculous conduct; your victuallers lay here empty for near six months, and the admiral would give no convoy because he had no admiralty orders on that head.'[1]

The delay in the prompt return of victuallers to Britain, although aggravated by the Arbuthnot-Clinton dispute, was caused above all by the shortage of naval escorts. Victuallers were often detained in ports other than New York because of the lack of convoy to Britain. For example, the army commander in the Windward Islands reported to the Treasury that there were six victuallers at Barbados which could not sail for Britain because there were no warships to escort them.[2] Captain Walter Young suggested to Middleton in 1780 that the escort problem could be solved only by getting the Admiralty to allocate a number of warships for the sole purpose of escorting victuallers regularly to and from the British Isles. Middleton, on 9 September 1782, told Lord Shelburne that large numbers of victuallers were being immobilized abroad due to a lack of convoys to Britain and that this problem could be solved if

Every commander abroad should have the strictest orders on this head, and next to attending the immediate service of the squadron, this should be the particular employment of frigates. If this service was properly conducted, we might discharge one third part of the transports now employed, and have every demand made better supplied than at present.[3]

The problem of procuring convoys for homeward-bound victuallers, however, plagued the transport service until the end of the war, for the Navy Board was confronted from 1779 to 1782 with a military situation which demanded the increase of the number

[1] PRO, ADM/1/486, f. 559; T/64/110, ff. 65–6; HMC, *American Manuscripts*, ii, 250; NRS, *Barham Papers*, i, 73–4; For an account of Clinton's many disputes and difficulties with navy officers, see William B. Willcox, *Portrait of A General: Sir Henry Clinton in the War of Independence* (New York, 1964), passim.
[2] PRO, T/1/577, Major General G. Christie to Treasury, Dec. 15, 1781.
[3] NRS, *Barham Papers*, i, 74; SP, 151, Middleton to Shelburne, Sept. 9, 1782.

of victuallers so that the British military position in the Western Hemisphere could be maintained.

From 1779 to 1782 there was a steady increase in the consumption of provisions by the British forces in the Western Hemisphere. It was only in the West Indies, however, that larger amounts of provisions were required because of the increase in the number of troops. There was a constant flow of troops from Britain to the Caribbean from 1779 to 1782, while the British forces on the North American mainland were not greatly reinforced during these years; even so, there was a marked increase in the consumption of provisions. For example, on 1 September 1779 the King's troops in Canada numbered 7968, while at the same time their commander, General Frederick Haldimand, was demanding that the Treasury dispatch to Canada enough provisions to feed 20,000 men.[1] The need to feed large numbers of Indians accounted for this discrepancy. At the beginning of 1779 George Rogers Clark seized the Illinois country, and Haldimand thought 'it is much to be apprehended that our Indian Allies have it in contemplation to desert us . . . altho' they continue to perform their attachment to the King, they frame excuses for not going to war, and discover, upon all occasions an indifference which indicates their intentions to forsake us'. During the summer of 1779 British influence among the Indians was further weakened by an American punitive campaign against the Six Nations in western New York. American forces entered the territory of the Six Nations and broke the power of the Long House by destroying the Indians' houses, crops, stores of food, and by forcing those Iroquois who survived to seek shelter at the British posts on the Great Lakes where they had to be fed out of the King's stores, for alienation of the Indians would jeopardize Upper Canada and the Canadian fur trade. As Haldimand warned Germain, the Indians 'will be forced into a neutrality, which with Indians, is little better than a declaration of war against the weakest party'.[2] The British forces in West Florida were confronted with a provision problem similar to the one caused by the Indians in

[1] PRO, CO/5/7, f. 716; T/64/115, pp. 80–2.
[2] PRO, CO/5/98, ff. 190–1, 284–6; CO/42/39, ff. 234, 358–9.

Canada. Approximately 1000 King's troops were in West Florida, but it was found because of the 'immense consumption of provisions by Indians, by artificers, and labourers, by victualling the transports, and by the maintenance of refugees, that the present contract for 3,000 men will only supply their present numbers, and should they be reinforced they cannot furnish provisions for the Indians'.[1] Clinton at New York did not have to feed Indians, but the consumption of provisions at that port was greatly increased by the need to feed Loyalists. On 20 December 1781 he requested that rations for an additional 6000 men be dispatched to New York during 1782 in order to feed the Associated Loyalists, 'as well as . . . the great number of helpless Refugees, who pour in upon us from all parts of this continent, and would inevitably perish for want of subsistence if not furnished with some support from the King's magazines'.[2]

While the number of troops in North America remained stable, there was a steady increase in the consumption of provisions brought about by the need to feed civilians and Indians. In November 1779 there were 43,390 King's troops in North America, and in January 1782 they numbered 44,431. In 1782, however, the army in North America was feeding 28,169 men over and above its strength, and the transport service had to convey from the British Isles to the army in North America enough rations to maintain 72,600 men, necessitating the employment of a considerably larger number of victuallers than would have been required to supply the army alone.[3]

At the beginning of 1778, after the French entry into the conflict, the whole conduct of the war was changed by the adoption of a strategy of dispersal. From Lexington and Concord until 1778 the British had, with the exception of the two invasions of America from Canada in 1776 and 1777, followed a strategy of concentration of force. Before the French entry into the war the number of troops in the West Indies had been almost negligible, while the attack on Charleston in 1776, the occupation of Rhode Island, and the campaign in East Florida

[1] PRO, CO/5/102, f. 150; CO/5/258, f. 153.
[2] PRO, T/64/111, ff. 9–10.
[3] Add. MSS., 38433, f. 43; PRO, ADM/108/4A, Dec. 29, 1781; WO/17/1155, Jan., 1782.

had been side-shows. The British army in the Western Hemisphere had always been concentrated in the northern colonies, but from 1778 until the end of the war the British forces were driven to greater dispersion. New York and Canada were held in force, while at the same time great numbers of troops were committed to the Caribbean and large-scale operations were conducted in the American South. Before the change from a strategy of concentration to one of dispersal, the bulk of the army's provisions were transported either to Quebec or the seat of the main army in the American colonies. After the adoption of a strategy of dispersal, large amounts of provisions had to be conveyed simultaneously to such widely separated places as Quebec, New York, Virginia, Charleston, Savannah, the Windward Islands, and Jamaica. The strategy of dispersal resulted in a greater length of time spent in passage, a larger number of coastwise voyages required of victuallers, and the circuitous routing of convoys.

The strategy of dispersal was inaugurated on 21 March 1778, when Germain issued orders to Clinton to evacuate Philadelphia, to reinforce the garrisons of Nova Scotia and the Floridas, and to dispatch a force of 5000 troops to seize St Lucia from the French.[1] The expedition from New York arrived at St Lucia on 12 December 1778, and by the end of the year had captured the island. The troops which had seized St Lucia formed the main British force in the Lesser Antilles, but this force did not remain concentrated, for on 1 April 1779 General James Grant, the commander of the army at St Lucia, was ordered by Germain to occupy and defend in force all the British Islands in the Lesser Antilles. By July 1779 the British troops at St Lucia had been dispersed among several islands. Eight hundred and twenty-nine soldiers were stationed on warships, 655 at Antigua, 1386 at St Christophers, and 1422 at St Lucia. Until the end of the war the King's troops in the Lesser Antilles remained dispersed in small detachments on various islands. For example, in July 1782 there were 407 troops at Barbados, 1119 at St Lucia, 790 at Antigua, and 152 artillerymen divided between several garrisons.[2]

---

[1] PRO, CO/5/95, ff. 95–102.
[2] PRO, CO/318/5, pp. 111–12, 255; CO/318/6, f. 144; CO/318/9, f. 225.

Not only were the British troops in the Lesser Antilles scattered, but Clinton's army on the American mainland was split up and dispersed along the entire length of the American coast from Nova Scotia to West Florida. At the same time that Grant's troops left New York for the West Indies, the garrison of Nova Scotia was reinforced from New York. The 3500 men which formed the reinforced garrison of Nova Scotia were not a concentrated force because, in addition to guarding Nova Scotia itself, they held a string of posts extending westward along the Maine coast to Castine. At the end of 1778, 1000 troops were dispatched from New York to reinforce Pensacola and nearly 3000 more were sent to East Florida to attack Georgia. At the beginning of 1779, therefore, Clinton had approximately 22,000 rank-and-file effectives deployed in New York and Rhode Island, while approximately 8500 were stationed in Nova Scotia, the Floridas, and Georgia.[1] The army in America was even further dispersed at the end of 1779 when Clinton invaded South Carolina with some 7500 troops drawn from the army at New York. To commit large numbers of troops to operations in the American South in effect created two main British armies in America. Thus, in May 1780 there were 15,549 rank-and-file effectives in the New York area, while another 13,721 were stationed in South Carolina, Georgia, and East Florida, all supplied mainly through the ports of New York, Charleston, Savannah, and St Augustine.[2] The opening by the British of major operations in Virginia at the end of 1780 led to a further division of the King's forces in America. By 1 May 1781 there were 12,257 rank-and-file effectives at New York; 8579 in East Florida, Georgia, and the Carolinas; and 4925 in Virginia.[3] In the first week of May Lord Cornwallis entered Virginia from North Carolina, and by 15 August 1781 the British forces in Virginia had increased to 7968 rank-and-file effectives.[4] In short, until the surrender of Cornwallis's army at Yorktown on 19 October 1781, there were three separate major British armies operating simultaneously in different regions of America. The British army in America remained dispersed until the end of the

[1] PRO, CO/5/7, f. 716; CO/5/97, f. 177.   [2] PRO, CO/5/99, f. 254.
[3] PRO, CO/5/102, ff. 104–5.   [4] PRO, CO/5/103, f. 133.

war, for on 1 June 1782, after the capture by the Spanish of
West Florida and the surrender of Cornwallis at Yorktown, there
were 15,350 rank-and-file effectives at New York; 8309 in South
Carolina, Georgia, and East Florida; and 3235 in Nova Scotia
and Maine.[1]

In 1778 when the strategy of dispersal was adopted, British
authorities both in London and abroad did not seem to understand that the policy would require increasing numbers of
victuallers to implement. But by 1781 this fact had begun to
become apparent. On 27 February Clinton informed Germain:

As the number of our Posts are now greatly increased, it is difficult
to ascertain the exact quantity of tonnage which may be wanted for
their supply, and such expeditions as I may have to under take; but
I beg leave to assure your Lordship, that I shall not fail to pay the
strictest attention to His Majesty's commands in keeping here no
more transports than what may be absolutely wanted for the King's
service.[2]

The Navy Board on 1 May 1781 wrote to the Principal Agent
for Transports in America that it was well aware that the
campaign in Virginia would require additional transport service
tonnage, 'but we are hopful that a succession may be kept up
[and that] their returns [to Britain] are regular'.[3] It was found,
however, that the victuallers could not be promptly and regularly returned to Britain from overseas because by its very nature
the strategy of dispersal brought about a detention of victualler
tonnage abroad.

The Navy Board and the Treasury attempted to limit the
number of victuallers required to support the dispersed British
troops in the Western Hemisphere by establishing a number of
central provision depots. On 4 November 1779 the Treasury
resolved 'that the Island of St Lucia should be made the
principal depot of provisions for the troops in the West Indies as
being the most Windward island', and directions were given to
the Navy Board to 'consign all the provisions intended for those
troops to the commanding officer of His Majesty's forces at

---

[1] PRO, CO/5/105, f. 242.   [2] PRO, CO/5/102, ff. 9–10.
[3] PRO, ADM/106/2605, May 1, 1781.

St. Lucia'.[1] Germain's office appears not to have approved of this plan, but William Knox was told by the Treasury on 29 April 1780 'that it is impossible for this Board to send out supplies of provisions to every island separately and for every small detached body of troops, but ... [the Treasury has] sent out a very ample supply to St Lucia, as the General Depot from whence the whole West India detachments must be supplied'.[2] At the suggestion of the Navy Board in the beginning of 1781 the same plan was adopted for the provisioning of troops stationed in Maine, Nova Scotia, Prince Edward Island, the Carolinas, and Georgia. On 23 January 1781 the Treasury, at the instigation of the Navy Board, resolved that 'the whole proportion of Provisions for Halifax and its Districts (except Newfoundland) to be sent to Halifax and transhipped; and that the same Rule be observed in respect to South Carolina and its districts'.[3] By establishing central provision depots at ports such as Halifax, New York, Charleston, and St Lucia, the Navy Board and the Treasury attempted to prevent the transport service's victuallers from being employed in coastwise voyages carrying provisions to outlying garrisons. Despite the best efforts of the Treasury and the Navy Board, a large number of victuallers had to be employed in directly supplying outlying garrisons. For instance, it was found in 1779 that Rhode Island could not continue to be supplied with provisions shipped on coasters through Long Island Sound from New York City because of the danger of capture by American armed vessels based in Connecticut. Clinton therefore ordered that victuallers be employed to provision Rhode Island, and in September 1779 the victuallers *Neptune* and *Hercules* were detached from a convoy off Sandy Hook and sent there under naval escort.[4]

The British forces in the Western Hemisphere were so widely dispersed that there were a number of garrisons, such as Pensacola, which could not possibly be provisioned from a central depot. Provisions could only be conveyed to Pensacola from

[1] PRO, T/29/49, f. 5; T/64/201, p. 46.   [2] PRO, CO/5/258, f. 116.

[3] PRO, ADM/108/4A, Jan. 23, 1781; T/64/201, p. 89.

[4] New-York Historical Society, Letter Book of Daniel Wier, Commissary General of the British Forces in America, Sept. 5, [30], 1779; PRO, ADM/1/489, ff. 234–5.

Britain by a circuitous route. In the fall of 1779 the victuallers *Baltick Merchant* and *Robert & Elizabeth* were dispatched to West Florida with provisions, first proceeding to Kingston, Jamaica, with the autumn West India convoy and then waiting at Jamaica for naval escort before going through the Channel of Yucatan to West Florida.[1] After unloading their cargoes, these vessels were forced to wait at Pensacola for naval escort either to Jamaica or New York in order to join a convoy bound for Britain. The necessity of having to provision small garrisons of British troops in such places as West Florida, the Mosquito Shore, Providence in the Bahamas, Bermuda, and Goree absorbed the services of a considerable number of victuallers.

Before the start of major military operations in the American South, most victuallers ran back and forth between Britain and New York, but after large numbers of the King's troops had been dispatched to Georgia and South Carolina, a number of ships had to proceed either to Savannah or Charleston. On 13 May 1779 the Navy Board therefore suggested to the Admiralty that convoys of victuallers bound to the army in America should take the 'Southern Passage instead of the direct one'.[2] In July 1779 a group of victuallers under the direction of Lieutenant Archibald Dow, Agent for Transports, left Cork for South Carolina, Georgia, and New York. The victuallers proceeded by the 'Southern Passage' to a point off 'Charles Town Bar' where Dow detached those ships bound for Charleston and Savannah before going himself with the remainder of the ships to New York. The victuallers left at Charleston and Savannah had orders 'to apply to the Senior Officer of his Majesty's Ships there for convoy to Europe ... but if none can be granted directly home, [they were] to take the benefit of the first that offers to join the ships ... at New York'.[3] On occasion convoys of victuallers with ships bound both for New York and ports in the American South did not proceed to New York by way of Charleston. On 19 October 1780 H.M.S. *Centurion* arrived at New York directly from the British Isles with a large convoy of

---

[1] NMM, ADM/B/199, Sept. 14, 1779; ADM/B/200, Oct. 11, 1779; ADM/N/249, Oct. 13, 1779.

[2] Navy Board to Admiralty, May 13, 1779, Barham MSS. at Exton Park.

[3] NMM, ADM/B/199, May 11, 1779; PRO, T/29/49, f. 255; T/64/200, p. 15.

victuallers, although fourteen days before the convoy reached New York H.M.S. *Camel* and twenty-six victuallers had parted from the convoy and proceeded to Charleston. Victuallers bound to Halifax sometimes went by way of New York. For example, three victuallers which arrived in America with the convoy under escort of H.M.S. *Centurion* were detached from the convoy off Sandy Hook and sent to Nova Scotia. Sometimes, however, victuallers going to Halifax accompanied Quebec or Newfoundland convoys. In 1781 the naval storeship *Recovery* and a number of army victuallers crossed the Atlantic with a Newfoundland convoy from which they and one of the escorts parted off Newfoundland in order to go to Halifax.[1] The necessity of dispatching victuallers bound both to Charleston and New York in one trans-Atlantic convoy greatly increased the length of time spent on the voyage to America from Britain. The routing of victuallers bound for Halifax via New York also led to the addition of hundreds of miles to a voyage. Naval authorities, however, had no other choice because the Royal Navy did not have enough escort vessels to supply the convoys required if the victuallers proceeding from Britain sailed directly to each garrison in America.

The stationing of British troops from Halifax to Pensacola, the entire length of the North American coast, led to the dispersal of victuallers, which in turn caused difficulties and delays in assembling convoys of empty ships for return to Britain. The empty victuallers had to wait for escort at the ports where they had unloaded and were then shuttled up and down the American coast until enough vessels had been assembled to warrant a convoy to Britain. On 23 July 1781 Captain Thomas Tonken reported to the Navy Board that a convoy of transports carrying troops and army equipment was being sent to Quebec from New York with orders to call at Halifax to pick up the empty victuallers at that port. From Halifax, the convoy, including the empty victuallers, was to go to Quebec where the troops and army equipment would be disembarked. The empty

---

[1] *Diary of Frederick Mackenzie: Giving a Daily Narrative of His Military Service as an Officer of the Regiment of Royal Welch Fusiliers during the Years 1775–1781 in Massachusetts, Rhode Island and New York* (Cambridge, Mass., 1930), ii, 668–70; PRO, ADM/49/2, f. 229; NMM, ADM/N/250, May 26, 1781.

transports, the empty victuallers from Halifax, and any empty victuallers at Quebec would then sail for Britain. At this time Tonken also reported to the Board that the victuallers at New York, while almost ready for sea, would not be immediately returned to Britain as the victuallers from Virginia and South Carolina and the transports with the 3rd and 13th Regiments had not yet arrived at New York. By 29 July 1781 Tonken had decided not to wait for the other ships and wrote to the Board: 'The Victualling transports being now ready to return to Cork . . . and no ships yet arrived from Virginia or Charles Town, I have taken the liberty of applying to Commodore [Edward] Affleck . . . for a convoy'.[1] These examples could be multiplied almost endlessly and it is clear that a large amount of victualler tonnage was immobilized in America as a result of the great delays caused by the difficulties in assembling empty victuallers from various American ports into convoys for return to the British Isles.

The Navy Board, despite the great obstacles it encountered, was highly successful from 1779 to 1782 in conveying the army's provisions to America. On 10 August 1782 the Adjutant General of the Hessian Forces wrote in his journal: 'Our store of provisions [at New York] has never been so plentiful as it now is.' By the summer of 1782 the Board had managed to amass a considerable store of provisions at New York, and the Treasury calculated that on 29 July 1782 there was at New York enough beef to make rations for 27,000 men for 763 days, enough flour for 357 days' rations, butter for 827 days' rations, rice and oatmeal for 816 days' rations, and 385 days' rations of pease.[2] Despite this achievement, the machinery for transporting the army's provisions overseas was threatened with ruin by the shortage of victualler tonnage in the British Isles at the end of 1782. By that time, it had become evident to the Board that it was impossible to charter additional victuallers and that unless the victuallers already in the transport service were returned at once to Britain, there would not be enough tonnage available to

[1] PRO, ADM/49/2, ff. 260–1.
[2] Bernhard A. Uhlendorf, trans. and ed., *Revolution in America: Confidential Letters and Journals, 1776–1784, of the Adjutant General Major Baurmeister of the Hessian Forces* (New Brunswick, N.J., 1957), 516–17; PRO, ADM/108/4A, Sept. 30, 1782.

transport the provisions required by the army overseas if the war continued into 1783. On 2 December 1782 the Navy Board wrote to Brook Watson, Commissary General at New York, warning him of 'the necessity of caution in the expenditure of provisions at New York & Halifax as we have not the least prospect of being able to provide for more stations than Quebec until the transports are returned from America'. On 13 December 1782 the Board requested the Treasury to issue directions to the 'Commanding Officers [abroad] for assisting each other as may be necessary to make up for any failure that may happen on this side [of] the water for want of transports which we by no means can procure'.[1]

The Commissioners of the Navy attempted to mitigate the victualler shortage in the British Isles by adopting such expedients as chartering neutral bottoms and sending provisions to Nova Scotia and Quebec on freight,[2] but such measures could never produce the tonnage needed to transport the provisions required by the British army overseas in 1783. The Navy Board could only procure the tonnage required to continue operations through the year 1783 by the immediate return of the victuallers from abroad—a requirement rendered impossible by the strategy of dispersal which absorbed victualler tonnage and by the failure of large numbers of officials to appreciate the importance of the victuallers to the British war effort. The Navy Board observed at the end of 1782: 'If all the shipping in Europe was employ'd in the service of the Army they would not prove sufficient, under this kind of mannagement.'[3]

[1] PRO, ADM/106/2610, Dec. 2, 13, 1782.
[2] E.g., PRO, ADM/106/2610, Nov. 12, 14, Dec. 5, 14, 1782.
[3] PRO, T/1/580, Navy Board to Treasury, Dec. 17, 1782.

CHAPTER IX

The Navy Board's Transports

AT THE OUTSET of the American War the British government realized that the bulk of the King's troops would
have to be raised and equipped in Europe and then
transported across thousands of miles of ocean to the scene of
battle. In addition, all reinforcements, replacements, and munitions required by the British forces in the Western Hemisphere
would have to be drawn from European sources. Thus Lord
Howe was only stating the obvious when he declared in 1778
that it was 'the transports, on which the subsistence of the army
immediately and entirely depends'.[1] Not only did the transports
convey from Europe all the men and materials necessary
for the prosecution of the war, but they also enabled the
British army to become a highly mobile amphibious force
capable of attacking any point which could be reached from
the sea.

During the American War two departments of the British
government were responsible for the conveyance of troops and
munitions. Ships in the service of the Ordnance Board carried
artillerymen, arms, engineer stores, and ammunition. The Navy
Board's transports carried infantry, cavalry, camp equipage,
army clothing, horses, quartermaster stores, Indian presents,
naval stores, and a variety of other items required by the
armed forces. But this division of labour between the two
departments was not hard and fast. On many occasions the
transport service carried artillerymen and arms.[2] Although the
cargoes, such as ammunition, carried by ordnance transports were extremely important, it was the transport service

---

[1] PRO, ADM/1/488, f. 256.
[2] E.g., NMM, ADM/N/250, Sept. 4, 28, 1781.

which bore the major burden of conveying troops and munitions.[1]

II

The British were at a serious geographical disadvantage during the American War. Hundreds of soldiers and scores of horses died at sea, the victims of a war of attrition against the Atlantic which the British army was forced to fight before it confronted a mortal enemy on the battlefields of America. Admiral James Gambier expressed the situation when he wrote, 'Our army . . . is healthy, brave, and zealous . . . [but] Twelve hundred leagues with its natural difficulties demand a solemn thought—the means and expense'.[2]

Only a small percentage of the soldiers lost at sea were captured or killed by the enemy. Periodically a transport separated from its convoy and was taken by the enemy, but an armed transport with a hundred soldiers on board was difficult for the average armed ship or privateer to attack successfully. Only twice during the war were large numbers of troops captured at sea by the enemy. In June 1776 four unescorted transports carrying 354 men of the 71st Regiment were captured by the Americans in the approaches to Boston Harbour, and in August 1780 six companies of the 99th Regiment en route to the West Indies were intercepted and captured off Spain by the Franco-Spanish fleet.[3] These two debacles were exceptions rather than the rule: it was disease and not the enemy which killed the King's troops on board transports.

The conditions under which the soldiers lived on transports were trying even by eighteenth-century standards. A Guards officer pungently described life on a transport as 'continued

[1] For an account of the Ordnance Board's shipping, see Edward E. Curtis, *The Organization of the British Army in the American Revolution* (New Haven, 1926), 120–34, 180–1.

[2] NRS, *Sandwich Papers*, ii, 299–300. The following paragraphs dealing with living conditions on the Navy Board's transports have appeared in a slightly different form in David Syrett, 'Living Conditions on the Navy Board's Transports During the American War, 1775–1783', *Mariner's Mirror* (Jan., 1969), lv, pp. 87–94.

[3] Accounts of these two actions may be found in William Bell Clark, *George Washington's Navy* (Baton Rouge, La., 1960), 160–5; Piers Mackesy, *The War for America, 1775–1783* (London, 1964), 357.

destruction in the foretops, the pox above-board, the plague between decks, hell in the forecastle, the devil at the helm'.[1] Captain Johann Hinrichs of the Jäger Corps, after a rough passage on a transport from New York to Charleston, declared: 'It may be safely said that the most strenuous campaign cannot be as trying as such a voyage.'[2] Being confined in a crowded transport for long periods of time was extremely tedious and nerve racking, and in the course of a voyage most men's tempers became short and some even went mad. Tempers became so frazzled on the transport *Unanimity*, which was proceeding to America in 1776, that in the middle of the Atlantic a duel was fought in which a cousin of the Landgrave of Hesse was killed.[3] Sergeant R. Lamb of the Royal Welch Fusiliers, while en route to Quebec in 1776 on the transport *Friendship*, recorded in his journal that during the passage there were two successful and one attempted suicides among the troops.[4]

During the American War troops were embarked on transports for a trans-Atlantic voyage at the rate of one man to every two tons of a ship's measured tonnage. That is, a transport measuring 200 tons would carry 100 men. For example, the Navy Board, upon receiving orders from the Admiralty 'to provide . . . for the conveyance of a corps of 700 men from Portsmouth to America', on 24 May 1779 assigned six transports with a total tonnage of 1531 tons to the task. Fourteen hundred tons of shipping were allotted for the troops and the extra 131 tons were for 'women & baggage'.[5] Although troops proceeding from Germany to Minorca were embarked at the rate of two tons per man, those being conveyed between other points in Europe were embarked at the ratio of one ton or one and one-half tons per man.[6] Depending on the length of the voyage, the embarkation of troops at the rate of one man to

[1] Quoted in Curtis, op. cit., 125.

[2] Bernhard A. Uhlendorf, trans. and ed., *The Siege of Charleston with an Account of the Province of South Carolina: Diaries and Letters of Hessian Officers from the von Jungkenn Papers in the William L. Clements Library* (Ann Arbor, Mich., 1938), 119.

[3] PRO, CO/5/93, f. 481.

[4] R. Lamb, *An Original and Authentic Journal of Occurrences during the Late American War, from its Commencement to the year 1783* (Dublin, 1809), 66–7.

[5] NMM, ADM/N/248, April 21, 1779; ADM/B/199, May 24, 1779.

[6] E.g., NMM, ADM/B/190, Aug. 11, 1775; ADM/N/245, Feb. 26, 1776.

every ton, one and one-half tons, or two tons of a ship's measured tonnage was a long established policy which had been followed during the Seven Years War.[1]

A shortage of transports was the usual cause for troops to be embarked at a lower rate than the standard ratio of men to tonnage.[2] Throughout the war German troops were crammed on board transports in German ports at rates which sometimes far exceeded one ton per man. Invariably at every major embarkation conducted in Germany more troops and equipment appeared at the port of embarkation than the authorities in London had anticipated. Units of German mercenaries had the tendency, despite a high rate of desertion, to increase in strength between the time when they were hired and when they embarked. This phenomenon was no doubt due to the fact that the German princes were paid by the British government according to the number of soldiers mustered into the King's service on board transports. When General William Fawcett, the commissary in charge of German Musters, had reached an agreement with a German prince for the hire of a unit of troops, he would then dispatch to London an account of the number of men hired and the name of the intended port of embarkation. This information was given to the Navy Board which would send to Germany the required number of transports. But between the time when the agreement was made and the time when the troops embarked, the strength of the unit would be enlarged by the German prince. The Board's calculations of the amount of tonnage required for German troops were further thrown off by the fact that many German infantry regiments, unlike British ones, contained artillery units.

The Navy Board's inability to predict the amount of tonnage required to embark German troops was a problem which persisted throughout the war. On 1 February 1777 Lord Suffolk ordered the Admiralty to have enough transports sent to Germany to pick up 1500 troops and suggested that 'it will be expedient to allot at least two ton to each man, as the numbers are most likely rather to exceed than fall short of what I have

[1] NMM, ADM/N/245, Jan. 27, 1776; SAN/T/1, Dec. 29, 1775.
[2] E.g., PRO, ADM/1/4148, f. 54.

specified'.[1] Fawcett solved this problem by disregarding the ratio of men to tonnage and leaving it to the Board to arrange for additional ships when the overcrowded transports arrived at Spithead. In April 1778 Fawcett squeezed 674 men of the Anhalt-Zerbst Battalion on board 526 tons of transports at Stade and then informed Lord Suffolk that 'they will be a little crowded . . . There being however no remedy for these inconveniences . . . they must submit to them till they get to Portsmouth'.[2] Sometimes the overloading of German troops on transports for the voyage between Germany and Spithead was disastrous. The East India Company on 30 January 1782 complained that twenty-two Hanoverian soldiers in its service had died as a result of overcrowding during this passage.[3]

Troops lived in crowded and uncomfortable quarters on board transports during the American War. The ships were only armed merchantmen of between 200 and 300 tons with holds compartmented into cabins. Each cabin contained a number of wooden two-tier 'Berths or Places of Repose'. Each tier held six soldiers.

The men were packed like herring. A tall man could not stand upright between decks, nor sit up straight in his berth. To every such berth six men were allotted, but as there were room for only four, the last two had to squeeze in as best they might. Thus the men lay in what boys call 'spoon fashion', and when they tired on one side, the man on the right would call 'about face', and the whole file would turn over at once; then, when they were tired again, the man on the left would give the same order, and they would turn back to the first side.[4]

When the ship rolled sharply, the soldiers' berths often collapsed.[5] For bedding each soldier was issued a sack of straw to serve as a mattress, a blanket, a pillow, and a coverlet.[6] There were abuses committed by the contractors who supplied the bedding, and in June 1776 two agents for transports complained

[1] PRO, ADM/1/4133, f. 32.
[2] PRO, ADM/1/4135, f. 87. For another example, see Add. MSS., 23651, f. 77.
[3] PRO, ADM/1/4147, f. 23.
[4] Edward J. Lowell, *The Hessians and other German Auxiliaries of Great Britain in the Revolutionary War* (New York, 1884), 56; PRO, ADM/1/4132, f. 68.
[5] E.g., Uhlendorf, op. cit., 111.   [6] PRO, ADM/1/4132, f. 68.

that the bedding on the transports under their command was 'infamously scanty; the pillows in particular not being above 7 inches by 5 at the most, resembling rather pincushions, but not so well stuffed; a whole set of bedding, consisting of mattress, pillow, blanket, and rugg hardly weigh all together . . . so much as seven pounds'.[1] In America the commanders of the army sometimes supplemented the Navy issue of bedding by allowing troops to bring part of their barrack bedding with them.[2]

The Navy Board was, despite some obvious shortcomings, satisfied with the system of putting troops on transports within cabins. When Vice Admiral Robert Roddam suggested that hammocks should be used instead of bunks, he was informed by the Board, 'We know from trial and experience that cabins are much cheaper to the publick than hammocks and much better adapted for Storeage and general Use.'[3] In addition to cabins, bunks, and bedding, the Board supplied the transports with equipment for cooking, vinegar, a 'Tin machine for sweetening water', candles, ladders, and lanterns. Sometimes battens were nailed across the deck beams in the transport's hold to make a place for the soldiers to store their arms and equipment during the voyage.[4]

The Victualling Board was responsible for supplying the provisions required by troops on transports.[5] The ship's owner fed the transport's crew. Civilians travelling on transports paid for their own food.[6] The Board of Ordnance paid for the provisions supplied to artillerymen and engineers.[7] The wages of all other troops, including Germans, were docked to pay for their provisions.[8]

---

[1] NMM, ADM/N/247, June 4, 1776; PRO, ADM/1/4132, f. 102.

[2] E.g., NYHSC, *Kemble Papers*, i, 373.

[3] NMM, ADM/BP/3, Dec. 7, 1782.

[4] PRO, ADM/1/4132, f. 68; ADM/106/2593, Aug. 25, 1775; ADM/106/3404, p. 112.

[5] Curtis, op. cit., 122.

[6] E.g., PRO, ADM/1/4141, f. 133.

[7] NMM, ADM/N/245, Feb. 10, 1776.

[8] E.g., NYHSC, *Transactions as Commissary for Embarking Foreign Troops in English Service from Germany with Copies of Letters relative to it. For the Years 1776-1777. By Charles Rainsford*, 359-60.

The Victualling Board had a complex set of administrative procedures for keeping track of all food consumed on transports so that the Navy could obtain payment for it. Attached to the end of all orders for the conveyance of troops received by the Navy Board was a statement declaring that 'as this is not a Naval Service, You are to solicit the Lords Commissioners of His Majesty's Treasury for money to [cover] the expence thereof, keeping a particular and distinctive account of the same'. Thus, the Victualling Board, on behalf of the Navy Board, would apply to the Treasury for payment for navy provisions consumed by troops when on transports.[1] The major defect in this system was that before the Victualling Board could pass the accounts of a transport or make a request for payment to the Treasury, it had to assemble all the receipts, accounts, and indents involved in the issuing and consumption of provisions. This exhaustive check was required in order to learn whether or not the masters and crews of transports were stealing government provisions, and to determine if the provisions consumed belonged to the army or navy. If the master or crew of a transport embezzled government provisions, the ship was mulcted, and the ship's freight would not be paid by the Navy Board until the ship's accounts had been audited by the Victualling Board. In addition, the Victualling Board could not claim payment from the Treasury for provisions supplied by the Commissary General's Department.

Whenever provisions were issued to a transport, an account of the transaction had to be dispatched to the Victualling Board in London.[2] The provisions appear to have been issued to the troops jointly by an officer of the transport and a representative of the army.[3] At the end of a voyage the commanding officer of the troops made out three receipts which stated the number of men provisioned, at what allowance, and for how many days. One of these receipts was given to the master of the transport, another transmitted to the War Office, and a third sent to the

[1] NMM, ADM/N/244, Aug. 1, 1775; PRO, ADM/106/2593, Sept. 25, Oct. 25, 1775.
[2] E.g., New-York Historical Society, Letter Book of Henry Davies, Agent Victualler of the Victualling Board at New York, Aug. 27, 1780.
[3] E.g., NYHSC, *Kemble Papers*, i, 342–3.

Victualling Office.[1] It was only when these receipts and the report of the official who had issued the provisions to the transport had reached London that the accounts of the ship's owner, the Victualling Board, War Office, and Treasury, could be audited and settled.

The Victualling Board did not approve of full rations being issued to troops on transports and refused to pass the accounts of those ships which had supplied soldiers with full rations.[2] As a result, Daniel Wier, the Commissary General in America, attempted to prevent army officers from ordering masters of transports to feed troops at full rations because the ship's freight would be docked.[3] Despite Wier's efforts, army commanders usually demanded that full rations be issued for several days before the commencement of an amphibious assault in order to improve the physical condition of their troops before committing them to battle. Masters of transports, being of low social status and not holding a King's commission, had no choice but to issue full rations when commanded to do so by a general officer. Because the Victualling Board consistently refused to allow full rations to be issued and deducted one-third of their cost from the ship's freight, the owners of transports were forced to subsidize amphibious landings in America by paying for one-third of the provisions consumed by the troops for several days before the beginning of the operation.

Troops on board ships of the transport service, except when proceeding to the East Indies or just before an amphibious operation in North America, received two-thirds rations.[4] The only item issued at the same rate on a transport as on land was rum. The Victualling Board defined a two-thirds ration as 'six soldiers are to have the same as four seamen'.[5] The master of the transport *James and William* at New York, for instance, was ordered on 17 February 1781 to provision soldiers at two-thirds ration according to the following table:

---

[1] E.g., PRO, WO/60/22–3.   [2] PRO, ADM/2/554, p. 390.
[3] New-York Historical Society, Letter Book of Daniel Wier, Commissary General of the British Forces in America, April 13, 1779.
[4] Troops en route to India received full rations by order of the King. PRO, ADM/1/4143, f. 103.
[5] PRO, ADM/108/1C, Sept. 2, 1782.

RULES to be observed by Masters and Commanders
of Transport Ships in victualling Land Forces

Table of Provisions for every six Officers and Soldiers

	Bread or flour Pounds	Beef Pounds	Pork Pounds	Butter Pounds	Pease Pints	Rice Pounds	Rum Gills
Sunday	4		4		2		8
Monday	4			$\frac{1}{2}$	3		8
Tuesday	4	7				1	8
Wednesday	4			$\frac{1}{2}$	2		8
Thursday	4		4		2		8
Friday	4			$\frac{1}{2}$	3		8
Saturday	4	7				1	8
Total	28	14	8	$1\frac{1}{2}$	12	2	56

When the soldiers were on two-thirds rations, the women
attached to the army were provisioned at the same rate except
'No Spirits are allowed to Women'.[1] Beer was issued at times to
German troops in place of rum.[2] It was, however, customary for
army officers to bring on board a supply of fresh provisions to
supplement the government issue rations.[3] Civilians and militia
were provisioned on transports at approximately the same rate
as troops except that they did not receive a rum ration, while
Negroes received a substantially lower ration than soldiers. All
children were given half rations.[4]

The greatest defect in the rations issued on transports was
the lack of vitamin C in the diet, a deficiency which reflected
the prevailing ignorance of basic nutrition and resulted in
countless cases of scurvy among the King's troops.[5] Compounding the medical problems caused by lack of vitamin C in the

[1] PRO, WO/60/23, Feb. 17, 1781.
[2] E.g., NMM, ADM/N/248, Jan. 12, 1778.
[3] E.g., PRO, CO/5/93, f. 481,
[4] All rules, regulations, receipts, and tables of rations for persons on board of
transports may be found in PRO, WO/60/22–23. PRO, ADM/7/565 contains a
complete account of all British troops provisioned on board of transports during
the years 1775–83.
[5] E.g., *Diary of Frederick Mackenzie: Giving a Daily Narrative of His Military Service
as an Officer of the Regiment of the Royal Welch Fusiliers during the years 1775–1781 in
Massachusetts, Rhode Island and New York* (Cambridge, Mass., 1930), ii, 585–6.

rations was the fact that the Victualling Board was almost incapable of providing provisions which were not at least half rotten. According to an historian of the Hessian forces,

The pork seemed to be four or five years old. It was streaked with black towards the outside, and was yellow farther in, with a little white in the middle. The salt beef was in much the same condition. The ship biscuit was often full of maggots. This biscuit was so hard that they [Hessian troops] sometimes broke it up with a cannon-ball, and the story ran that it had been taken from the French in the Seven Year's War, and lain in Portsmouth since. Some time they had groats and barley, or by way of a treat, pudding made of flour mixed half with salt water and half with fresh water, and old, old mutton fat. The water was all spoiled. When a cask was opened 'it stank between decks like Styx, Phlegethon, and Cocytus all together.' It was thick with filaments as long as your finger and they had to filter it through cloth before they could drink it.[1]

The Victualling Board issued bad provisions with such regularity during the eighteenth century that rotten food was an integral part of life on board the King's ships.

During the American War a substantial number of troops died or became sick on the voyage from Europe to the Western Hemisphere. The first contingent of German troops to arrive at New York in 1776 lost only about a score of men, but scurvy broke out in the last days of the voyage and many soldiers were sick when they disembarked. The second contingent of Brunswick troops to arrive at Quebec in 1776 lost nineteen men during the voyage and had 131 sick on arrival in Canada. At the end of August 1779 Admiral Marriot Arbuthnot arrived at New York from Europe with a convoy, which having lost 100 men on the passage, carried 3868 rank-and-file. Of this number 795 men were sick with 'a malignant jail fever' which, according to Clinton, 'soon spread itself among the rest of my army and sent above 6000 of my best troops to hospital'. When the 85th, 92nd, 93rd, and 94th Regiments, consisting of 2300 men, arrived at Jamaica in August 1780, 168 men were dead and

---

[1] Lowell, op. cit., 56–7.

780 sick.[1] Out of fourteen regiments with a total strength of 8437 men sent to the West Indies between October 1776 and February 1780, 932 men died during the passage. The average death rate among these fourteen regiments on the voyage to the West Indies was 11 percent of the total number of men embarked.[2] While the average mortality rate among troops on the passage to North America was not this high, it probably averaged at least 8 percent of the total number of men embarked.

Horses as well as men died on board the ships of the transport service. In the summer of 1776 out of 950 horses embarked at Portsmouth, 412 died on the voyage to New York. Sir William Howe lost most of the horses which embarked with his army at New York in the summer of 1777 for the invasion of Pennsylvania. On Clinton's expedition to South Carolina in 1779–80 every horse which was embarked at New York died en route to Charleston, and General Benedict Arnold (in British service) reported that in 1781 half the horses in his command died on the voyage between New York and Virginia.[3] Because of the great difficulty in transporting horses by sea, the British never had enough horses in America to mount all their cavalry. Large numbers of cavalrymen, although trained and equipped to fight on horseback, had to serve as infantry.[4] It is clear that the necessity of having to cross vast stretches of sea in order to reach the battlefields of the American War inflicted a large number of casualties on the British forces. But despite the cost in men and horses, it was the ability to convoy armies across oceans and

---

[1] PRO, ADM/1/487, f. 49; CO/5/98, f. 243; Max von Eelking, *The German Allied Troops in the North American War of Independence, 1776–1783*, trans. J. G. Rosengarten (Albany, N.Y., 1893), 94; Bernhard A. Uhlendorf, trans. and ed., *Revolution in America: Confidential Letters and Journals, 1776–1784, of Adjutant General Major Baurmeister of the Hessian Forces* (New Brunswick, N.J., 1957), 213; William B. Willcox, ed., *The American Rebellion: Sir Henry Clinton's Narrative of His Campaigns, 1775–1782, with an Appendix of Original Documents* (New Haven, 1954), 140–1; William B. Willcox, *Portrait of A General: Sir Henry Clinton in the War of Independence* (New York, 1964), 283–4; J. H. Fortescue, *A History of the British Army* (London, 1902), iii, 341.

[2] Add. MSS., 38345, ff. 16–17.

[3] PRO, CO/5/93, f. 499; Curtis, op. cit., 126–7.

[4] E.g., Mackesy, op. cit., 134; Eelking, op. cit., 107.

support them beyond the seas which enabled the British to fight the American War.

III

The greatest troop movement carried out by the transport service was the dispatch of reinforcements to North America at the beginning of the war. In the winter of 1775–76, the service was called upon to assemble from such widely separated points as southern England, the Clyde, Ireland, Germany, and the Mediterranean approximately 27,000 infantry, a regiment of cavalry, 950 horses, and a vast mass of military equipment. This force had then to be transported across the Atlantic to New York and Quebec and landed on a hostile continent. No military operation of this size and scope had ever before been attempted.

The government, by dispatching to North America a huge force, intended to crush the American rebellion in one massive campaign and it was realized as early as 25 August 1775, 'that the success of the War in America absolutely depends upon a considerable army being there early in the Spring [of 1776]'.[1] On 9 October 1775 General Howe wrote from Boston that the reinforcements for America should be dispatched in such a way that 'they may be expected here about the time I should wish the campaign [of 1776] to open, in the middle or latter end of April'; and on 16 January 1776 Howe warned 'that if a respectable supply of troops from Europe does not arrive soon in the spring, another defensive campaign, I conclude, will be the consequence'.[2] Lord Rawdon, at the beginning of 1776, said that the Americans could not resist for more than one campaign 'if you give us the necessary means to carry on the war with vigour'.[3]

During the summer of 1775 the British forces in Europe were redeployed, and the army in America was reinforced. On 30 March 1775 six transports carrying marines sailed from Plymouth for Boston. At the same time the Navy Board started to make arrangements for the transport of the 3rd and 11th Regiments from Plymouth to Cork and the 22nd, 40th, 44th, and 45th Regiments from Ireland to New York. These troop

---

[1] G, no. 1699.   [2] PRO, CO/5/92, f. 312; CO/5/93, ff. 33–4.
[3] HMC, *Hastings MSS.*, iii, 167.

movements began in April 1775. In the middle of April the 17th
Light Dragoons was dispatched from Ireland to Boston, and in
the summer of 1775 the transport service conveyed the 17th,
27th, 28th, 46th, and 56th Regiments and a year's supply of
clothing for the army in America from Cork to Boston.[1] At the
same time the British decided to reorganize their Mediterranean
garrisons in order to release troops for service in America. On
4 August 1775 orders were issued to the Board to dispatch
transports to Stade to carry five Hanoverian regiments to the
Mediterranean. Three Hanoverian regiments were to be sent to
Gibraltar to relieve three British regiments, and the other two
were to replace two British regiments at Minorca. The transports which took out the German troops were to return to the
British Isles with the British regiments. Three days later the
Board was directed to carry a unit of 425 Invalids to Minorca
which was to replace the 25th Regiment on that island. In this
service the Board employed twenty transports with a total
tonnage of 6007 tons. Although the Hanoverians and Invalids
were supposed to embark at the beginning of September, they
were not in fact taken on board till 6 October. These delays
were partly caused by alterations in the number and type of
Invalids and the change from Stade to Ritzebüttel as the port of
embarkation for the Hanoverian troops. Although the transports' departure was delayed, they had a fast passage, and the
majority of them were back in Britain with troops from the
Mediterranean garrisons by the middle of February 1776.[2]

Between 1 January and 30 September 1775 the Board deployed seventy-five ships with a total tonnage of 27,242 tons to
convey reinforcements to America and to effect the changes in
the Mediterranean garrisons.[3] These were preliminary troop
movements leading up to the dispatch of reinforcements to
North America in 1776.

The British originally intended to crush the revolt in the

---

[1] NMM, ADM/B/189, April 13, 15, 19, 28, May 5, 1775; ADM/N/244, Aug. 1,
7, 9, 1775; Fortescue, op. cit., iii, 154, 173.
[2] NMM, ADM/B/190, Sept. 12, 1775; ADM/B/191, Feb. 21, 1776; ADM/N/244,
Aug. 4, 7, Sept. 8, 13, 1775; PRO, ADM/1/4130, ff. 68, 94; ADM/3/81, ff. 140–1;
Uhlendorf, *Revolution in America*, 4.
[3] NMM, ADM/B/190, Nov. 30, 1775.

American colonies in a single campaign by concentrating a massive army before New York in the spring of 1776, but the principle of concentration of force was abandoned even before preparations for the campaign had begun in Britain. In the fall of 1775 reports arrived in London from Governor Josiah Martin of North Carolina stating that the settlers in the back country were strongly Loyalist and that with assistance from Britain the Loyalists could regain control of the province for the Crown. The government at first planned to support the Loyalists in North Carolina by sending them arms and by asking Howe to dispatch a small body of troops to that region.[1] But as more and more reports arrived in Whitehall of Loyalist activity in the American South, the government increased the amount of aid to be dispatched until a shipment of arms to North Carolina grew into a major expedition. The plan that finally emerged in October 1775 called for the 32nd and 36th Regiments to be taken from Portsmouth to Cork to reinforce Ireland, while the 15th, 37th, 53rd, 54th, and 57th Regiments and some artillery escorted by seven warships were to sail from Cork on 1 December in order to reach North Carolina in the first months of 1776, at which time the Loyalists were to rise against the Americans. General Henry Clinton, who was at Boston, was to meet the force off Cape Fear and take command of it.[2] By the beginning of November the Board had assembled twenty-one transports with a total tonnage of 5959 tons to move the two regiments from England to Ireland and the five regiments from Cork to North Carolina. At this point, however, a number of delays occurred which proved fatal to the expedition. The Ordnance Board failed to produce ordnance transports promptly and one of the warships of the escort was found to be in need of repair. The eight transports with the 32nd and 36th Regiments did not sail from Portsmouth until 12 December, and once in the Channel met head winds and bad weather which delayed their arrival in Ireland.[3]

---

[1] Mackesy, op. cit., 43–4; Eric Robson, 'The Expedition to the Southern Colonies, 1775–1776', *English Historical Review* (Oct., 1951), lxvi, 538–40.
   [2] NMM, ADM/N/244, Oct. 19, 1775; PRO, ADM/1/4130, f. 120.
   [3] NMM, ADM/B/190, Nov. 8, Dec. 12, 1775; Robert Wilden Neeser, ed., *The Dispatches of Molyneux Shuldham* (New York, 1913), 34; Robson, op. cit., 545.

While the 32nd and 36th Regiments were proceeding to Cork, a number of alterations were being made in the composition of the expedition. On 25 October the 28th Regiment and seven companies of the 46th Regiment were added to it. These troops had already been dispatched to North America, but their transports were forced by bad weather to put back into Milford Haven. By 8 January 1776 all the infantry had embarked, but the expedition did not sail until 12 February because the arrival of the naval escorts at Cork was delayed. A few days after leaving Cork the expedition ran into bad weather. The convoy dispersed, and three transports carrying elements of the 57th, 54th, and 37th Regiments were forced back to the British Isles. It was not until the first weeks of May that the whole expedition, after a rough passage from Ireland, assembled off Cape Fear.[1]

The expedition to North Carolina in the winter of 1776 was ill-conceived, badly executed, and a waste of time, ships, and men. The force from Cork arrived months too late to assist the North Carolina Loyalists. Expecting earlier assistance they had, according to plan, rallied to the Royal Standard in January, only to be crushed by the Americans on 27 February 1776 at the battle of Moore's Bridge. Clinton, upon learning of the Loyalist defeat, compounded the debacle by using the force from Cork to make an abortive attack on Fort Moultrie at the entrance of Charleston Harbour before joining the main British army at New York on 2 August.[2]

While the expedition to the Carolinas was being prepared, news reached London of the American invasion of Canada. On 23 December 1775 dispatches arrived from General Guy Carleton reporting that the bulk of the British forces in Canada had been destroyed and that the Americans had overrun all of the Province of Quebec except the city of Quebec with its small garrison and weak fortifications. The news forced the government to change its plans for the campaign of 1776. It was now resolved that Quebec must be relieved and Canada reconquered at the first opportunity and that this operation would

[1] NMM, ADM/B/191, March 1, 1776; ADM/N/244, Dec. 9, 1775; Robson, op. cit., 544, 545, 547, 548, 553.

[2] PRO, ADM/1/487, f. 37; Willard M. Wallace, *Appeal to Arms: A Military History of the American Revolution* (New York, 1951), 88–96.

take priority over the dispatch of forces for the invasion of New York.[1]

On 26 December 1775 Lord George Germain and Admiral Hugh Palliser, the only Lord of the Admiralty in London at the time, met to arrange for the immediate relief of Quebec and agreed to dispatch a small advance force to succour Quebec 'as early as is practicable'. Accordingly, H.M.S. *Isis*, three frigates, three victuallers, and transports carrying the 29th Regiment sailed from the Nore on 10 February 1776. This force broke the American siege of Quebec on 6 May when H.M.S. *Isis* and a frigate reached the city after pushing through the melting ice of the St Lawrence River.[2] This operation marked the opening of the campaign of 1776.

At the end of December 1775, while the relief of Quebec was being organized, the government began to issue the orders to assemble the shipping needed to carry across the Atlantic the men and materials for the main campaign in North America. On 21 December the Admiralty, on Lord Suffolk's orders, directed the Navy Board to charter enough transports to carry 5000 men. Suffolk warned Sandwich on 25 December: 'The transports for 5,000 men already ordered won't be quite sufficient for the Brunswick, Waldeck and Hanau troops—in all probability there will be 2,000 of the Scotch-Dutch to be provided for in the first instance, and then ten or twelve thousand Hessians, besides what men go from hence or from Ireland.' Three days later, on 28 December, Suffolk ordered that transports be provided for an additional 12,000 men. This order was transmitted to the Board the next day with directions to ballast the ships with coal and fit them at the rate of two tons per man. The Board, which was not informed for what purpose transports were required, was only told that it would 'have due notice of the time & Place of Embarkation with such other Particulars as may be necessary for your information'. While Suffolk was providing for the conveyance of German troops, Germain was planning for the movement to North America of British troops. On 7 January 1776 the Admiralty was directed to order the

---

[1] Mackesy, op. cit., 56–7.

[2] NMM, ADM/N/245, Feb. 10, 1776; SAN/T/7, Dec. 27, 1775; Mackesy, op. cit., 57, 80; Wallace, op. cit., 84–7.

Board to hire shipping to carry 10,000 infantry, one regiment of cavalry, and 1000 draught horses, and on 13 February shipping was ordered to be provided to carry to Quebec the materials to build six sloops and 800 bateaux. All the vessels employed in these tasks were to be ballasted with coal.[1]

The government's basic plan, as William Eden, an under secretary of state, explained it to Sandwich on 5 February 1776, was to convey 27,480 infantry, the 16th Light Dragoons, and 1000 horses from Europe to North America in time to open a campaign against the Americans in the spring. This force would be dispatched to North America in four groups. The first group was to consist of 7580 British and German infantry which would be carried to Quebec in 15,800 tons of shipping. The second division would be sent to America in 27,000 tons of transports and consist of 8200 Hessians, 3500 Highlanders, and 1000 Guards. The third body of troops to be dispatched would be 3800 German infantry which were to go to Canada on 6400 tons of transports. The fourth division would be made up of 4000 Hessians, the 16th Light Dragoons, and 1000 horses which would proceed to America in 28,000 tons of shipping. The government thought that the whole movement could be carried out with 77,200 tons of transports.[2] This estimate, however, did not take into account the need to transport recruits, camp equipage, and clothing, nor did it anticipate the numerous alterations and additions to the plan which were subsequently made. In addition, the government's scheme did not take into consideration the time factor. If the campaign was to be decisive, it was imperative that the forces from Europe arrive in North America early in the spring giving them the entire summer and fall of 1776 to subdue the Americans. The success of the campaign of 1776 depended absolutely on the ability of the Board to procure and fit-out quickly the required shipping. At every turn, however, the dispatch of troops was held up by a shortage of ships.[3] The delays due to the difficulties of procuring transports

---

[1] Sandwich MSS., file 8, box 4, bundle 17, no. 26, at Mapperton; NMM, ADM/N/244, Dec. 21, 29, 1775; ADM/N/245, Jan. 7, Feb. 13, 1776; SAN/T/1, Dec. 25, 1775; PRO, ADM/1/4130, f. 170.
[2] NMM, SAN/T/1, Feb. 5, 1776.
[3] For an account of the efforts to obtain transports in 1776, see above, pp. 90–3.

would not in themselves have been decisive, but the government had also to overcome delays imposed by weather and the miscarriages that were bound to occur in coordinating the movement of troops, stores, transports, and warships taking part in numerous embarkations at such widely separated points as Germany, southern England, the Clyde, and Cork.

In the first months of 1776, the government thought that it could carry out the plan for the campaign in North America despite the difficulties which would result from the great size of the enterprise. On 11 January 1776 Sandwich wrote to the King saying that there would be trouble finding the transport tonnage required, but that he believed 'we shall be ready in time with all the transports that are wanted'.[1] And on 1 February Germain informed Howe that he thought, 'the reinforcement for the army under your command will be embarked before the end of March, and that the armament intended for Quebec will be ready much sooner'.[2] Less exalted officials, however, were not so optimistic. Palliser was openly dismayed: 'we are now required to provide (as it were instantly) more transports than the greatest number employed in the last war, which were years growing to the number'. The most he could promise was 'that the utmost that can be effected by zeal, duty, and money, will be done'.[3]

The Board was in turmoil during the first months of 1776. This confusion was due in part to the way in which Germain and Suffolk drafted their orders for the procurement of transports. Between 21 December 1775 and 7 January 1776 the Commissioners of the Navy had received orders to provide enough shipping to convey 27,000 infantry, one regiment of cavalry, and 1000 horses, but they were not informed of the places of embarkation, destination, or the names of the units. The secretaries of state planned to give the Board this information at a later date in a series of supplementary directives, but by the time the secretaries began to issue these supplementary directives, a number of alterations and additions had been made in the original plan. The result was that the Board, when it received orders to transport a unit of troops, did not know if the

---

[1] G, no. 1809.   [2] PRO, CO/5/93, f. 16.   [3] NRS, *Sandwich Papers*, i, 97.

unit in question was part of the 27,000 men for whom ships had already been ordered or an addition to that number.

Throughout the winter and spring of 1776 Germain put forth schemes which diverted tonnage from the central task of transporting troops from Europe to North America. On 9 March he ordered the Board to dispatch transports to St Vincent to embark the 6th Regiment and convey it to America where the private soldiers of the regiment were to be made into replacements. At the same time he ordered the Board to send transports to Grenada to pick up and bring back to England the officers, non-commissioned officers, and invalids of the 48th Regiment. The Commissioners, however, refused to divert tonnage from the task of transporting troops across the Atlantic and suggested that the shipping needed to collect the 6th Regiment and the remnants of the 48th Regiment be supplied from North America. This suggestion was accepted by the government.[1] The decision to abandon Germain's plan for removing troops from the West Indies was a wise one, for it was of far greater importance to dispatch complete combat units to North America in the spring of 1776 than to tie up ships in a long three-legged voyage in order to provide Howe with a few hundred replacements.

Confusion was created when from time to time the orders received by the Board for supplying transports were radically changed without notice. On 17 January the Board was directed to supply transports to carry the 3rd, 9th, 11th, 24th, 34th, 53rd, and 62nd Regiments from Cork to Canada.[2] But on 10 February these orders were altered. The 3rd and 11th Regiments were not to be embarked and the 21st Regiment at Plymouth and the 31st Regiment in Scotland were to be dispatched to Canada in their place.[3]

Another obstacle encountered by the Board in its efforts to dispatch troops overseas in 1776 was harassment by the Customs Service. In the fall of 1775 the Commissioners of Customs were requested to permit transports to enter and leave British ports

[1] NMM, ADM/B/191, Jan. 24, Feb. 22, 1776; ADM/N/245, Jan. 20, 1776; ADM/N/246, March 9, 1776; PRO, ADM/1/487, f. 37; ADM/1/4131, ff. 81, 88.
[2] NMM, ADM/N/245, Jan. 17, 1776.
[3] NMM, ADM/N/254, Feb. 10, 1776.

without 'entry or Clearance' through customs. This permission was refused, and the only concession made to military necessity was that

Transports having only Soldiers on board with nothing more than their necessary Baggage and Equipage, are considered as being in Ballast, and therefore the usual Forms are despens't with, but it would furnish Opertunities to the greatest frauds if *Loaden Ships* were to be released from the Rules and Examinations of the Customs.[1]

The crowning blow came when the Customs Service made known its attitude towards coal on board transports. The Navy Board had orders to ballast all ships dispatched to North America with coal. The Commissioners of Customs required that the Board obtain warrants from the Treasury in order to export coal without paying a tax. In March 1776 the Customs Service demanded that all coal being used for ballast by transports then in the Thames be unloaded so that it could be measured in order to determine how much 'London duty' each vessel had to pay. This demand, if complied with, would have forced the Board to remove the ballast from ships which had been hired at ports, such as Newcastle, and arrived at Deptford for fitting-out already ballasted with coal. In order to prevent the Commissioners of Customs from bringing the transport service to a halt, the Board was forced to appeal to the Treasury to intervene. The affair ended when the Commissioners of Customs agreed that for the purpose of collecting the London duty they would accept the Board's account of the amount of coal on each ship in the Thames. The coal incident of 1776 did not put an end to the obstructiveness of the customs officials, for they continued to harass the transport service throughout the war.[2]

Despite confusing directives and the obstructionism of the Customs Service, the Navy Board had, by 2 February 1776, managed to assemble at various British ports 101 transports con-

---

[1] PRO, T/1/516, Customs Board to Treasury, Oct. 20, 1775.
[2] NMM, ADM/B/191, March 7, 1776; ADM/N/246, March 23, 1776; PRO, T/1/516, Customs Board to Treasury, Aug. 8, 1775; T/29/45, ff. 40–41. For other examples of harassment of the transport service by the Customs Service, see NMM, ADM/B/191, April 11, 13, 16, 24, 1776.

sisting of 38,996 tons. It was intended that the bulk of this tonnage be used to carry the first group of troops to Canada, but the fitting-out of the ships at Deptford was hindered by the severe winter of 1776.[1] Between 22 January and 14 February, nineteen transports with a total tonnage of 6461 tons were assigned to carry the 2932 men of the Brunswick and Hanau Regiments to Canada.[2] The transports, drawn from those fitting-out at Deptford, arrived in the Elbe River in time to complete the embarkation by 26 March and arrived at Spithead on 30 March. The force sailed from Spithead on 3 April and was joined at sea by transports carrying the 21st Regiment which had embarked at Plymouth.[3]

The Board marshalled shipping from all over the British Isles to transport the eight British regiments which accompanied the first echelon of German troops to Canada. At the beginning of April the 21st Regiment at Plymouth boarded five transports with a total tonnage of 1323 tons and sailed in time to join the convoy with the Brunswick and Hanau troops in the Channel.[4] The 31st Regiment began its voyage to Canada even before the German troops and the 21st Regiment had embarked. At the end of February this unit left the Clyde on eight transports for Cork, where it arrived in time to join the six regiments being dispatched from Ireland to Canada.[5] To convey to Canada from Ireland the six British regiments, which had a total strength of 2972 rank-and-file, the Board amassed at Cork thirty-four transports with a total tonnage of 9149 tons. Thirteen of these ships came from the Thames, four from Plymouth, and thirteen from Portsmouth. The ships from Portsmouth had just been refitted after returning from Gibraltar and Minorca. On 7 April the forty-two transports carrying the six regiments from Ireland and the 31st from the Clyde left Cork and joined at sea on 20 April the convoy with the 21st Regiment and the Brunswick and Hanau troops. The arrival on 20 May of the first group of reinforcements from Europe and of the 47th Regiment from

[1] NMM, ADM/B/191, Feb. 2, 1776.
[2] NMM, ADM/B/191, Jan. 22, Feb. 14, 1776.
[3] NMM, ADM/N/246, March 18, April 1, 1776; Eelking, op. cit., 88–9.
[4] NMM, ADM/B/191, Feb. 11, April 13, 1776; ADM/N/246, April 12, 1776.
[5] NMM, ADM/B/191, Feb. 16, 1776.

Howe's army brought the number of troops in Quebec to more than 11,000 men.[1]

In March 1776, the Board began to assemble the shipping required to carry the troops to be used in the invasion of New York. Two regiments of Highlanders, a detachment of Guards, a division of Hessians, and a year's supply of camp equipage for the forces already in America were to be sent from Europe as soon as possible after the departure of the first reinforcement for Canada. Their dispatch was delayed, however, by the shortage of transport tonnage in Europe.[2] The 42nd and 71st Regiments of Highlanders consisting of 3466 officers and men were the first to leave Europe in 1776 to reinforce Howe's army. The Highlanders were embarked on thirty-three transports in the Clyde and sailed for America on 27 April under escort of H.M.S. *Flora*. On 5 May the convoy was scattered by a storm off the Scilly Islands. Only nine transports remained under escort of H.M.S. *Flora* after this storm, while the rest proceeded independently towards Boston which was their destination. Twenty of the transports which had separated from the H.M.S. *Flora* were intercepted at sea by British warships and sent into Halifax, but four ships not knowing that Boston had been evacuated were captured by the Americans.[3]

On 7 February 1776 the Board was ordered to provide transports to carry 8392 Hessian troops who were to embark on 20 March for America. In the next weeks the Board received orders to dispatch to America with the Hessians 1103 Guards, 200 tons of army equipment, a year's supply of camp equipage for twenty-six battalions of British infantry, several score of British recruits, and 100 tons of army medicines.[4] Great efforts were made to execute these orders, but the shortage of shipping retarded and curtailed the troop movement. On 23 February the Board informed the Admiralty that it did not have the

---

[1] NMM, ADM/B/191, Feb. 20, April 16, 1776; PRO, CO/5/7, ff. 295, 340; WO/25/1145, April 15, 1776; Fortescue, op. cit., 178; Neeser, op. cit., 175-6; Eelking, op. cit., 88-9.

[2] PRO, CO/5/93, ff. 69-70.

[3] NMM, ADM/N/245, Feb. 21, 22, 1776; PRO, ADM/51/360, April 27, May 5-8, 1776; NRS, *Naval Miscellany*, i, 119; Neeser, op. cit., 257-8, 273; Clark, op. cit., 160-5.

[4] NMM, ADM/N/245, Feb. 7, 9, 19, 23, 1776; ADM/N/246, March 4, 18, 1776.

transport tonnage required to embark the Hessians in Germany at the rate of two tons per man, and suggested that the Hessians be embarked at the rate of one and one-half tons per man for the passage to Spithead; the Board hoped to have additional tonnage available to be able to transport them from Spithead to America at the rate of two tons per man. The Board also wanted eighty-six tons of baggage per Hessian regiment left behind and the number of women allowed to each regiment cut from ninety to forty-five. If these measures were not adopted the Board warned, 'we cannot give them hopes of its being in our power to dispatch a greater number of transports for the Weser with the probability of their arrival there by the time fixed upon than will admit of receiving twelve of the seventeen Regiments which are to compose this embarkation of 8,392 men'.[1] These suggestions were accepted by the Admiralty.[2]

By 19 March twenty-two transports had sailed from Deptford for the Weser and an additional thirty-two ships were scheduled to depart from the Thames between 19 and 21 March for Germany. On 21 and 22 March the Hessians were mustered into the King's service, and on 23 March the troops began to board transports. It was found, however, that the Hessians did not number 8392 men as had been specified but rather 9100 men and that each regiment had a huge quantity of baggage. Also, each general officer in the Hessian service wanted to take a private carriage to America. Attempts were made by George Marsh, the Clerk of the Acts who was in Germany at the time, to charter extra tonnage in Hamburg, but the German ship-owners were unwilling to risk their ships on a wartime voyage to America. The result was that Rall's and Mirbach's Regiments and 154 men of Kyphausen's Regiment had to be left behind. The Hessians sailed for Spithead on 16 April and arrived in England at the beginning of May.[3]

While the Hessians were embarking in the River Weser, the Board was assembling at Spithead the tonnage necessary to embark the Guards, camp equipage, military stores, and to

[1] NMM, ADM/B/191, Feb. 23, 1776.
[2] NMM, ADM/N/245, Feb. 26, 1776.
[3] NMM, ADM/B/191, March 19, 29, 1776; Eelking, op. cit., 24.

carry the Hessians to America at the rate of two tons per man. Twenty-nine transports were ordered to proceed to Spithead in time to arrive at that anchorage by the end of April from Deptford, Dunkirk, Plymouth, Bristol, Liverpool, Cork, and Whitehaven.[1] At Spithead during the first week of May, the Guards embarked and some of the Hessians were rearranged on board transports in order to be embarked at the rate of two tons per man. At the same time 1500 sets of clothing for the marines in America were loaded on the ships along with eighty-two flat-bottom boats and 131 wagons. Again, because of the shortage of ships, 107 wagons and nine casks of camp equipage had to be left at Portsmouth. The Hessians, Guards, camp equipage, and stores sailed from Spithead on 7 May on board seventy transports, two storeships, two ordnance transports, and nine Navy victuallers under a heavy naval escort, and arrived at Staten Island on 12 August.[2] The concentration of troops at Staten Island in August 1776 formed an army of 25,000 men which 'for its numbers, is one of the finest that ever was seen'.[3]

During April 1776 the Board began to assemble the shipping necessary to convey the second group of reinforcements to America and Canada. The 16th Light Dragoons, 950 horses, 4200 Hessians, and 680 Waldeckers were to be sent to America, and 2148 Brunswick and Hanau troops were to be dispatched to Canada. The force going to America was to have priority over the troops for Canada. It was planned to carry the German troops from Germany to Spithead on two British transports which were dispatched to Germany from Portsmouth, eleven Dutch transports with a total tonnage of 4624 tons which were fitting-out at Deptford, four Dutch transports consisting of 2920 tons fitting-out at Amsterdam, and six other Dutch transports being fitted-out in Hamburg. In order to speed up the movement of German troops to Spithead, the Admiralty directed that the transports sail independently. It was not until 22 June, however, that all the Germans had arrived in England

---

[1] NMM, ADM/B/191, March 19, April 10, 1776.
[2] NMM, ADM/B/191, April 30, 1776; ADM/B/193, May 8, 1776; ADM/N/246, April 26, 1776; ADM/N/247, May 13, 1776; PRO, ADM/1/487, ff. 51–2; NRS, *Naval Miscellany*, i, 112.
[3] HMC, *Rutland MSS.*, iii, 6.

where they embarked for the Atlantic crossing at the ratio of one man to every two tons of shipping.[1] While the German troops were being moved from Germany to Spithead, the shipping required to transport the 490 officers and men of the 16th Light Dragoons and 950 horses was also being assembled. This task was completed in late June, and the second echelon of reinforcements for Canada and America departed from Britain in the early summer. The Brunswick and Hanau troops arrived at Quebec on 14 September, and the second division of Hessians, the Waldeckers, the 16th Light Dragoons, and the horses arrived off Sandy Hook on 18 October 1776.[2]

On 22 August 1776 the campaign intended to quell the American revolt in one massive blow began, when 6000 soldiers waded ashore at Gravesend on Long Island. The summer was nearly over, and although the campaign lasted for more than three months and defeat after defeat was inflicted upon the Americans, there was not enough time left before winter brought the campaign to a halt to catch and destroy in battle an enemy so skilful at retreating and running as were the Americans. In December a disintegrating Continental Army, which had been driven from New York and New Jersey, retreated across the Delaware River into Pennsylvania, while the British, as was the custom of the eighteenth-century European armies, ended the campaign and went into winter quarters without having achieved a decisive victory. It was the late start of the campaign more than any other factor which prevented the British from destroying Washington's army during 1776, for there is little doubt that if it had not been for the onset of winter, the British would have followed the deteriorating American army into Pennsylvania and destroyed it. This failure was not caused by any act of oversight or neglect on the part of the transport service. On the contrary, the conveyance of over 27,000 infantry, a regiment of cavalry, and 950 horses from Europe to North America in the space of nine months was a stupendous

[1] NMM, ADM/B/191, April 10, 24, 27, 1776; ADM/B/193, June 18, 22, 1776; ADM/N/246, April 19, 27, 1776; ADM/N/247, May 11, 1776.

[2] NMM, ADM/B/193, May 16, 20, 30, June 22, 1776; ADM/N/247, June 22, 1776; Eelking, op. cit., 45, 94; Edward H. Tatum, Jr, ed., *The American Journal of Ambrose Serle* (San Marino, Calif., 1940), 125.

administrative achievement which would not again be equalled until the twentieth century.

The blame rests rather with those who formulated British strategy. The government had originally intended to smash the revolt in America in one campaign to be opened in the early spring by a massive invasion of New York. This campaign was to take priority over all other military commitments in 1776. But when the news of the loss of Quebec reached Whitehall, the government decided that the recovery of Quebec had to take precedence over the invasion of New York. This choice between New York and Canada was made necessary by the lack of shipping for the simultaneous invasion of New York and relief of Canada. The government's mistake in 1776 was to allow the expedition to the southern colonies to sail after it had learned of the American conquest of Quebec. There was time to stop this expedition from leaving the British Isles, for the news of the American siege of the city of Quebec arrived in England on 23 December 1775, and the expedition to the southern colonies did not depart from Cork until 12 February 1776. If this expedition had been prevented from sailing, the transport service would have had the tonnage available to send over twenty empty transports to Boston or reinforce Howe's army simultaneously with the first group of reinforcements for Canada.

The shortage of transports in America also hindered British efforts to invade New York early in the spring of 1776. Even if the British army had been promptly reinforced with the six regiments which were sent to the southern colonies, it is very doubtful that the campaign could have opened before the end of spring because there was not enough tonnage in America to move the army to New York. However, this problem could have been solved if the ships which were employed on the expedition to the southern colonies had been sent to Howe empty, for then the British would have had the transports required to withdraw from Boston. Throughout the winter of 1775–76 the British wished to evacuate Boston and shift their army to New York, but were prevented from doing so by a shortage of transports. On 27 November 1775 there were forty-seven transports in America of which seventeen vessels were employed collecting provisions, wood, and forage for the support of the army. By

20 January 1776 the number of transports in America had increased to sixty-one with a total tonnage of 19,765 tons, but it was calculated that a further 8597 tons were required to embark the British forces at Boston.[1] The British expected to make up this tonnage deficiency by taking into the King's service a number of ships which were dispatched with provisions to Boston, but these vessels were driven to the West Indies by the weather and never arrived in Massachusetts. Because of the transport shortage, the British either had to remain in Boston or remove their army from the town in two groups—an extremely dangerous operation to be carried out in the face of the besieging American army. The British thus decided to remain in Boston until they had collected enough tonnage to evacuate the town in one movement. On 4 March, however, the Americans occupied Dorchester Heights and forced the British to evacuate Boston. The British left Boston on St Patrick's Day in seventy-eight ships with a total tonnage of 21,933 tons. On these ships were crammed helter-skelter 8908 troops, 924 Loyalists, and a huge quantity of military equipment and stores. 'Never was an Army so Crowded in Transports, owning to the want of Shipping.' The shortage of ships forced the British to leave behind large quantities of stores.[2] On 21 March 1776 Howe wrote from Nantasket Road informing the government:

I am justly sensible how much more . . . it would be to His Majesty's Service if this army was in a situation to proceed immediately to New York; but the present condition of the troops crowded in transports without regard to conveniences, the inevitable dissortments, stores & all the incumberances with which [it is] clogged, effectively disable me from . . . any offensive operations.[3]

Howe proceeded to Halifax in order to sort out his army in a friendly port and embark the troops in combat order for the assault on New York. By 7 May the requisite amount of shipping had been collected to mount the assault on New York, but the force was further delayed at Halifax waiting for provisions. It was not until 1 July that the 9000 men of Howe's army began

---

[1] PRO, ADM/1/4131, ff. 3–4; ADM/1/4132, f. 4.
[2] PRO, ADM/1/484, f. 480; CO/5/93, ff. 94–5, 162, 166–72; Add. MSS., 21680, f. 100.
[3] PRO, CO/5/93, f. 89.

landing on Staten Island at the entrance of New York Harbour. After capturing Staten Island at the beginning of July, the British operations in the New York area halted until the arrival of the Guards, Hessians, and camp equipage from Europe on 12 August because Howe would not begin operations without new camp equipage.[1]

The British bid for a decisive victory in the campaign of 1776 failed owing to bad generalship and the sheer size and complexity of the operation. Too few ships were available at any one time to convey the thousands of troops, the hundreds of horses, and the great mass of stores and equipment required to carry out the operation. It was also beyond the power of the government in the eighteenth century to control and coordinate the movement of scores of transports and thousands of troops in such widely separated places as Germany, England, Ireland, Scotland, the Mediterranean, and North America. Compounding the other difficulties was the government's diversion of resources from the main operations, which were the reconquest of Quebec and the invasion of New York, into peripheral projects. Insurmountable administrative difficulties when coupled with the government's lack of strategic insight and the sluggish and mediocre generalship displayed by Clinton, Carleton, and Howe had a disastrous effect on the outcome of British operations in 1776. The amazing thing about the British effort in 1776 is not that it failed, but rather that so huge and complex an operation came so close to succeeding.

IV

After the dispatch of the great reinforcement to North America in 1776, the transport service continued to play a major role in the British military effort. Throughout the war the Navy Board employed transports to convey men and materials around the shores of the British Isles. Transports carried seamen[2] and naval stores between various British ports.[3] The transport service was also used to move prisoners of war between various

---

[1] PRO, CO/5/93, ff. 153–4; HMC, *Stopford-Sackville MSS.*, ii, 37–8; NYHSC, *Kemble Papers*, i, 359–60; Mackesy, op. cit., 82–3.

[2] E.g., PRO, ADM/106/3385, p. 46.

[3] E.g., PRO, ADM/106/2595, May 29, 1777; ADM/106/2601, Sept. 7, 9, 1779.

places of confinement in Britain and to France for exchange.[1] The large number of transports always in British ports during the American War provided the government with a cheap and easy means of conveying men and material between various points in Britain.

The movement of troops and army equipment between ports in the British Isles by the transport service was of far greater importance than the *ad hoc* conveyance of seamen, naval stores, and prisoners of war. Every major reinforcement dispatched overseas during the American War was coupled with or preceded by major troop movements in Britain involving the redeployment of forces on garrison duty and the conveyance of troops intended for foreign service to the British port from which they were to be dispatched abroad.

The troop movements in the British Isles conducted by the transport service in 1778 were typical of the kind of reshuffling of forces which took place constantly in Britain during the American War. On 31 January 1778 Germain ordered the Navy Board to convey 800 recruits from the Clyde to America and 500 recruits from Chatham to America. By 4 February the transport service had three transports at Gravesend to carry the 500 recruits from Chatham to Spithead where they were to await convoy for the Atlantic crossing. At the same time the Board ordered another three transports at Cork to proceed to the Clyde where they would be joined by the transport *Resolution* to embark the 800 Highland recruits intended for America.[2] On 13 February the Board was directed to transport 9500 more troops from Britain to America, 6500 of them to be embarked in the Clyde. On 28 March, however, Germain cancelled the embarkation of the Highland troops for America and directed that the 70th Regiment and a number of soldiers belonging to the 42nd Regiment embark at the Clyde for Nova Scotia, two regiments be sent from Scotland to Ireland, and one company of the 42nd Regiment and two companies of the 71st Regiment totalling 332 officers and men be conveyed from the Clyde to Cork from whence they would proceed to Newfoundland. The

---

[1] E.g., NMM, ADM/B/197, Dec. 23, 1778; ADM/N/249, Aug. 12, 1779.
[2] NMM, ADM/B/195, Feb. 4, 21, 1778; ADM/N/248, Feb. 2, 14, 1778; PRO, ADM/1/4135, f. 17.

three companies of Highlanders being sent to Newfoundland were drawn from the 800 recruits which Germain had ordered on 31 January to be sent to America. In the early summer of 1778 the two regiments were moved from Scotland to Ireland, and the 70th Regiment and attached members of the 42nd Regiment departed from the Clyde for Nova Scotia. On 5 April the transports *Preston* and *Resolution* sailed from Greenock for Cork with the three companies of the 42nd and 71st Regiments en route to Newfoundland. The remainder of the 800 recruits at the Clyde, originally intended to be sent to America, sailed to Spithead on three transports where they arrived on 18 June to serve as marines in the Channel Fleet.[1]

Simultaneously with the troop movements ordered by Germain, the Board conducted, on the orders of Lord Weymouth, Secretary of State for the Southern Department, another series of troop movements. On 17 March 1778, following instructions from Weymouth, the Admiralty directed the Board to provide transports for the conveyance to Gibraltar of the Manchester Regiment from Liverpool and 800 recruits from the Thames. The Manchester Regiment was originally intended to be sent to St Augustine and was included in the orders issued to the Board on 13 February to provide for the conveyance of 9500 men to America. At the end of March, these orders were again changed; the Manchester Regiment was not to embark at Liverpool, but rather at Portsmouth, and in addition to the 800 recruits a number of Hanoverians and eighty more British were to embark in the Thames. By 20 April the service had collected five transports at Portsmouth, one at the Nore, and five others at Blackslake to embark the troops bound to Gibraltar and the Manchester Regiment was embarked at Portsmouth at the beginning of May. But it was not until the second week of June that the transports from the Thames arrived at Portsmouth and the combined force sailed for Gibraltar.[2] On 7 April 1778 Weymouth ordered yet another series of troop movements. The Board was required to dispatch transports to Fort St George in

[1] NMM, ADM/B/196, March 28, April 13, 25, 27, June 9, 18, 1778; ADM/N/248, Feb. 13, March 6, 28, April 10, 27, May 11, 13, June 10, 1778.
[2] NMM, ADM/B/196, April 20, 21, 1778; ADM/N/248, March 17, 24, 27, April 22, May 11, 1778.

Scotland to embark 1000 men of Mackenzie's Regiment of Highlanders and carry them to the Channel Islands. On 20 April seven transports sailed from the Nore for Scotland. On 11 August, almost before Mackenzie's Regiment had arrived in the Channel Islands, the Board was directed to send transports to Leith in order to carry 1167 officers and men of the Seaforth Highlanders to Guernsey and Jersey. After the disembarkation of the Seaforth Highlanders, the transports were to embark Mackenzie's Regiment and carry it to Spithead. While the transports were proceeding along the east coast of Britain to Leith to embark the Seaforth Highlanders, Weymouth, on 22 August, ordered the Board to provide ships to carry 600 recruits from Kinsale to Chatham. The Navy Board issued directions on 16 September for a transport at Spithead and two transports at Plymouth to perform this service. The movement was not carried out by these ships, however, because Lord Amherst, who was impatient with the Board, ordered the army to hire its own shipping for the task. The last major troop movement in Britain carried out by the transport service in 1778 was ordered by the Admiralty on 13 December: the Board was directed to provide transports to carry 500 troops from Chatham to Spithead 'with the greatest of expedition'. On 19 December the troops embarked at Chatham on three transports, and on 23 December sailed for Spithead.[1] The redeployment of troops in the British Isles carried out by the transport service in 1778 in response to the French entry into the war demonstrated the great mobility given to the British forces by extensive utilization of sea-borne transport.

The majority of British troops intended for service overseas, with their personal equipment and regimental baggage, were embarked at various British ports on the Board's transports. However, most of the King's troops sent to India during the conflict were carried on East India Company ships, and some 8500 men were carried as passengers to the Caribbean on ships belonging to the London West India merchants.[2] Special

[1] NMM, ADM/B/196, April 10, 20, 1778; ADM/B/197, Sept. 16, Oct. 5, Dec. 14, 17, 23, 1778; ADM/N/248, April 7, 13, 15, Aug. 11, 15, Oct. 8, Dec. 13, 19, 1778.
[2] For an account of these arrangements, see above pp. 67-9, 71-6.

arrangements also had to be made by the Board to meet the unique problems encountered in transporting German troops, naval stores, military equipment, and Indian presents.

One of the most important tasks of the transport service was to convey to North America recruits and stores belonging to German forces in British service. Under the terms of the agreements between the British government and the German princes, it was the responsibility of the princes to provide the recruits and equipment required by the German units in America.[1] At the beginning of each year the Secretary of State for the Northern Department, after receiving reports of the number of German recruits and the amount of stores to be dispatched by the various German princes to their forces in North America, would issue orders for the Board to provide the necessary shipping. For example, the Board was directed on 10 February and 5 March 1778 to provide transports to embark at Bremen 567 Anspach and Hanau recruits, 180 Waldeck recruits, and 300 Hessian recruits, and at the same time 450 Brunswick recruits and 674 Anhalt-Zerbst troops which were just entering the British service were to be embarked at Stade. It was also understood that an unknown quantity of stores would be accompanying these troops. The Board assigned six transports at Harwich to proceed to Bremen to embark the recruits at that port and another ten transports were sent from the Thames to Stade to pick up the contingents from Brunswick and Anhalt-Zerbst. The transports arrived in Germany at the beginning of April and the embarkation at Bremen was completed on 6 April and that at Stade on 14 April. The transports then proceeded to Spithead to join convoys for the passage to North America. It was discovered, however, that there was not enough tonnage at either Bremen or Stade to embark all the German troops, stores, and equipment at the rate of two tons per man. Thus, the Navy Board was directed to supply additional transports at Spithead for the passage to North America. At this time the Board was also directed to have the transports carrying the Brunswick, Anhalt-Zerbst, and Hanau troops join a convoy proceeding to Canada, while the ships with Waldeck, Anspach, and Hessian

[1] Eelking, op. cit., 17.

recruits were to join a convoy going to America.[1] These move-ments were typical of the effort made throughout the war to convey recruits and stores to the German forces in North America.

The necessity of having to convey German recruits and stores to America and Canada presented the government with a tactical problem in the dispatch of convoys. The Germans usually could not be embarked before March, and in most cases they did not board transports before April. Each year, therefore, the government had to decide whether or not to have the trans-ports bound for America and Canada with British troops and stores wait at Spithead for the Germans. If they were so detained the combined force of British and German recruits usually could not depart from Europe before the middle of May, and any delay in embarking the German troops would postpone the departure until later in the summer with the result that the campaigning season in North America would be almost over before any recruits arrived from Europe. If, however, the British recruits and stores were dispatched to America and Canada without waiting for the Germans, the number of con-voys required would be doubled from two to four. This would have presented such problems that in most cases the first of these alternatives was adopted despite the disadvantage of delay which it contained.

German troops were always accompanied by excessive quantities of baggage, clothing, and equipment and this created extra problems for the Navy Board. In 1779 such a vast amount of material appeared at the port of embarkation with the German recruits that a special ship had to be chartered to carry it to Spithead.[2] In 1781 the Board became suspicious of the large amount of stores which accompanied German recruits to North America each year, and on 21 May ordered the Principal Agent for Transports to search the ships carrying them when they arrived at New York, 'The Board having great reason to apprehend from the large quantity of baggage & stores ship'd ... that it cannot consist wholly of necessaries for the troops

---

[1] NMM, ADM/B/195, Feb. 12, 1778; ADM/N/248, Feb. 10, 21, March 5, April 23, 27, May 8, 1778; PRO, ADM/1/4135, f. 95.
[2] NMM, ADM/N/249, March 8, 1780.

but that merchandize or articles of trade are ship'd with it for private emolument'.[1] Despite the delays that the late arrival at Spithead of German recruits and stores imposed on the sailing of convoys for North America and the many problems caused by German baggage and stores, more than 8500 recruits and thousands of tons of stores belonging to the German forces were transported across the Atlantic during the American War.

Most naval stores were shipped overseas by the Navy Board from Royal Dockyards in the Thames in naval storeships or specially fitted, heavily armed transports. A large number of naval storeships employed during the American War were large merchant ships, usually ex-East Indiamen which had been purchased by the government and manned by personnel of the Royal Navy.[2] Because there was never an adequate number of storeships in the Navy, many transports were also used to carry naval stores. Although naval storeships, and transports serving as naval storeships, were usually large, heavily manned, and well-armed, groups of soldiers were often carried to help defend them.[3]

A single naval storeship or transport was capable of carrying a vast assortment of stores. The naval storeship *Green Island*, for instance, unloaded at Antigua in January 1780 a cargo from Woolwich Dockyard which consisted of 3500 tiles and 'Three hundred and Sixteen Tons, Two hundred Weight and Thirteen Pounds' of assorted naval stores consisting of a large quantity of marine ironmongery, tools, blocks, deadeyes, cables, rope, flags, fifty-six masts, paint, tar, and pitch.[4] Sometimes naval storeships and transports employed as naval storeships carried mixed cargoes of naval stores and army equipment.[5]

The transport service was also responsible for conveying camp equipage and clothing to the British armies stationed overseas, each unit in the British army receiving a complete new issue

[1] PRO, ADM/106/2605, May 21, 1781.

[2] E.g., PRO, ADM/106/2595, Feb. 14, 1777; ADM/106/2598, Nov. 4, 1778; ADM/106/2599, March 24, 1779.

[3] E.g., NMM, ADM/B/198, March 11, 1779; ADM/N/248, March 30, 1779; PRO, ADM/1/4135, f. 2; ADM/106/2596, Dec. 30, 1777; ADM/106/2606, Oct. 22, 1781.

[4] PRO, ADM/49/2, ff. 123-7.

[5] E.g., NMM, ADM/B/199, Aug. 18, 1779; ADM/N/249, Sept. 5, 1780.

annually. The War Office calculated that the average regiment of infantry on the regular establishment required twenty tons of clothing per year. There were, however, some large regiments such as the 42nd Regiment which received twenty-five tons, and the 71st and 72nd Regiments which needed thirty tons each. In 1779 the War Office planned to supply seven British regiments, including the 72nd at Gibraltar and Minorca, with 150 tons of clothing. In the same year it was calculated that sixteen British infantry regiments, 17th Light Dragoons, the detachment of Guards, and the troops under the Convention of Saratoga in America would require 443 tons of clothing; the British troops in Canada would need 223 tons; and the ten regiments of infantry in the Lesser Antilles required 200 tons of clothing.[1] The conveyance of army clothing to troops overseas generally required that one or two ships be sent every year to each major theatre of operations.

The transport service also conveyed camp equipage consisting of personal equipment, other than arms and ammunition, required by troops in the field. The following articles, for instance, were sent as camp equipage to America and the Lesser Antilles in 1780:

	Lesser Antilles	America[2]
Private tents with poles, pins, etc.	4,826	4,875
Bell tents with poles, pins, etc.	132	392
Drum cases	220	520
Powder bags	110	266
Hatchets	1,826	4,922
Kettles and bags	1,826	4,892
Canteens	8,412	22,858
Haversacks	8,412	22,420
Camp colours	132	312
Axes		6
Scythes		240
Lots Forage Cords For the 17th Light		240
Picket ropes Dragoons		30
Water buckets		48
Great mallets		12
Picket posts		180

[1] PRO, WO/1/682, f. 523; WO/1/890, ff. 182–3.
[2] PRO, WO/34/124, ff. 236–8. This document is also printed in Mackesy, op. cit., 527.

In 1780 the *Arwin Galley* carried a consignment of 170 tons of camp equipage to the Lesser Antilles and the *William and Elizabeth* 463 tons to America.[1]

From time to time the transport service also conveyed other kinds of military stores. For example, on 4 March 1777 the transports *St Helena* and *Springfield* were assigned to carry ordnance stores to the Caribbean and the transport *Vernon* was ordered on 26 August 1779 to convey a cargo of vinegar and 'articles of barrack furniture' to New York.[2] Indian presents, however, were the most common type of military stores other than clothing and camp equipage carried by transports. These goods were mostly sent to the American South and to Canada on transports which, because of the large quantity of explosives in this type of cargo, had magazines specially constructed in their holds.[3] In the summer of 1780 the transport *Content* carried to Pensacola a typical load of Indian presents weighing 150 tons valued at £6665 3s 2½d which among other things consisted of clothing, ironmongery, paint, kettles, six casks of flints, ninety-six cases of guns, forty barrels of bullets, thirty casks of lead, and 400 quarters of gunpowder.[4] The conveyance of Indian presents required two to four ships a year.

Although relatively few vessels of the transport service were used to carry army stores, they presented a vexing problem. The safety of these cargoes was of the utmost importance. If large quantities of military stores were captured at sea by the enemy, American forces would be able to take the field employing captured British equipment. This was dramatically illustrated by an incident early in the war. On 27 November 1775 the ordnance transport *Nancy* was brought into Cape Ann, Massachusetts, as a prize. The commander-in-chief of the American forces, General George Washington, thought the event an 'instance of Divine favour', for her cargo consisted of a huge quantity of munitions.[5] During the summer of 1776, in

[1] NMM, ADM/N/249, March 21, 1780; HMC, *American Manuscripts*, ii, 115.
[2] NMM, ADM/B/194, March 4, 1777; ADM/B/199, Aug. 30, 1779; ADM/N/249, Aug. 26, 1779.
[3] E.g., NMM, ADM/N/248, March 9, 1779; ADM/B/198, March 10, 1779.
[4] NMM, ADM/N/249, July 4, 1780; PRO, ADM/1/4143, f. 76.
[5] John C. Fitzpatrick, ed., *The Writings of George Washington* (Washington, 1931), iv, 128n, 130.

order to prevent a repetition of the *Nancy* affair, Lord Amherst and Lord Barrington proposed that the government employ warships to carry military equipment and munitions, by removing the lower tier of guns from two-decked warships and using the empty lower gun-deck to carry stores.[1] This proposal was rejected by the Admiralty on technical grounds, but it seems likely that the real reason was an understandable aversion to having a large part of the Royal Navy converted into glorified army storeships. After the rejection of the Amherst-Barrington plan, it was the government's policy, as explained by Sandwich to Lord Howe in a letter of 17 October 1776, to ship military stores in armed transports. Sandwich specified that these ships were to be large and 'armed with upwards of 20 guns, and manned with a proportionable number of seamen, besides parties of [army] recruits, which will make them stronger than any rebel cruizer I have yet heard of; this in my opinion is the most judicious & indeed the only method of conveying these valuable cargos with safety'.[2]

The Board had great difficulty procuring the type of ship necessary to put Sandwich's policy into effect, and for the most part relied for the safety of the cargoes of military stores on the ability of the transports to keep company with their naval escorts. On 9 August 1776 Germain directed that all shipments of clothing to the army in North America must be sent on heavily armed vessels capable of defending themselves against American cruisers. Three days later the Board informed the Admiralty that it had loaded a year's supply of clothing for the army in Canada, along with twenty soldiers, on board the armed transport *Mellish* which was armed with six 3-pounders and six swivel guns, and added that 'in the present scarcity of Shipping it was with difficulty [that the *Mellish* was] procured, and should [it] not be thought proper for the purpose, we have reason to believe others capable of mounting Guns sufficient to make a better deffence cannot be procured in time'. In the fall of 1776 the *Mellish* sailed from Britain under escort of H.M.S. *Richmond*, but en route to Canada separated from the warship

[1] PRO, ADM/1/4132, f. 48.
[2] The Earl of Sandwich's Private Letters, ii, 19–20, at Mapperton.

and was captured.[1] When the news of this loss reached the London officials responsible for supplying the British army they became determined not to let the Admiralty and Navy Board continue to send military stores in ships as easily captured as were the *Nancy* and *Mellish*.

The problem of protecting military stores en route to the army came to a head in the summer of 1777, when a dispute arose over whether or not the 234-ton transport *Arwin Galley*, armed with two 6-pounders and twelve 4-pounders, was a fit vessel to carry 160 tons of army clothing to Canada. When Germain forbade the use of this vessel because it would in his opinion be inviting a repetition of the *Nancy* and *Mellish* disasters, the Navy Board maintained that it did not have a more heavily armed ship available. Because the Board proved unable or unwilling to provide a stronger ship, Germain made arrangements for the transport service, without the Board's knowledge, to charter the *Adamant* which he considered to be a suitable ship for the task. The Board agreed reluctantly to the employment of the *Adamant*, but made it clear to Germain that in future it would not tolerate his interference in the affairs of the transport service. As a result of this ultimatum, Germain used Treasury victuallers to carry camp equipage to North America in 1777, but with the expansion of the conflict into a world war in 1778, he was forced to employ vessels of the transport service on terms laid down by the Board. After the dispute with Germain concerning the *Adamant*, the Board always attempted to use the most heavily armed transports possible, but thought 'that the providing ships of force for carrying stores etc. abroad is attended with a very considerable expence to Government and in our Opinion the Utility of it is not . . . adequate to the expence as it in general consists only of a few additional guns without any addition of men, and is therefore of very little service in case of losing the convoy'.[2]

The inability of the transport service to dispatch punctually from Europe the reinforcements, naval and army stores, and

[1] NMM, ADM/B/193, Aug. 12, 1776; PRO, ADM/1/4132, f. 41.
[2] David Syrett, 'Lord George Germain and the Navy Board in Conflict: the *Adamant* and *Arwin Galley* Dispute, 1777', *Bulletin of the Institute of Historical Research* (Nov., 1965), xxxviii, 163–71; NMM, ADM/B/199, May 24, 1779.

recruits required by the forces overseas had a profound effect on the conduct of the war. Many warships overseas were constantly in a state of disrepair because naval stores failed to arrive from England.[1] The failure of army reinforcements, recruits, and camp equipage to arrive in America in the early spring on several occasions prevented the beginning of military operations until the greater part of the campaigning season had passed. In 1776 Howe stopped operations before New York for more than a month waiting for the arrival of camp equipage, and in 1777 he again delayed the opening of the campaign until 19 June, apparently waiting for camp equipage and recruits. A second group of recruits arrived at New York on 24 September 1777, and Clinton maintained that 'had the reinforcement from Europe arrived in time to enable me to make the move [against the Highlands of the Hudson] sooner, I had little doubt that even the attempt might have so alarmed the enemy as to have called off some part of the multitude opposed to our northern army [Burgoyne], and have thereby eased its retreat'. In 1781 Clinton put off and then cancelled an assault on Rhode Island because the reinforcements from Europe which he considered essential to the success of the operation did not reach New York until 11 August.[2] It is debatable whether Howe and Clinton were justified in not beginning operations until the annual supply of camp equipage and recruits had reached America, but nevertheless the uncertain and often tardy arrival of reinforcements and stores made the planning and execution of military operations extremely difficult.

There were many reasons for the sporadic and often late departure from Europe of men and materials. One of the greatest difficulties was the necessity of having to formulate military policy at Whitehall for the next year's campaign without knowing the outcome of the previous year's operations. As Germain noted on 21 August 1777: 'the issue of the present

---

[1] E.g., NYHSC, *Letter-Books and Order-Book of George, Lord Rodney*, i, 97–8, 273–5; NRS, *Barham Papers*, i, 60–1, 64.

[2] PRO, CO/5/94, ff. 180, 194, 210–11; HMC, *Stopford-Sackville MSS.*, ii, 37–8; HMC, *Various Collections*, vi, 131; Troyer Steele Anderson, *The Command of the Howe Brothers during the American Revolution* (New York, 1936), 241, 276; Willcox, ed., *Sir Henry Clinton's Narrative*, 72, 74; Willcox, *Portrait of A General*, 402, 413, 415.

Campaign in North America cannot be known here in time to prepare for the Operations of another'. Orders for assembling the shipping necessary for the dispatch of reinforcements and stores in the spring to the Western Hemisphere had to be issued to the Navy Board in the preceding December, while the outcome of the previous year's campaign was not fully known at Whitehall until February or March.[1]

One of the results of this lack of up-to-date information was that often men and materials were sent to the wrong place. In 1779, for example, just after ten regiments left North America for the Caribbean, a transport arrived at New York with clothing and camp equipage belonging to these units. Through a series of blunders these stores remained in the hold of the transport *Hopewell* at New York for more than a year before being forwarded to the West Indies. When 326 recruits from Cork arrived at New York in the summer of 1781, it was discovered that 256 of them belonged to units in the West Indies and another nine men were members of the 44th Regiment in Canada.[2]

The necessity of having to issue orders for the dispatch of men and stores overseas without adequate intelligence often led to indecision and delay. On 5 March 1780 the government ordered that transports be sent to Germany to embark the German recruits for the army in America. But orders for providing shipping for the British recruits to America were not issued at this time because 'Lord Amherst wished to wait to settle the recruits for N. America and the Leeward Islands till he saw more of the intentions of France'. Germain agreed that 'they cannot embark till France's intention concerning invasion are known, but I see no inconvenience in making preparations'. Orders were, therefore, issued to the Board on 24 April to provide conveyance for 2000 British recruits to New York. By the time the 'intentions of France' became clear and the transports with the British recruits joined those with the German recruits for departure to America, it was summer and further delays

[1] PRO, ADM/1/4134, f. 43.
[2] PRO, ADM/108/1B, Oct. 8, 1781; CO/5/8, f. 200; CO/5/101, f. 222; WO/1/683, f. 613.

were then imposed by the threat of French naval operations in the Western Approaches with the result that the recruits did not reach New York until October.[1]

The need to issue directions for the provision of transports on the basis of scanty intelligence sometimes resulted in the government, upon receipt of new information, radically altering its directives. On 16 December 1776 the government ordered that the Board supply transports to carry 2000 British recruits to America, but on 10 February 1777, after the Board had procured and fitted the transports, Germain directed that ships would be required for only 1000 men.[2] On 11 December 1778 Lord Suffolk directed that transports be provided in Germany to embark 1400 German troops for conveyance to North America. On 11 February 1779 the Board was directed to dispatch at once to Dort in Holland enough tonnage to embark 200 of the 1400 Germans, plus 'camp equipage, clothing & other stores for other troops already in America'. The following day the Board sent to Dort the transports *Minerva* and *Sally* to collect the 200 troops and the stores, informing the Admiralty at the same time that by 15 February eleven other transports would be assembled at the Nore for the conveyance of the remainder of the Germans to America. On 26 March, however, after the transports had sailed for Germany, the Board was told that instead of 1200 Germans to be embarked there were 1700 with the result that 1000 additional tons of shipping would be required to carry out the movement.[3] On 3 December 1781 the Board sent one of many complaints about this state of affairs to the Admiralty, stating 'how impracticable it is for us to provide at a moments warning for services that under the most favourable circumstances require time & preparation'.[4] Middleton thought that the confusion was caused by the government not having a plan for the conduct of the war, and he informed Germain: 'I am frequently a witness of delays that could not

[1] PRO, ADM/1/4141, f. 61; NMM, ADM/N/249, April 24, 1780; HMC, *Various Collections*, vi, 166–7; Mackesy, op. cit., 357.

[2] NMM, ADM/B/194, Jan. 21, 1777; PRO, ADM/1/4133, f. 39.

[3] NMM, ADM/B/198, Feb. 12, March 27, 1779; ADM/N/248, Feb. 11, March 26, 1779; PRO, ADM/1/4137, f. 69.

[4] PRO, ADM/106/2606, Dec. 3, 1781.

possibly happen if any degree of plan was laid down, and communicated in the first instance to those who are to be entrusted with the execution of it.'[1] Despite protests and complaints by the Board, however, preparations and plans for the conveyance of men and material overseas were throughout the war constantly disrupted by repeated alterations in the directives it received from the government.

The practice of manning the Royal Navy by impressment was one of the greatest obstacles encountered by the Navy Board. From the entry of France into the war in 1778 until the end of the conflict, hundreds of ships of the transport service were immobilized in British waters when their crews were impressed. On 10 February 1779, for example, the Board complained to the Admiralty that the crews of twelve transports which were en route to Germany had been impressed in the Thames. Captain Walter Young, Agent for Transports at Deptford, reported to the Board on 27 June 1779 that 'several of the transports men have been pressed, and that if a stop is not put to this matter in future, it will be impossible for him to get the transports from Deptford'.[2] The transport service was essential to the prosecution of the war, yet officers of the Royal Navy constantly impeded its operations by impressing the crews of its ships which was one of the most illogical aspects of the British war effort.

Impressment also greatly hampered the efforts made by the Board to charter additional tonnage and jeopardized the legality of the charter parties of the ships in service. On 11 July 1782 the Board informed the Admiralty: 'we are under the necessity of keeping many of them [transports] in the service contrary to the owners inclinations and should the pressing their men be urged against us in a case of litigation on their refusing to refit their ships for continuance in service it might frustrate our endeavours'.[3] The Board attempted to prevent impressment by issuing protections to seamen of the ships in the transport service, but the Admiralty did not recognize the validity of the Navy

---

[1] NRS, *Barham Papers*, ii, 44.
[2] NMM, ADM/B/198, Feb. 10, 1779; PRO, ADM/106/2600, June 27, 1779.
[3] PRO, ADM/106/2609, July 11, 1782.

Board protections, and officers of the Royal Navy did not respect them.[1] As a result, the Board was forced to employ persuasion to prevent or mitigate the damage caused by impressment. On 27 July 1779 the Board informed Captain Charles Hamilton 'that by means of his having impressed the men from the Hartford transport in Dec last the public has been put to upwards of £400 expence by her detention: And therefore desire he will in future be more cautious how he suffers men to be impressed from ships under contract with this Board'.[2] At times appeals were made to high-ranking Navy officers for men who had been impressed to be returned to the Board's vessels.[3] At other times appeals were made to officials of the Impress Service.[4] It was to the Admiralty, however, that the Board directed most of its complaints, appeals, and protests about the impressment of seamen from its ships. In addition to persuading the Admiralty to order the return of men who had been impressed, the Board at times also prevailed upon it to issue orders to prevent the pressing of men from the vessels of the transport service.[5] But regardless of these appeals and protests the practice continued until the end of the war.

The dates on which troops and stores could be dispatched from Europe to the British forces overseas were dictated by climatic conditions in both Europe and the Western Hemisphere. Troops and stores could not be sent to the West Indies to arrive between August and December, which was the hurricane season. It was impossible to conduct military operations during the hurricane season, and any troops remaining in the West Indies during this period would be decimated by disease. In the fall and winter of 1780, for instance, 1100 men of the garrison of Jamaica died. Most trade and military convoys, therefore, departed from Britain in the winter so that they could arrive in the Caribbean well after the end of the hurricane

---

[1] Roland Greene Usher, Jr, *The Civil Administration of the British Navy during the American Revolution*, 91–9. See also above, p. 19.

[2] PRO, ADM/106/2600, July 27, 1779.

[3] E.g., PRO, ADM/106/2597, April 4, May 19, 1778.

[4] E.g., PRO, ADM/106/2601, Oct. 15, 1779; ADM/106/2602, March 17, 1780.

[5] E.g., NMM, ADM/N/248, Feb. 13, 1779; ADM/N/249, Sept. 5, 1780; ADM/N/250, Oct. 29, 1781; PRO, ADM/106/2609, July 19, 1782.

season. Thus, in the winter of 1780–81 convoys were scheduled
to sail for the West Indies between the end of October and the
beginning of April. Middleton, however, thought that naval
stores should be dispatched to the West Indies at an earlier date
despite the dangers posed by hurricanes, because 'A convoy at
the later end of October will not be in time for storeships
intended for the Leeward Islands. Such supplies must not be
confined to general convoys, as has been the practice hitherto,
otherwise the squadron will remain inactive, and no exertion
on our part will be able to prevent it.'[1]

Weather also played an important role in determining the
time of departure from Britain of ships bound for Quebec, for
they had to arrive in Canada when the St Lawrence River was
free from ice. On several occasions transports proceeding to
Canada had to be diverted to New York or Halifax because
they departed from Britain so late that they failed to reach the
St Lawrence before winter closed the river to navigation.[2]

The government always attempted to dispatch forces and
stores to North America in the early spring so that they would
reach the armies in the field before the beginning of the campaign. With the entry of France into the war and the advent of
major naval operations in the English Channel in 1778, the
departure of soldiers and stores in the early spring became
imperative. If the North American convoys did not leave
European waters before the enemy battle fleet put to sea, they
would become caught in the summer naval operations in the
Channel. On 25 December 1781 Middleton declared in a
memorandum that the convoys 'Must collect early at the Nore,
Spithead, and Cork, and be dispatched before the combined
fleet take their station westward', and that the following schedule
should be adhered to:

The Quebec fleets at Cork and Spithead should sail so early in
March . . . the West Indies and America ones getting away at the
same time . . . But if the whole are detained till the enemy are at
sea, the whole is obstructed; the accumulation becomes so great at

[1] NMM, ADM/N/250, Jan. 25, 1781; NRS, *Sandwich Papers*, iii, 302; Fortescue,
op. cit., iii, 341.
[2] E.g., PRO, CO/5/100, ff. 65–6.

Spithead and Cork, that they cannot get to sea under a considerable time; winds are lost; the summer passes on; the days shorten; and separation becomes unavoidable; capture is added to our other disappointments.[1]

The weather in Europe, however, tended to frustrate attempts to dispatch forces to North America in the early spring. The embarkation of German troops on many occasions could not take place until the rivers of northern Europe were free of ice, since many of these troops travelled by boat down the Rhine, Elbe, and Weser to the ports of embarkation. As a result, most major embarkations of German troops did not take place until March.[2] The delays brought about by ice in European rivers were minor when compared to those caused by the necessity of having to collect and form into convoys at Spithead or Cork scores of ships from a dozen different points in Germany and the British Isles in the face of adverse winds. Almost every major military convoy dispatched overseas during the American War was composed of ships which first had to proceed from various ports of embarkation to the place where the convoy was formed. The ports through which troops embarked for overseas were so located that invariably a component of any given convoy was forced to proceed to the convoy's rendezvous against the wind. For example, if the wind was blowing from the east, vessels going from Germany or the Downs to join a convoy at Spithead would have a fair wind, but ships leaving the Thames or coming from Plymouth or Cork to join the same convoy would be forced to proceed against the wind. If the wind was from the west the reverse would be true. In an effort to prevent the delays caused by adverse winds, Middleton suggested:

I would exclude Chatham in all cases of expedition, and confine embarcations to the western ports. The same objections hold good against sudden equipments of every kind in the river Thames, as it is impracticable to get either stores or transports sent round at short notice.[3]

[1] NRS, *Barham Papers*, ii, 39.
[2] For an account of the routes and methods used by German troops to reach ports of embarkation, see Lowell, op. cit., 46–56.
[3] NRS, *Barham Papers*, ii, 45.

The government did not accept the Comptroller's advice, and throughout the war the departure of ships for overseas was delayed by the necessity of having to assemble convoys in the face of adverse winds.

Many of the delays and frustrations could have been avoided if a reserve of transport tonnage had been maintained in Britain. In the first three years of the war the government never attempted to form and maintain such a reserve. After the build up of British forces in North America in 1776, the Board was directed to discharge all unemployed transports in Britain, and even as late as 9 July 1778, the Admiralty ordered the discharge of any transports for which there was no immediate use.[1] It is evident that the government never completely understood the administrative and strategic possibilities inherent in the existence of a large reserve of transport tonnage in Britain. On 15 December 1778 the Board nevertheless suggested that,

Having frequently received directions of the Right Honorable the Lords Comm. of the Admiralty to provide transports for small parties of troops, or for baggage, clothing &c. and having also had occasion of late to make use of some of the transports to carry naval stores from the River Thames to the Western yards; we desire you will please to submit to their Lordships whether they may not think it adviseable to retain a certain quantity of tonnage in pay to answer any emergency.

The following day the Admiralty authorized the Board to maintain as a reserve 1000 tons of transports in the Thames and another 1000 tons at Portsmouth.[2] On 19 August 1779 the Admiralty, in a belated response to the threat of invasion posed by the presence of the Franco-Spanish fleet in the Channel, informed the Board:

We do hereby desire and direct you to keep three thousand tons of transport vessels at Plymouth, three thousand tons at Portsmouth, and one thousand tons at Blackslake, and to have them in constant

[1] NMM, ADM/B/196, July 8, 1778; ADM/N/249, July 9, 1778; PRO, ADM/1/4132, f. 59.
[2] NMM, ADM/B/197, Dec. 15, 1778; ADM/N/248, Dec. 16, 1778; PRO, ADM/106/2598, Dec. 15, 1778.

readyness for service, in case it should be necessary to transport troops from one part of the coast to another.[1]

During the winter of 1779–80 the reserve of transport tonnage was gradually reduced because of a shortage of vessels in the service, the need to provide victuallers, and the government's failure to understand the military advantage of such a reserve. In an undated memorandum submitted to Germain, Middleton indicated some of the advantages to be gained by maintaining in Britain a strategic reserve of transports and troops as an existing amphibious striking force. Middleton wanted

ten gunboats, thirty bateaux in frame, and as many flat boats, with every necessary material to be provided at leisure and lodged at Portsmouth; 10,000 tons of coppered transports, with a proportionate number of coppered victuallers, to be kept in constant readiness at Spithead, and as much provisions in store at Cowes as will serve 5,000 men for six months. To this preparation I would add every kind of artillery and ammunition that may be necessary for a distant expedition and loged at the gun-wharf at Portsmouth. This preparation brings everything within a narrow compass and will enable you [Germain] to embark six regiments in forty-eight hours. The opportunity of a favourable wind will be seized and the object of the expedition probably gained before the enemy is apprised of it.[2]

But Middleton's plan for the formation of a strategic amphibious reserve based at Spithead was never put into effect, and the process of collecting troops, transports, and stores for dispatch overseas remained until the end of the war a lengthy and laborious task, imposing numerous delays on military operations.

V

It was recognized almost from the beginning of the conflict that large numbers of transports would have to be permanently stationed in America. On 22 February 1776 the Admiralty directed Admiral Molyneux Shuldham, the British naval commander in America, to take command of all ships of the trans-

[1] NMM, ADM/N/249, Aug. 19, 1779.
[2] NRS, *Barham Papers*, ii, 46.

port service in American waters, 'With the Authority either to return or discharge them as he shall think fit'. The Admiral was further instructed 'to detain such Number as shall, under all Events, be Necessary for the removal of his Majesty's Troops from place to place as the Commander in Chief of these troops shall think necessary and proper'.[1] General Howe complained to Germain that putting transports under the control of the Navy would impede operations by making the army dependent upon the Navy for its sea-borne transport. Clinton objected so strongly to the Navy's control of the transports that in 1780 he sent his quartermaster general, William Dalrymple, to London to demand that control of transports be turned over to the army.[2] Despite the complaints of the generals, the transports in America remained under the Navy's direction throughout the war.

The transports supported the British effort in North America in a variety of ways. Their crews provided a pool of trained seamen from which the Navy in North America could draw reinforcements.[3] Large numbers of vessels of the transport service were used as hospital ships, prison ships, flags of truce, and guard ships,[4] as well as to carry military cargoes on coastal voyages.[5]

The transports in America made it possible for the British army to become a highly mobile amphibious striking force capable of attacking any point that could be reached from the sea. The operations which culminated in the occupation of Rhode Island in 1776, the invasion of Pennsylvania in 1777, the seizure of St Lucia in 1779, and the capture of Charleston in 1780 were all staged and mounted from New York. And throughout the war British amphibious raiding forces carried on transports ranged up and down the American coast. The mere existence of large numbers of fully equipped transports at

[1] PRO, ADM/1/4131, f. 55.
[2] HMC, *Stopford-Sackville MSS.*, ii, 35; Willcox, *Portrait of A General*, 355.
[3] E.g., NRS, *Sandwich Papers*, i, 171–2; Uhlendorf, *Revolution in America*, 190.
[4] E.g., PRO, ADM/106/2605, May 1, 1781; ADM/108/1B, Jan. 2, 1782; NYHSC, *Letter-Books and Order-Book of George, Lord Rodney*, ii, 779; French Ensor Chadwick, ed., *The Graves Papers* (New York, 1916), 115.
[5] E.g., PRO, ADM/1/488, ff. 207, 421; *Diary of Frederick Mackenzie*, i, 253, 255, 259, 263.

New York placed the Americans at a tactical and strategic disadvantage. On 5 November 1776 Frederick Mackenzie noted in his journal,

Transports sufficient for the reception of near 15000 men on the shortest notice are now almost ready in the harbor of New York; and are victualled, watered, and nearly ready to proceed to Sea. There destination is not known, but it is generally imagined an Expedition against some place of consequence is intended. The preparation of these vessels may be with a view to deceive and alarm the Enemy, and by putting them under apprehensions for places at a distance, prevent them from sending reinforcements to Washington's Army. If it is intended to send troops from hence, it by no means follows that because transports for 15000 men are prepared, so many will embark. This may also be done in order to deceive the Rebels.

As the Rebels have good intelligence of what we are doing, it must alarm them when they are informed that so large a fleet is ready to put to Sea, and has nothing to do but take the troops on board, which might be done in a few hours. The uncertainty where the Storm would fall, must keep a considerable part of the Country in a state of constant preparation, occasion much expense, and harrass the Country people by being kept away from their families and employments.[1]

The strategic quandary in which British amphibious capabilities periodically placed the Americans was dramatically illustrated by the impact which the water-borne movements of Howe's army in 1777 had on George Washington. In the summer of 1777 the Continental Army was immobilized in New Jersey because the British at New York could either launch an amphibious assault up the Hudson River or at any point on the American coast to the north or south of New York. On 2 July 1777 Washington wrote to Jonathan Trumbull: 'There is a great Stir among their Shipping; and in all probability, their next Movement will be by water, though it is impossible to decide with certainty to what Place.' Between 9 and 11 July 14,000 British troops embarked on transports in Lower New York Bay, and on 22 July Washington wrote to General Philip

[1] *Diary of Frederick Mackenzie*, i, 97.

Schuyler: 'I cannot give you any certain account of Genl. Howe's intended Operations. His conduct is puzzling and embarrassing, beyond measure; so are the informations, which I get. At one time the Ships are standing up towards the North River. In a little while they are going up the Sound, and in an hour after they are going out of the Hook.' Howe's army sailed from Sandy Hook on 23 July, and Washington still could not discern the intentions of the British. On 25 July Washington wrote to the President of the Continental Congress: 'The amazing advantage the Enemy derive from their Ships and the Command of the water, keeps us in a State of constant perplexity and the most anxious conjecture. We are not yet informed of their destination, nor can any plausible conclusions be drawn respecting it; at least not such as appears satisfactory.' Howe's intention to attack Philadelphia did not become clear until the beginning of August when the British briefly appeared off the Capes of the Delaware before proceeding to the Head of the Elk.[1] When properly utilized, the amphibious mobility given to the British army in North America by the transport service was a major strategic and tactical advantage.

The great importance of transports to the conduct of military operations in the Western Hemisphere resulted in large numbers of these vessels being detained overseas. For instance, on 3 April 1779 there were ninety-seven transports with a total tonnage of 27,025 tons employed in America. The small number of ships which returned to Britain from overseas were usually unfit for service,[2] a situation that led the Board to believe that the problem of the shortage of transport tonnage could be solved, or at least mitigated, if ships were correctly deployed in America and all unnecessary tonnage was promptly sent to Europe.[3] This, however, was a false assumption, for the shortage of transports was caused above all by the inability of the Board to charter enough tonnage. The number of transports in service during the last years of the war actually decreased from 192

[1] Fitzpatrick, op. cit., viii, 331, 335, 355–6, 414, 449, 453–4, 470.
[2] E.g., PRO, ADM/1/488, ff. 479–80; ADM/1/489, ff. 278–9; ADM/106/279, April 9, 1778; ADM/108/1C, July 3, 1782.
[3] E.g., NMM, ADM/BP/1, Oct. 10, 1781.

with a total tonnage of 59,015 tons on 31 December 1780, to 125 with a tonnage of 37,725 tons on 31 December 1782.[1]

The shortage of transports first became apparent at the beginning of 1780, when on 15 January the Navy Board discovered that it could not supply transports to carry 272 invalids to the Channel Islands because, due to the 'scarcity of ships in the River Thames and other circumstances the sending of transports on that service at this time will be a means of impeding orders we are already under to provide for other embarkations'.[2] The situation did not improve in 1781, for on 1 March the Board told the Admiralty, 'We shall use our best endeavours' to find ships to carry clothing to the army in North America, but 'We are apprehensive however from the great scarcity of shipping at home & the heavy demand already made for the American service, & no ships yet returned from Carolina & New York that it will be out of our powers to comply with it in so short a notice'. The shortage of transports again became apparent when, on 2 April 1781, the Admiralty ordered a regiment of 1000 men to be carried from Spithead to the Channel Islands and another regiment conveyed from Jersey back to Spithead; the Board had only enough transports to move 800 men, and was forced to conduct the operation with the assistance of victuallers and tenders.[3]

By 1782 the shortage of transports was so acute that the North government's policy of conducting large-scale military operations on the American mainland was no longer feasible. On 14 January 1782, the Board informed the Admiralty that 'from the scarcity of shipping nothing but early & punctual convoys to insure a speedy return [to Britain of transports] can enable us to get through the service of this year'.[4] Upon receiving orders to provide transports to carry 500 German recruits to America, the Board on 18 February 1782 had to inform the Admiralty:

---

[1] An account of the number of ships and their tonnage which appear to have been in service at the end of each year during the present war, [undated], Barham MSS. at Exton Park.

[2] NMM, ADM/B/200, Jan. 15, 1780; ADM/N/249, Jan. 14, 1780.

[3] NMM, ADM/N/250, April 2, 5, 9, 1781; PRO, T/1/567, Navy Board to Admiralty, March 1, 1781.

[4] PRO, ADM/106/2607, Jan. 14, 1782.

'We shall do everything in our power to procure them [transports] but the losses we have met with in America & the detention of others . . . renders it impossible to say when they can be ready.' Again on 22 February 1782 the Board, after being directed to transport 2700 British army recruits to North America, was forced to report: 'it is not in our power for these services under three months at least as we have not one transport unappropriated nor a prospect of getting any new ones & therefore propose as the ships return from America to refit such as are proper for this service & to send the recruits by the different convoys as they can be got ready to receive them.'[1] At the beginning of 1782, the shortage of tonnage had reduced the Board to depending on the spasmodic return to Britain of worn-out ships from overseas in order to procure the vessels required to transport the minimum number of men necessary to make good the casualties suffered in the previous campaign in North America.

The consequences of the perilous condition of the transport service in 1782 were spectacularly shown by the evacuation of America. On 4 March 1782 the House of Commons passed a resolution calling for the end of offensive operations in America, and on 20 March Lord North resigned. A week later the Marquis of Rockingham became First Lord of the Treasury at the head of a government committed to ending the war. Upon taking office, the new government planned to withdraw from America and redeploy part of the army in the Caribbean so that it could enter into peace negotiations with a display of strength in the West Indies. On 4 April General Sir Guy Carleton was directed to go to New York and take command of the British forces in North America with orders to evacuate New York, Charleston, Savannah, and if necessary, St Augustine, and to send as many troops as possible to the Caribbean. Carleton was also directed to treat the Loyalists with his 'tenderest and most honourable care giving them every assistance and prudent assurance of attention in whatever other parts of America in His Majesty's possession they chuse to settle'. Orders were sent to the army commanders in the West Indies to

[1] PRO, ADM/106/2607, Feb. 18, 22, 1782.

communicate with Carleton at New York, and the naval commander in America was placed under the direct command of the new Secretary of State for Colonies, Lord Shelburne. The ministry, however, neglected to inform the Navy Board of its intention to withdraw from America.[1]

The news arrived in London on 18 May that the Royal Navy had won naval superiority in the Caribbean in the Battle of the Saints. This victory suggested vast offensive possibilities to the government, for if the army could be withdrawn from America and thrown into the West Indies, the British might be able to go to the peace conference in possession of a great Caribbean prize such as Cuba or Puerto Rico. This course of action was proposed on 21 May and on 5 June Shelburne wrote to Carleton suggesting that because of the Battle of the Saints, 'we may now be in a condition to carry on an offensive war in the West Indies'. It was not, however, until 7 August that the ministry 'agreed to send directions to Sir Guy Carleton to evacuate New York, and as an active scene of war was to be opened in the West Indies, to transport the greatest part of the army there'.[2] The success of this scheme depended on the formulation of a plan to utilize the existing shipping for the transfer of troops from America to the Caribbean. But no such plan was forthcoming, and the ministry did not take any of the practical steps necessary to put its policy into effect.

A clear and logical plan for the evacuation of America was an absolute necessity because of the size and complexity of the operation. On 1 March 1782 there were 15,240 rank-and-file effectives at New York, 7588 in South Carolina, 1624 in Georgia, and 541 in East Florida. At each of these bases there were large quantities of stores and military equipment which either had to be removed or destroyed. Moreover, in areas controlled by the British many Loyalists had to be evacuated. The overall military situation in 1782 further complicated the evacuation of America. While the British were confined to four mutually dependent bridgeheads in America (New York, Charleston,

---

[1] PRO, ADM/1/4147, f. 96; CO/5/106, ff. 1–5; Mackesy, op. cit., 474–5; I. R. Christie, *The End of North's Ministry, 1780–1782* (London, 1958), 340–69.

[2] PRO, CO/5/106, ff. 30–1; Bedford Record Office, Grantham MSS., L/29/600.

Savannah, and St Augustine), American military intentions and capabilities after Yorktown, especially in the South, were obscure, and the British were confronted with the possibility that the withdrawal might have to be conducted in the face of enemy attack. The British, therefore, could not evacuate America piecemeal, but from military necessity had to leave each bridgehead in one movement. In addition, the transport service had to provide the ships necessary to meet the logistical requirements of the West Indies, Canada, and Gibraltar simultaneously with the evacuation of America.[1]

At the end of March, Middleton, who had learned from the newspapers of the government's intention to evacuate America, submitted to Lord Keppel, the new First Lord of the Admiralty, a detailed plan for the evacuation. The Comptroller estimated that at least 85,000 tons of shipping, which was not available, would be needed to withdraw simultanously from all the posts in America. He therefore proposed to evacuate New York first and then to withdraw from the American South. In order to assemble as quickly as possible the 40,000 or 50,000 tons of shipping which he thought would be needed to evacuate New York, Middleton suggested that orders be sent immediately to Halifax, Charleston, St Lucia, and Jamaica for every victualler, storeship, and transport in these ports to be dispatched to New York. At the same time the victuallers at Cowes and Spithead under orders to proceed to Halifax and Quebec should be directed to go to New York after their cargoes had been discharged. Orders should also be issued calling for the immediate dispatch to New York of the materials required to convert victuallers and storeships into transports, and the victuallers bound for America with army provisions should be directed to go to the West Indies, and after discharging their cargoes, sail for New York. Middleton thought that if this plan was put into effect at once, New York could be evacuated by September.[2]

Middleton's plan for the evacuation of America was ignored. The ministry apparently did not address itself to military problems during the summer of 1782, for it made almost no

[1] PRO, CO/5/104, ff. 131–2, 162; CO/5/105, ff. 59, 75–6.
[2] NRS, *Barham Papers*, ii, 47–50.

effort to speed up the evacuation of America. Among the very few steps taken by the ministry to expedite the withdrawal from America was Shelburne's order of 8 May directing that the transports being collected to carry 2700 recruits to America be used instead to convey American prisoners to New York for exchange. It was not until 2 October that the Cabinet directed 'that every transport that could be got should be sent to Sir Guy Carleton, for the purpose of evacuating New York'. The ministers then contradicted themselves by resolving at the same meeting to send an expedition to Buenos Aires—a project of doubtful value, but one which would require transports. On 25 October the government had another flight of fancy when it decided to attempt to gain American assistance in withdrawing from America in return for a British invasion of West Florida and a pledge not to attack 'this season' any French West Indian possessions.[1] In this fashion the opportunity of taking the offensive in the Caribbean made possible by the Battle of the Saints was lost because of the government's inability to address itself to the problem of collecting the tonnage necessary to withdraw from America.

The effects of the government's inaction and lack of planning were pointed out at the end of 1782 by Middleton in a memorandum in which he noted that he had submitted a scheme for the evacuation of America within days after the change of government

and had any attention been paid to it, the whole of the New York garrison would have been moved this year, and Charleston early in the ensuing one; but suffering three months to elapse without coming to any resolution on it, and permitting the victuallers and transports to lay unnecessarily at Spithead, and after all to sail for Quebec, Canada and the West Indies, without any view to an object of this magnitude that had been ordered to be carried into

---

[1] PRO, ADM/1/4148, f. 14; Bedford Record Office, Grantham MSS., L/29/670, 667. Ironically the idea of American assistance in withdrawing from the United States in return for a British invasion of West Florida originated with John Jay, one of the American commissioners in Paris for negotiating a peace treaty with the British, who for unknown reasons preferred to have the British in West Florida to the Spanish. See Richard B. Morris, *The Peacemakers: The Great Powers and American Independence* (New York, 1965), 344–6.

execution, is scarcely credible. Sending out, or not preventing the navy board from sending provisions and stores to garrisons that were to be removed, and by that means adding to the difficulty and losing the use of the transports when the scarcity of shipping would admit of no recruit at home, must appear equally extraordinary. From these circumstances, and not sending early information to the commanding officer in the Leeward Islands for providing stores, there are between 2000 and 3000 tons of shipping lying at this time, loaded with provisions, at Charleston; 5700 at New York, and in all probability 7000 at the Leeward Islands; so that we have 18,000 tons of shipping lying idle, at a time when we do not know where to get a single ship; and 12,000 of them have been sent to New York and Charleston with provisions after a resolution was taken to abandon them, and with a quantity in store equal to 15 months' consumption.[1]

Soon after his arrival in America Sir Guy Carleton discovered that his instructions were totally irrelevant. On 7 May 1782 there were in America only forty-four transports with a total tonnage of 13,027 tons. Three of these vessels were hospital ships, while the others were engaged in transporting the 19th and 30th Regiments to the Caribbean. Because of the shortage of transports in America, Carleton decided to disregard his instructions, and on 14 May he wrote a dispatch informing the government that it was 'impossible' to evacuate America quickly and send a considerable force to the Caribbean. Believing that Charleston and Savannah were 'at the mercy of the first enemy who shall approach them', Carleton planned instead to withdraw the troops at Charleston, Savannah, and St Augustine to New York.[2]

Savannah was the first British post in the American South to be evacuated, because tonnage for the simultaneous evacuation of Savannah, Charleston, and St Augustine was not available. Carleton evacuated Savannah first because it was the weakest post; he planned to withdraw later from Charleston, and to depart from St Augustine last because it was a strong position.[3] Every available transport in America, amounting to 11,014 tons of shipping was employed to evacuate Savannah on 11 July 1782. This tonnage proved to be insufficient, and despite the

[1] NRS, *Barham Papers*, ii, 77-8.   [2] PRO, CO/5/106, ff. 25-8.
[3] HMC, *American Manuscripts*, ii, 494-5, 500, 520.

assistance of ships chartered by the Royal Lieutenant Governor
of Georgia, there were not enough vessels to remove all the
troops, stores, and Loyalists. As a result many Loyalists were
forced to make their way overland or in small craft to St
Augustine.[1]

With the arrival at New York on 10 August of some of the
troops withdrawn from Georgia, Carleton discovered that the
transports employed in the evacuation of Savannah had been
scattered, for of the 11,014 tons of transports used in the evacuation, 4797 tons were sent to New York, 2699 tons went to
Charleston, 1880 to St Augustine, and 1638 tons to Jamaica.
Before the next evacuation could take place, the shipping which
was employed in the withdrawal from Savannah had to be
reassembled at Charleston, and an additional 20,000 tons had
to be obtained, for it was estimated that the evacuation of
Charleston would require at least 30,000 tons of shipping. On
15 August Carleton warned the government that 'unless more
shipping can be procured this cannot take place in eighty two,
nor the evacuation of New York in eighty three; in the mean
time each post stands exposed . . . without being able to assist
any other'.[2]

During the summer and fall of 1782 the government began to
respond to Carleton's dispatches and Middleton's memoranda
by ordering transports to assemble at New York. On 5 June
1782 Shelburne informed Carleton that he had ordered twenty
victuallers and transports en route to the West Indies to proceed
to New York after discharging their cargoes. The commander
of the British forces in Canada was directed on 31 July to send to
New York all the vessels of the transport service in Quebec. In
response to this directive, twenty-three transports left Quebec
on 10 October for New York. At the end of July General Edward
Mathew sent the transports which had brought the 19th and
30th Regiments to Antigua back to America, while at the same
time Carleton and the naval commander in America, Admiral
Robert Digby, were searching American ports for shipping to

---

[1] PRO, CO/5/106, ff. 166–9; HMC, *American Manuscripts*, iii, 28–9, iv, 146;
Kenneth Coleman, *The American Revolution in Georgia, 1763–1789* (Athens, Ga.,
1958), 145.
[2] PRO, CO/5/106, ff. 166–9.

evacuate Charleston. By the beginning of December the tonnage necessary to evacuate Charleston had been assembled with great effort from points as distant as New York, the West Indies, St Augustine, Halifax, and Quebec.[1]

On 14 December 1782, 6300 rank-and-file, many tons of stores and provisions, and thousands of Loyalists with their slaves embarked at Charleston on a fleet of 129 transports, victuallers, and storeships amounting to 35,785 tons. The British ships left Charleston on 18 December and off the bar 'the different divisions of transports separated and sailed for the places of their destination'. Forty-eight vessels went to New York, twenty-nine to Jamaica, twenty to England, fifteen to St Augustine, nine to Halifax, five to St Lucia, one as a cartel to Havana, and two were lost.[2] Thus, the ships which had been collected with such difficulty for the evacuation of Charleston were dispersed, and the laborious process had to be repeated on an even larger scale before the evacuation of New York could be undertaken.

The evacuation of New York in 1783 was a huge task. On 10 January 1783 there were 20,010 rank-and-file effectives at New York as well as large quantities of stores and provisions. In addition the 7900 men who had been captured at Yorktown would also have to be removed from America, while the removal of thousands of Loyalists from the city tended to make the evacuation resemble a migration rather than a military operation. It has been estimated that more than 10,000 Loyalists left New York before the evacuation got underway officially, and the Commissary General's Office reported that in the course of the withdrawal 27,009 Loyalists were transported to Nova Scotia, 1328 to Canada, and 941 to Abaco.[3] To conduct the evacuation of New York Carleton and Digby had collected by 16 January 1783 eighty-six transports, victuallers, and storeships with a total tonnage of 26,512 tons. Although sixty-two

[1] PRO, ADM/1/490, f. 139; CO/5/106, ff. 44–5; CO/5/107, ff. 120, 247, 253–4; CO/42/42, ff. 198–9; CO/42/43, f. 204; CO/318/9, ff. 194, 242–3; HMC, *American Manuscripts*, iii, 45.

[2] PRO, CO/5/107, f. 251; CO/5/108, ff. 72–3, 76.

[3] PRO, CO/5/108, f. 134; CO/5/111, ff. 118–19; Oscar Theodore Barck, *New York City during the War of Independence* (New York, 1931), 214–15.

transports and victuallers amounting to 15,915 tons were also expected at New York by the spring from the West Indies, St Augustine, and Halifax,[1] 148 ships with a total tonnage of 42,427 tons was inadequate to withdraw from New York in one movement as had been done at Savannah and Charleston.

The task of evacuating New York was considerably simplified when news arrived in America early in 1783 that the preliminary treaty of peace had been signed by the United States and Great Britain. The end of hostilities in America quickly followed the news of the preliminary peace treaty and made possible the withdrawal of the British from New York in echelons. In addition, naval escort was not required for all departing transports. These advantages were somewhat offset by the anti-Loyalist measures enacted by the Americans in 1783 which caused hundreds of additional Loyalists to seek the protection of the British at New York. The end of the war also resulted in the necessity of having to employ shipping in tasks other than the evacuation of New York. On 10 April 1783, in an effort to save money, the government ordered all German troops in North America returned at once to Europe for immediate discharge from the King's service. Twenty-five transports were thus employed in August 1783 to carry the 4286 German troops in Canada to Europe, and at the same time other transports were used to remove the German troops from Nova Scotia. Also, four transports which had gone to Nova Scotia from New York in September with Loyalists were needed to withdraw to Europe the garrison of Castine which had been ceded to the United States. Shipping had to be spared as well to evacuate St Augustine which had reverted to Spain under the terms of the peace. This operation was carried out in the early fall of 1783.[2]

In April 1783, with about 40,000 tons of shipping, the evacuation of New York began. During April approximately 4000 Loyalists and troops, as well as three shiploads of provisions, left New York for Nova Scotia, and a large quantity of ordnance and stores were sent to the West Indies. But on 12 April

[1] PRO, CO/5/108, ff. 45, 105, 107.
[2] PRO, CO/5/109, ff. 396–7; CO/42/44, ff. 55–6, 58–9, 176; CO/318/10, ff. 73–4; HMC, *American Manuscripts*, iv, 57, 274, 277, 356, 378–9.

Carleton warned the government: 'A considerable increase of shipping will be necessary to accomplish the entire evacuation of this place [New York] in the course of the summer'. Anticipating Carleton's warning, the government on 16 April directed all warships in the West Indies with orders to return to Britain to proceed instead to New York to assist with the evacuation. These orders arrived in the Caribbean after the ships had already sailed for England.[1]

Despite the great shortage of shipping, throughout the summer of 1783 a steady stream of men and material left New York. On 15 and 17 June, for instance, 1274 troops embarked for Europe and 2472 Loyalists left for Nova Scotia. In order to save transport tonnage, 1500 German troops were sent to Europe in July on three ships of the Royal Navy and the prizes *South Carolina* and *La Sybille*, and on 13 August an additional 4000 Germans departed from New York for Europe in a mixed fleet of transports and warships.[2] The evacuation of New York, however, was prolonged by the shortage of ships, for although the Navy Board took the unprecedented step of offering to charter ships at the rate of 13s 'ready money' per ton, it could only scrape together 14,000 tons to send to America in the early summer of 1783. In order to save tonnage, Carleton was forced to make the Loyalists leave all their personal possessions behind, and in the last days of British rule auctions became an every day event in New York. In a further effort to save shipping, it was ordered on 1 September that in future only destitute Loyalists could be evacuated on government ships. Despite these harsh measures, however, the rate of the withdrawal depended totally on the speed with which shipping became available. On 6 October Carleton was able to report that all the provincial forces had left New York, that all the stores and artillery were embarked, and that 'almost all those loyalists who expected assistance from government in removing from hence, are provided with shipping and gone to different parts of Nova Scotia. The troops now here destined for Europe, only wait the return of a sufficient

[1] PRO, ADM/1/490, f. 259; ADM/1/4150, f. 35; CO/5/109, ff. 100–3, 181–3, 202, 208, 214.
[2] PRO, ADM/1/490, ff. 297, 312; CO/5/110, ff. 30–4, 74, 110.

number of transports, when the final embarkation will take place, which the Admiral thinks cannot be completed before the first week in December.' By 22 November only 1930 troops remained in New York, and on 28 November Carleton, on board H.M.S. *Ceres* off Staten Island, was able to report that 'His Majesty's troops, and such of the Loyalists as chose to emigrate, were on the 25th instant, withdrawn from the City of New York, in good order, and embarked without the smallest circumstance of irregularity or misbehaviour of any kind'.[1]

VI

Transports were an integral part of the British armed forces, for these ships carried to the battlefields of the American War the great bulk of men and materials necessary for the prosecution of the conflict. By giving the King's forces the means of becoming a highly mobile amphibious striking force, transports, especially in America, gave the British a great strategic and tactical advantage. Hundreds of the King's troops, however, died from scurvy on the long passage to the Western Hemisphere, and it was found nearly impossible to dispatch ships with troops and stores from Britain so that they arrived in America at the beginning of the campaigning season. Despite numerous obstacles, such as impressment of transport seamen and harassment by the Customs Service, the Navy Board was able to convey a great army to North America in 1776 and to maintain it there until 1783, while at the same time transporting to the West Indies, Mediterranean, and India the men and material necessary to meet the challenge posed by the entry of the European powers into the war. But the demands of a world war and the failure, after 1780, of the Navy Board to procure the tonnage necessary to meet the demands of Britain's deteriorating military position in America imposed a crushing burden on the transport service. By 1782 the shortage of ships had reduced the transport service to a point where it could not supply tonnage for amphibious operations or meet the logistical

[1] PRO, ADM/1/940, ff. 316–17; CO/5/109, ff. 181–3; CO/5/111, ff. 49–50, 194, 212; Encouragements given to the owners of transports in the employ of the Navy Board from 1776 to 1782, [undated], Barham MSS. at Exton Park; Barck, op. cit., 214.

requirements of the British forces. The weakness of the transport service at the end of the American War was illustrated by Britain's inability to redeploy its forces from America to the West Indies and by the length of time required to evacuate America.

CHAPTER X

Shipping and the American War:
A Conclusion

THE ATLANTIC OCEAN and the inability to think in terms of logistics were two of the most formidable obstacles confronting the British during the American War. Every biscuit, man, and bullet required by the British forces in America had to be transported across 3000 miles of ocean. Those responsible for formulating British policy, however, failed to come to terms with this, the most basic logistic problem of the war.

At the root of all logistical problems lay the inability to perceive the simple fact that a sufficient amount of transport service tonnage was an absolute prerequisite for almost every type of military operation. There was during the American War a simple interrelation and interaction between strategy, logistics, and shipping which geography imposed upon the British effort, but this was not seen in Whitehall, and only dimly perceived at the Navy Office.

The effects of this failure to understand the relationship between strategy, logistics, and shipping resources permeated almost every aspect of the British conduct of the war. The resolve to dispatch a large army in 1776 to crush the Americans in one campaign was predicated upon the assumption that it would arrive in America early in the spring. The government never attempted to determine whether the transports required to carry out this movement were available; instead it dispersed its already inadequate shipping resources in subsidiary projects, causing the army to arrive in America months late. Compounding this failure was the fact that in 1776 the British army was sent to North America without the ministry understanding that in all probability the troops would have to be provisioned from

Britain, and that this task would require thousands of tons of victuallers. In 1778 the British embarked on a strategy of dispersal in the Western Hemisphere, not realizing that this would require a large number of transports and victuallers to support the King's forces, and that inadvertently the effects of the already existing shipping shortage would be greatly intensified. In 1782 the government ordered that the army be evacuated from America and redeployed in the West Indies without knowing that the tonnage necessary to conduct this movement, and simultaneously supply the forces in the West Indies and Canada, was just not available. When it became apparent that the British army could not be quickly withdrawn, few steps were taken to provide the necessary ships, and as a result the army was stranded in America. Because there was almost no exchange of information between the ministers who formulated military policy and the Navy Board which provided the shipping necessary to carry it out, most British military efforts during the American War were planned on the assumption that there would always be enough transports, victuallers, and storeships to put any scheme into effect, when in fact the required amount of tonnage was seldom readily available.

It was the difficult task of the Commissioners of the Navy to reconcile the government's often extravagant military plans with the realities of the shipping situation. The Navy Board, greatly overworked and in many respects ill-constituted to manage the transport service, was only a subordinate department of the government. The Commissioners were rarely consulted by the ministry concerning the availability of the shipping required to put a policy into effect, and they could only officially communicate with other departments of the government, save for the Treasury, through the confused medium of the Admiralty. The administrators of the transport service were bureaucratically isolated, for after 1776 the Admiralty was not interested in shipping problems and the Treasury could not be depended upon in a crisis. The extent of this isolation can be seen by the fact that the transport service only learned of the government's resolve to evacuate America when Sir Charles Middleton read of it in the newspapers. In this position of isolation and weakness, the Commissioners were subjected to an

endless deluge of orders, communications, and directives which
in many cases were totally unrealistic, contradictory, and subject to alteration without notice. If possible, the Navy Board had
to transform this disordered mass of paper into the transports,
storeships, and victuallers necessary to carry the ministry's
military policy into effect.

Despite bureaucratic confusion, continual harassment by the
Customs Service, and the impressment of the crews of its ships,
the Navy Board was highly successful at administering the
transport service. Under the competent leadership of the
Comptroller of the Navy, Maurice Suckling, and after 1778 of
the brilliant administrator Charles Middleton, the Board collected an able corps of agents for transports which formed the
nucleus of the machinery which enabled it to run the transport
service effectively. Utilizing the facilities of the Royal Dockyards, the Board set up a workable system of measuring,
inspecting, and supervising the fitting-out of ships entering the
service. In addition, the Board was able to expand the scope of
the transport service's operations to meet the challenge presented by the entry of the European powers into the conflict and
to take over the task of conveying army provisions in 1779. After
assuming this last responsibility, the Board, with the support of
the Treasury, instituted numerous reforms and completely
overhauled and reconstructed the entire process of inspecting,
receiving, and shipping provisions. This was a considerable
administrative achievement to have been carried out in the
midst of a world war. The administrative machinery set up
during the American War by the Navy Board was very effective
and efficient, and made the transport service one of the best-run
organizations in the British government.

The Navy Board, while able to administer the transport
service efficiently, was unable in the last years of the war to
procure a sufficient number of ships to meet the requirements
of the British war effort. The transport service's shortage of ships
in this period brought the British to the edge of catastrophe. At
the end of 1782 the Navy Board did not have the tonnage
necessary to meet the logistical requirements of the British army
in North America during 1783. If the war had continued into
1783 the British government would have had to face the

possibility that the army in America at best might become the eighteenth-century 'Gardeners of Salonika' and at worst be starved into submission. As it turned out, even with the advent of peace at the beginning of 1783, the shortage of ships resulted in the immobilization of the army in America.

The government might well have been able to avert the threat of military disaster brought about by the deficiency of ships if it had heeded the repeated warnings of the Navy Board and taken some action to solve the problem. In 1776, when the shipping was being assembled to carry the army to North America, the ministry successfully coordinated and supervised the efforts of the various government departments to charter vessels. When it became apparent, however, in the last years of the war that the transport service was unable, under the existing circumstances, to charter additional ships, the government took no action. From 1780 onwards the Navy Board submitted memorandum after memorandum on the tonnage shortage to the Admiralty and the Treasury and stated repeatedly that if more ships were not immediately found, the logistical support of the British forces overseas would collapse. According to the Navy Board, the shipping shortage was caused by the failure to deploy effectively the tonnage already in service and by the inability of the government to formulate and put into effect a rational ship procurement policy. The Board thought that ships were being kept abroad unnecessarily by local commanders, and over and over again asked the ministry to order the return of the vessels to the British Isles. The government issued such orders to the overseas commanders, but the ships were not returned to Britain. The Navy Board could not charter additional tonnage after 1780 because the weakness of the Navy's credit did not permit it to offer competitive rates of freight, and it was constantly outbid for ships by the Ordnance and Victualling Boards. Ironically, it did not occur to anyone to suggest that the shipping problem could be solved by providing the transport service with the financial resources to enable it to offer competitive freight rates. The situation was a preposterous one, for, as the Commissioners of the Navy pointed out, it was madness for three different government departments to be forcing freight rates up by competing against each other for ships. They had suggested on several occasions to the ministry that either the procurement policies of the three departments be coordinated or that the Navy Board be given control of all the shipping under charter to the government. The ministry did not take any action on the shipping crisis and ignored all suggestions by the Board for reform and rationalization of the methods employed to charter ships. Thus, the Navy Board was left unassisted to grapple with a problem which, if left unsolved, could only lead to military disaster.

In the absence of support from the ministry, the Navy Board attempted with its own resources to solve or at least mitigate the problems caused by the shipping shortage. The Board relieved the transport service of some of its burden by entering into a number of short-term agreements with shipowners. Large quantities of naval stores were transported on ships under short-term space charters. Agreements were also made with the London West India merchants for the conveyance of some 8500 men as passengers on West Indiamen to the Caribbean. The East India Company was prevailed upon to provide transportation for men and materials bound for India. The Board at various times was also able to charter shipping on a short-term basis to carry cargoes, such as oats, to North America. Attempts were made as well to utilize the ships of the transport service to the fullest possible extent. The Board introduced a number of measures that reduced the amount of time spent by victuallers in British ports by streamlining the entire process of loading and dispatching ships. The short-term agreements for the conveyance of men and goods, and the introduction of measures to increase the efficiency of its shipping, greatly lessened the burden of the transport service. Only the procurement of additional ships under long-term charter, however, would have had a decisive effect on the tonnage shortage. When it became apparent that additional tonnage could not be found and that the ministry would not reform or alter the government's ship procurement policy, the Board instituted the precaution of keeping every ship in service even against the will of the owners, and was forced to resign itself to the disastrous prospect of having to operate the service with an ever-decreasing number of ships.

The achievements of the transport service during the American War were prodigious. In the course of the war the service transported thousands of men to the far corners of the North Atlantic Basin. During 1776, for example, the Board's transports carried over 27,000 troops to North America; between October 1776 and March 1780 the Board arranged for the conveyance of over 8000 men to the West Indies; over 29,000 German troops were transported across the Atlantic during the war; and in 1783 some 29,000 Loyalists were withdrawn from New York by the ships of the transport service. Cargoes of military clothing, stores, camp equipage, Indian presents, and army provisions conveyed by the transport service amounted to millions of tons by the end of the war. The Navy Board, for instance, supplied the bulk of the shipping which was employed to carry provisions and stores in the three reliefs of Gibraltar, and in 1782 the transport service had to carry to North America enough provisions to feed 72,000 men. As well as transporting the bulk of the men and material necessary for the conduct of the war, the ships and men of the transport service played a major role in numerous military operations. The transports stationed in America provided the British forces with the ships to conduct large-scale amphibious operations, and the transport service turned the British army into a highly mobile amphibious striking force. It was the ships of the transport service that carried the forces that invaded New York, Rhode Island, Pennsylvania, South Carolina, and St Lucia. The transport service even took part in such obscure operations as the invasion of Nicaragua, and men drawn from transports served in such distant and unlikely places as Lake Champlain. By any standards, the achievements of the transport service during the American War rank among the greatest military and administrative feats of the eighteenth century.

APPENDIX A

Number and tonnage of transports and victuallers in the transport service during the American War[1]

Date	Number and tonnage of transports	Number and tonnage of victuallers	Total number of ships	Total tonnage
Dec. 31, 1775	132 transports with a total tonnage of 49,997 tons		132	49,997
July 1776	416 transports with a total tonnage of 128,427 tons		416	128,427
Dec. 31, 1776	347 transports with a total tonnage of 102,063 tons		347	102,063
Dec. 31, 1777	247 transports with a total tonnage of 72,835 tons		247	72,835
Dec. 31, 1778	201 transports with a total tonnage of 57,107 tons		201	57,107
Dec. 31, 1779	221 transports with a total tonnage of 64,754 tons	97 victuallers with a total tonnage of 29,263 tons	318	94,017

[1] Undermentioned in an account of the number of ships and their tonnage which appear to have been in service at the end of each year during the present war, [undated], Barham MSS. at Exton Park; SP, vol. 145, transports hired at different periods by the Navy Board, [1777].

APPENDIX A

Date	Number and tonnage of transports	Number and tonnage of victuallers	Total number of ships	Total tonnage
Sept. 31, 1780	207 transports with a total tonnage of 61,703 tons	134 victuallers with a total tonnage of 40,527 tons	341	102,230
Dec. 31, 1780	192 transports with a total tonnage of 59,015 tons	154 victuallers with a total tonnage of 45,732 tons	346	104,747
Dec. 31, 1781	157 transports with a total tonnage of 50,621 tons	212 victuallers with a total tonnage of 62,519 tons	369	113,140
Dec. 31, 1782	125 transports with a total tonnage of 37,725 tons	193 victuallers with a total tonnage of 57,446 tons	318	95,171 [1]

[1] Plus 5000 tons of shipping borrowed from the Board of Ordnance. PRO, ADM/106/2607, 25 March 1782.

APPENDIX B

Freight rates

Date when a change in the freight rate took effect	Rate of freight per month per ton of a ship's measured burden	Concessions made by the Navy Board to shipowners which were not increases of the rate of freight
Before the out-break of hostilities	9s[1]	
Nov. 5, 1775	10s[2]	
Dec. 1775	11s[3]	
Jan. 26, 1776		Allowance for arming of trans-ports[4]
April 1776	12s 6d[5]	
June 12, 1776	11s[6]	
March 10, 1778	12s	Allowance made for the number of guns over and above the number called for in the ship's charter party.[7]
Jan. 4, 1779	11s 6d[8]	
Jan. 28, 1779	12s[9]	

[1] Add. MSS., 38343, f. 7.   [2] NMM, ADM/B/194, Jan. 3, 1777.   [3] Ibid.
[4] Encouragements given to the owners of transports and victuallers in the employ of the Navy Board from 1776 to 1782, [undated], Barham MSS. at Exton Park.
[5] SP, vol. 145, Prices and Tonnage of Transports hired by the Navy Board between Nov. 1, 1775, and Nov. 4, 1776, as sent to the Treasury [on] Jan. 3, 1777.
[6] Encouragements given to the owners of transports . . . Barham MSS. at Exton Park.
[7] PRO, ADM/106/2597, March 10, 1778; Encouragements given to the owners of transports . . . Barham MSS. at Exton Park.
[8] PRO, ADM/106/2599, Jan. 4, 1779.
[9] PRO, ADM/106/2599, Jan. 28, 1779.

Date when a change in the freight rate took effect	Rate of freight per month per ton of a ship's measured burden	Concessions made by the Navy Board to shipowners which were not increases of the rate of freight
May 24, 1780		Reduction of the number of men from seven to six per hundred tons of a ship's measured burden and the number of cables from four to three. This change in the charter parties was calculated by the Navy Board to be equal to an increase in the freight rate of one shilling per ton.[1]
Oct. 5, 1780		Ships which are taken or destroyed by the enemy to be paid for in ready money.[2]
Nov. 6, 1780	12s 9d	The Navy Board grants two months' withheld freight to those ships which had been overseas for more than a year and are being refitted for further service.[3]
May 4, 1782		All ships which have one year's freight due upon arriving in Britain are permitted to sign new charter parties and are to be paid all the freight due on the old charter party.[4]
Summer, 1783	13s in ready money[5]	

[1] PRO, ADM/106/2603, May 24, 1780; Encouragements given to the owners of transports . . . Barham MSS. at Exton Park.

[2] PRO, ADM/106/2604, Oct. 5, 1780; SP, vol. 151, Navy Board to Admiralty, Aug. 30, 1782.

[3] PRO, ADM/106/2604, Nov. 6, 1780. This freight increase at first applied only to those ships just entering the service and those ships which were being refitted for further service after returning from overseas. However, on May 3, 1782, the increase was extended to every ship in the transport service. PRO, ADM/106/2608, May 3, 1782.

[4] Encouragements given to the owners of transports . . . Barham MSS. at Exton Park; PRO, ADM/106/2608, May 4, 1782.

[5] Encouragements given to the owners of transports . . . Barham MSS. at Exton Park.

BIBLIOGRAPHY

(A) MANUSCRIPTS

Public Record Office

ADM/1/484–90, Commander-in-Chief in America to Admiralty.
ADM/1/3913–14, East India Company to Admiralty.
ADM/4130–50, Secretary of State to Admiralty.
ADM/1/4288, Treasury to Admiralty.
ADM/1/4328, 4330, War Office to Admiralty.
ADM/1/5168, Orders in Council.
ADM/2/554, Secretary of the Admiralty to Public Officials and Admirals
ADM/3/81–96, Admiralty Minutes.
ADM/7/299, Solicitors Opinions.
ADM/7/565, List of all British personnel provisioned on board transports, 1775–83.
ADM/49/2, Documents relating to transports and tenders employed during the American War.
ADM/49/3, 4, 5, 6, Musters of transports in America.
ADM/49/7, Documents relating to expenses.
ADM/49/125, Papers relating to transports.
ADM/49/134–5, Register of orders to dockyards.
ADM/51/360, Log of H.M.S. *Flora*.
ADM/95/95, Navy Board book of warrants.
ADM/106/250, Chatham, Sheerness, Deal, Harwich officials relating to transports.
ADM/106/279–80, Promiscuous letters as to transports.
ADM/106/2593–611, Navy Board Minutes.
ADM/106/3318–20, 3385–6, 3402–5, Deptford Dockyard Letter Books.
ADM/106/3525–6, Papers relating to the charge of transports.
ADM/106/3529–30, Papers relating to the survey of transports.
ADM/108/1A, 1B, 1C, 4A, Transport Department in letters.
C/66/3776, Letters Patent.
CO/5/7–8, Dispatches and Miscellaneous.
CO/5/92–111, Dispatches, America.
CO/5/258, Treasury to American Secretary of State.
CO/42/36–44, Dispatches, Canada.
CO/318/5–10, Dispatches, Leeward Islands.
HCA/8/1, Assignation Book.
HCA/32/437, Instance Papers.

T/1/516, 541, 545, 555, 560, 563, 564, 567, 569, 570, 573, 575, 577, 580, Miscellaneous papers.

T/29/45–53, Treasury minutes.

T/64/104, Treasury to Commissary General in Canada.

T/64/105, Treasury to Commander-in-Chief in Canada.

T/64/107, 119, Treasury to Commander-in-Chief in America.

T/64/109–12, Commander-in-Chief in America to Treasury.

T/64/114, Commissary General in America to Treasury.

T/64/115, Commander-in-Chief in Canada to Treasury.

T/64/120, Deputy Commissary General in Georgia to Treasury.

T/64/200, Navy Board to Treasury.

T/64/201, Treasury to Navy Board.

WO/1/682–3, Secretary of State to Secretary at War.

WO/1/890, War Office Statistics.

WO/17/1155, Monthly Returns.

WO/25/1145, Embarkation Returns.

WO/34/124, Amherst papers.

WO/60/22–3, Rules, regulations, accounts and receipts for Provisioning troops on transports.

British Museum

Haldimand Papers, Add. MSS., 21680.

Liverpool Papers, Add. MSS., 38205, 38208–10, 38212, 38342–3, 38345, 38375.

Rainsford Papers, Add. MSS., 23649, 23651.

Robinson Papers, Add. MSS., 37834.

New-York Historical Society

Letter book of Henry Davies, Agent Victualler of the Victualling Board at New York.

Letter book of Daniel Wier, Commissary General of the British Forces in America.

West India Committee

Minutes of the West India Committee 1778–83.

National Maritime Museum

ADM/B/189–200, Navy Board to Admiralty.

ADM/BP/1–3, Navy Board to Admiralty.

ADM/N/244–50, Admiralty to Navy Board concerning the transport service.

SAN/T/1–7, Transcripts of the papers of the Fourth Earl of Sandwich made by the Navy Records Society.

William L. Clements Library, University of Michigan, Ann Arbor, Michigan

Shelburne Papers, volumes 145, 146, 151.

Commonwealth Relations Office Library
Miscellanies Letters Sent, volumes 21–6.
Miscellaneous Letters Received, volumes 60–71.

Exton Park, Oakham, Rutland
The papers of Lord Barham.

Mapperton, Beaminster, Dorset
The papers of the Fourth Earl of Sandwich.

Transcripts of the Grantham Papers
Copies of the Grantham MSS. from the Bedford Record Office lent to the author by Professor I. R. Christie.

(B) PERIODICALS

Annual Register, vol. viii.
Daily Advertiser.
Court and City Register for the Year 1757 (London, n.d.).
Court and City Register for the Year 1762 (London, n.d.).
Court and City Register for the Year 1764 (London, n.d.).
Court and City Register for the Year 1765 (London, n.d.).
Gentleman's Magazine, vol. lvi.
London Gazette.
Morning Chronicle and London Advertiser.
Public Advertiser.
Royal Kalendar (London, 1778).
St James Chronicle.

(C) PRINTED PRIMARY SOURCES

BAIN, JAMES, ed., 'The Siege of Charleston; Journal of Captain Peter Russel, December 25, 1779, to May 2, 1780', *American Historical Review* (April, 1899), vol. iv.
BIDDULPH, VIOLET, ed., 'Letters of Robert Biddulph, 1779–1783', *American Historical Review* (Oct., 1923), vol. xxix.
BURNEY, WILLIAM, ed., *A New Universal Dictionary of the Marine; Being, A Copious Explanation of the Technical Terms and Phrases usually employed in the Construction, Equipment, Machinery, Movements, and Military, as well as Naval, Operations of Ships; with such Parts of Astronomy, and Navigation, as will be found useful to Practical Navigators, Illustrated with a variety of modern designes of shipping &c. together with a separate views of the Masts, Yards,*

Sails, and Rigging. To which is annexed A Vocabulary of French Sea-Phrases and Terms of Art, collected from the best authorities. Originally compiled by William Falconer (London, 1815).

CARTER, CLARENCE EDWIN, ed., *The Correspondence of General Thomas Gage* (New Haven, 1933).

CHADWICK, FRENCH ENSOR, ed., *The Graves Papers* (New York, 1916).

COLE, ARTHUR HARRISON, ed., *Industrial and Commercial Correspondence of Alexander Hamilton Anticipating His Report on Manufactures* (Chicago, 1928).

CUTTER, WILLIAM RICHARD, ed., 'A Yankee Privateersman in Prison in England, 1777–1779', *The New England Historical and Genealogical Register* (April, 1876), vol. xxx.

FITZPATRICK, JOHN C., ed., *The Writings of George Washington* (Washington, 1931–44).

FORTESCUE, SIR JOHN W., ed., *The Correspondence of King George the Third from 1760 to December 1783* (London, 1927–8).

HISTORICAL MANUSCRIPT COMMISSION, *Report on American Manuscripts in the Royal Institution of Great Britain* (London, Dublin, and Hereford, 1904–09).

——, *Report on Manuscripts of the Late Reginald Hastings, Esq., of the Manor House, Ashby de la Zouche* (London, 1928–47).

——, *Fourteenth Report: The Manuscripts of His Grace The Duke of Rutland, K.G., preserved at Belvoir Castle* (London, 1894).

——, *Report on the Manuscripts of Mrs. Stopford-Sackville, of Drayton House, Northamptonshire* (London and Hereford, 1904–10).

——, *Report on the Manuscripts in Various Collections* (London, Dublin, and Hereford, 1901–14).

LAMB, R., *An Original and Authentic Journal of Occurrences during the Late American War, from its Commencement to the year 1783* (Dublin, 1809).

LODGE, HENRY CABOT, ed., *André's Journal* (Boston, 1903).

LYDENBERG, HARRY MILLER, ed., *Archibald Robertson, Lieutenant-General Royal Engineers, His Diaries and Sketches in America, 1762–1780* (New York, 1930).

MACKENZIE, FREDERICK, *Diary of Frederick Mackenzie: Giving a Daily Narrative of His Military Service as an Officer of the Regiment of Royal Welch Fusiliers during the years 1775–1781 in Massachusetts, Rhode Island and New York* (Cambridge, Mass., 1930).

NAVY RECORDS SOCIETY, *Letters and Papers of Charles, Lord Barham* (London, 1907–11).

——, *Letters and Papers of Admiral the Hon. Samuel Barrington* (London, 1937–41).

——, *The Private Papers of John, Earl of Sandwich* (London, 1932–38).

——, *The Naval Miscellany* (London, 1902).

——, *Letters written by Sir Samuel Hood (Viscount Hood) in 1781-2-3* (London, 1895).

——, *The Keith Papers* (London, 1927–45).

NEESER, ROBERT WILDEN, ed., *The Dispatches of Molyneux Shuldham* (New York, 1913).

NEW-YORK HISTORICAL SOCIETY COLLECTIONS, *Transactions as Commissary for Embarking Foreign Troops in the English Service from Germany with Copies of Letters relative to it. For the Years 1776–1777. By Charles Rainsford* (New York, 1880).

——, *The Kemble Papers* (New York, 1884–85).

——, *Proceedings of A Board of General Officers of the British Army at New York, 1781* (New York, 1916).

——, *Letter-Books and Order-Book of George, Lord Rodney* (New York, 1932).

PARLIAMENTARY PAPERS, *The Fifth Report of the Commissioners on Fees, &c. of Public Offices* (n.p., 1806).

ROBSON, ERIC, ed., *Letters from America, 1773–1780* (Manchester, 1951).

SCULL, G. D., ed., *Memoir and Letters of Captain W. Glenville Evelyn of the 4th Regiment ('King's Own,') from North America, 1774–1776* (Oxford, 1879).

TATUM, EDWARD H., ed., *The American Journal of Ambrose Serle* (San Marino, Calif., 1940).

UHLENDORF, BERNHARD A., trans. and ed., *The Siege of Charleston, with an Account of the Province of South Carolina: Diaries and Letters of Hessian Officers from the von Jungkenn Papers in the William L. Clements Library* (Ann Arbor, Mich., 1938).

——, *Revolution in America: Confidential Letters and Journals, 1776–1784, of Adjutant General Major Baurmeister of the Hessian Forces* (New Brunswick, N.J., 1957).

WILLCOX, WILLIAM B., ed., *The American Rebellion: Sir Henry Clinton's Narrative of His Campaigns, 1775–1782, with an Appendix of Original Documents* (New Haven, 1954).

(D) SECONDARY WORKS

ANDERSON, TROYER STEELE, *The Command of the Howe Brothers during the American Revolution* (New York, 1936).

BARCK, OSCAR THEODORE, *New York City during the War of Independence* (New York, 1931).

BARRINGTON, SHUTE, *The Political Life of William Wildman, Viscount Barrington* (London, 1814).

BINNEY, J. E. D., *British Public Finance and Administration, 1774–92* (Oxford, 1958).

BRIDENBAUGH, CARL, *Cities in Revolt, Urban Life in America, 1743–1776* (New York, 1955).

BROOKE, JOHN, *see* NAMIER.

CHRISTIE, I. R., *The End of North's Ministry, 1780–1782* (London, 1958).

——, 'Private Patronage versus Government Influence: John Butler and the Contest for Control of Parliamentary Elections at Saltash, 1780–1790', *English Historical Review* (April, 1956), vol. lxxi.

CLARK, WILLIAM BELL, *George Washington's Navy* (Baton Rouge, La., 1960).

C[OKAYNE], G. E., ed., *The Complete Baronetage* (Exeter, 1900–06).

C[OKAYNE], G. E., and GEOFFREY H. WHITE, *The Complete Peerage* (London, 1953), vol. xii.

COLEMAN, KENNETH, *The American Revolution in Georgia, 1763–1789* (Athens, Ga., 1958).

CURTIS, EDWARD E., *The Organization of the British Army in the American Revolution* (New Haven, 1926).

DAVIES, C. S., 'The Administration of the Royal Navy under Henry VIII: the Origins of the Navy Board', *English Historical Review* (April, 1965), vol. lxxx.

DAVIS, RALPH, *The Rise of the English Shipping Industry in the Seventeenth and Eighteenth Centuries* (London, 1962).

DONOUGHUE, BERNARD, *British Politics and the American Revolution: The Path to War, 1773–75* (London, 1964).

EELKING, MAX VON, *The German Allied Troops in the North American War of Independence, 1776–1783*, trans. J. G. Rosengarten (Albany, N.Y., 1893).

FAYLE, C. ERNEST, *see* WRIGHT, CHARLES.

FORTESCUE, J. W., *A History of the British Army* (London, 1902), vol. iii.

GRAHAM, G. S., 'Considerations on the War of American Independence', *Bulletin of the Institute of Historical Research* (May, 1949), vol. xxii.

JAMES, W. M., *The British Navy in Adversity* (London, 1926).

JOHN, A. H., 'The London Assurance Company and the Marine Insurance Market of the Eighteenth Century', *Economica* (May, 1958), vol. xxv.

JOHNS, A. W., 'The Principal Officers of the Navy', *Mariner's Mirror* (Jan., 1928), vol. xiv.

LOWELL, EDWARD J., *The Hessians and other German Auxiliaries of Great Britain in the Revolutionary War* (New York, 1884).

MACKESY, PIERS, *The War for America, 1775–1783* (London, 1964).

MADARIAGA, ISABEL DE, *Britain, Russia, and the Armed Neutrality of 1780* (London, 1962).

MORISON, SAMUEL ELIOT, *John Paul Jones: A Sailor's Biography* (London, 1959).

MORRIS, RICHARD B., *The Peacemakers: The Great Powers and American Independence* (New York, 1965).

NAMIER, SIR LEWIS, *The Structure of Politics at the Accession of George III* (London, 1957).

NAMIER, SIR LEWIS, and JOHN BROOKE, *The History of Parliament: The House of Commons, 1754–1790* (London, 1964).

[NATIONAL MARITIME MUSEUM], *The Commissioned Sea Officers of the Royal Navy, 1660–1815* (n.p., 1954).

PARES, RICHARD, *King George III and the Politicians* (Oxford, 1953).

———, *A West-India Fortune* (London, 1950).

———, *War and Trade in the West Indies, 1739–1763* (London, 1936).

PATTERSON, A. TEMPLE, *The Other Armada* (Manchester, 1960).

ROBSON, ERIC, *The American Revolution* (London, 1955).

——, 'The Expedition to the Southern Colonies, 1775–1776', *English Historical Review* (Oct., 1951), vol. lxvi.

RUTHERFORD, G., 'Sidelights on Commodore Johnstone's Expedition to the Cape', *Mariner's Mirror* (July, 1942), vol. xxviii.

SHAW, WM. A., *The Knights of England* (London, 1906).

STRYKER, WILLIAM S., *The Battles of Trenton and Princeton* (Cambridge, Mass., 1898).

SYRETT, DAVID, 'Lord George Germain and the Navy Board in Conflict: the *Adamant* and *Arwin Galley* Dispute, 1777', *Bulletin of the Institute of Historical Research* (Nov., 1965), vol. xxxviii.

——, 'The West India Merchants and the Conveyance of the King's Troops to the Caribbean, 1779–1782', *Journal of the Society for Army Historical Research* (Autumn, 1967), vol. xlv.

——, 'Living Conditions on the Navy Board's Transports during the American War, 1775–1783', *Mariner's Mirror* (Jan., 1969), vol. lv.

USHER, ROLAND GREENE, JR, *The Civil Administration of the British Navy during the American Revolution* (unpublished University of Michigan Ph.D. thesis, 1942).

WALLACE, WILLARD M., *Appeal to Arms: A Military History of the American Revolution* (New York, 1951).

WICKWIRE, FRANKLIN B., *British Subministers and Colonial America, 1763–1783* (Princeton, N. J., 1966).

——, 'Admiralty Secretaries and the British Civil Service', *Huntington Library Quarterly* (May, 1965), vol. xxiii.

WILLCOX, WILLIAM B., *Portrait of A General: Sir Henry Clinton in the War of Independence* (New York, 1964).

WILLIAMS, M. J., *The Naval Administration of the Fourth Earl of Sandwich, 1771–82* (unpublished Oxford Ph.D. thesis, 1962).

WRIGHT, CHARLES, and C. ERNEST FAYLE, *A History of Lloyd's* (London, 1928).

WRIGHT, GEOFFREY H., *see* C[OKAYNE].

INDEX

Abaco, Bahamas, 238
Adamant merchant ship, chartered by Germain, 218
Admiralty, 2, 6, 8, 9, 11–15, 23, 24, 31–3, 38, 44, 49, 51, 67, 71, 92–3, 98, 137, 140, 163, 217, 223; secretaries of, 6–7; Middleton on, 7; lack of interest in transport service and Navy Board, 9–10, 18–20; arrangements for the conveyance of troops and stores to India, 72–6; attitudes towards transport of army provisions, 129, 154; fails to provide convoys, 154–160; approves reserve of transports, 226–7; control of transports in America, 226–7
advertisements for shipping, 64–5, 81–2
Æolus transport, 42
Affleck, Commodore Edward, 179
Africa, 4, 5, 139
Agents for Transports, 33, 69, 71, 168; appointment, pay, and previous experience, 38–9; professional status, promotion, employment, 40–1; at Deptford, 42; at Portsmouth, 42–4; at Cork, 44–6; duties of, 47–57; not available, 58; to investigate loss of ships, 83; to oversee the fitting-out, measurement, and appraisal of ships, 116; to issue licenses, 116; to report loss of provisions, 153. *See also* Bourmaster, Chads, Dow, Harris, Parrey, Young, Principal Agent for Transports
America, 41, 48, 63, 70, 94, 114, 116, 128–9, 132, 172, 173, 206, 209, 210, 213, 216, 221, 234; excessive freight rates to, 63; ships built in, 77; nature of warfare in, 125–6; logistical problems of British forces in, 128–9; provisions sent to, 131–2; troops in, 139; provisions for, 147, 154, 156, 157; army dispersed in, 174–5; amphibious operations in, 188; reinforcements for, 192, 197, 204–5; shortage of transports in, 206–7; clothing and camp equipage for troops in, 215–16; importance of transports in, 227–30; number of transports in, 230, 236; end of offensive operations in, 232; evacuation of, 232–41
America transport, 48
Amherst, Lord, 68, 211, 217, 220
Amory, Isaac, 56
Amsterdam, 204
Angerstein, J. J., 80
Anhalt-Zerbst troops, 212
Ann transport, 50, 53
Ann victualler, seized by customs officials, 165
Annabella transport, recapture and condemnation of, 84–5
Anspach troops, 212
Antigallican transport, 50
Antigua, 64–5, 66, 165, 214; troops at, 173
Apollo transport, 56
appraisals, 118–19
Aquidnek Island, R.I., 127
Arbuthnot, Admiral Marriot, 53, 54, 85, 190; dispute with Clinton, 169–70
Argo transport, 48

18—S.A.W. 261

army, shipping belonging to, 52; deployed at, 139, 173–5; to be redeployed in West Indies, 232–3; number of troops at New York, Charleston, Georgia, and East Florida, 233

army clothing, transportation of, 214–5

army stores, safe conveyance of, 216–18

Arnold, General Benedict, 191

Arwin Galley transport, 216; dispute over, 218

Ashly River, S.C., 54

Associated Loyalists, 172

Atkinson, Richard, 130, 135

Baltick Merchant victualler, 177

Baltic timber trade, 101

Barbados, 165; victuallers detained at, 170; troops at, 173

Barrack Master General's Department, shipping of at New York, 52

barrels, defective, 142

Barrington, Lord, 8, 122–3, 217

Bateman, William, 27, 30

Bay of Fundy, 122, 169

bedding, 185–6

Belfast, 58

Belle Isle, 85

Bermuda, 9, 177; transports at, 55

Betsey transport, 48, 57

Betsy victualler, 46

Blackslake, 210, 226

Blackwall, 33

Blast warship, 41

Board of Ordnance, *see* Ordnance Board

Boston, 14, 84, 121, 122, 127, 129, 182, 192, 193, 194; capture of transports at, 202; withdrawal from, 206–7

Bourmaster, Captain John, 39, 40–1, 51, 53

Bradley, Lieutenant, 50

Bremen, 212

Brest, 58

Brett, Timothy, 26, 30

Brilliant ordnance transport, 10

Bristol, 59, 91, 107, 108, 204

British merchant marine, number of ships in, 77

Bronx, N.Y., 123

Brown Hall merchant ship, chartered to carry stores to Halifax, 65–6

Brunswick, Duke of, 40

Brunswick troops, 196, 204, 205, 212; embarkation of, 201

Buchanan, John and George, 14–15

Butts, William, 81

Cabinet, 1, 15; working of, 1–5

cabin passengers, fare of, 68

Camel warship, 178

Camilla warship, 126

Campbell, Brigadier General Archibald, 52, 165

camp equipage, 202, 203, 204, 208, 219; freight for, 68; conveyance of, 215–16

Canada, 32, 33, 34, 63, 64, 172, 173, 190, 201, 204, 206, 212, 213, 216, 217, 220, 227, 234, 235, 238, 239; troops in, 139, 171; provisions for, 143, 147, 148; trade convoys to, 156; increased consumption of provisions in, 171; American invasion of, 195; troops embarked for, 199; reinforcements for, 209; clothing for troops in, 215

Cape Breton, 12, 34, 127

Cape Fear, N.C., 194, 195

Caribbean, *see* West Indies

Carleton, General Sir Guy, 164, 195, 208, 233, 235, 236, 237, 238, 240; sent to New York to evacuate America, 232

Carter, Lieutenant Robert, 166

Castine, Me., 174, 239

Cato merchant ship, chartered to carry stores to Antigua, 65

Centurion warship, 177, 178

Ceres warship, 241

Chads, Captain Henry, 39, 52

Channel Islands, 211, 231

Charleston, 48, 54, 127, 172, 173, 177, 178, 179, 183, 195, 228, 232, 234, 235, 236, 239; provision depot at, 176; evacuation of, 237–8

Charlestown, *see* Charleston

charter party, 31; enforcement of the terms of, 37–8; number of men required by, 56

Chassers, 49

Chatham, 209, 211

Chatham transport, 48

Cherry, George, 144, 145, 148, 149, 150

Chester, Pa., 126

Chesterfield warship, 22

China trade, 63n

Clark, George Rogers, 171

Cleveland merchant ship, 109

Clinton, General Sir Henry, 51, 53, 70, 71, 157, 158, 170n, 172, 173, 174, 175, 190, 191, 194, 195, 208, 219, 228; complains of late arrival of provisions, 157; ordered to return victuallers to England, 162–3; dispute with Arbuthnot, 169–70

Clyde, the, 192, 198, 201, 202, 209, 210

coasters, hiring of, 61–2

Colden, Cadwallader, 127

Collingwood, Lieutenant, 50

Commissary General's Department, shipping at New York, 52

compensation, paid for ships lost, 82–6; paid for ships taken into the King's service, 85–6; paid in cash, 99

Connecticut, 176

Cononicut Island, R.I., 127

Content transport, 216

contracts, penalty clause in, 148–9; enforcement of, 148–54

contractors, 142, 143; agents of at Cork, 150–1; complaints against, 150–2

convoys, 130–1, 135, 137, 139, 140, 143, 145, 155, 156, 161; economic effects of, 79; Admiralty's failure to provide, 154–60; for victuallers, 160–1, 169–70; mix-ups of, 165–6; lack of escorts for, 178; difficulties assembling for return to England, 178–9; tactical problem of dispatching to North America, 213; schedules of, 223–5; effects of adverse winds upon, 225

Cope and Bignell, 80

Cope and May, 80

Cork, 13, 14, 39, 45–7, 48, 50, 59, 98, 132, 133, 140, 141, 143, 165–6, 177, 179, 192, 193, 194, 198, 199, 204, 206, 209, 210, 220, 224, 225; duties of agent for transports at, 41, 44–6; victuallers at, 45–6, 113, 115; John Marsh appointed agent victualler at, 144; receipt and dispatch of provisions at, 143, 147, 150–1; convoys from, 154–5, 160–1; victuallers delayed at, 155–6, 157; embarkation at, 201

Cornwall, Charles, 130; plan for managing army provisions, 133–4

Cornwallis, Lord, 174, 175

Countess of Darlington transport, 50

Cowes, 42, 44, 145, 160, 161, 234; provision depot at, 144, 147; contractors' agents at, 151

Cumming, Lieutenant William, 40, 49

Customs Service, 13; harassment by, 115–16, 165, 199–200; reduces procedures for victuallers, 146

Dalling merchant ship, chartered to carry stores to Antigua, 65

Dalrymple, William, 87, 228

Darby, Pa., 126

Davis, Thomas, 35

Dawson, William, 116, 119

Day, Nathaniel, 154

Deal, 59

Delaware River, 124, 126, 205

demurrage, 68, 70–1, 161

Deptford, 13, 14, 33, 43, 44, 47, 66, 91, 107, 115, 116, 200, 201, 203, 204; duties of agent for transports at, 41; inspecting, surveying, appraising, and refitting ships of the transport service at, 108–10, 117–18, 118–20; impressment at, 222

Deptford Dockyard, 20, 21, 25, 26, 29, 33, 41, 68

Dickinson, Lieutenant, 50

Digby, Admiral Robert, 51, 164, 237, 238

dockyards, appointments in, 18–19; officials of supervise transport service shipping, 58–9

Dolphin warship, 29

Donkin, Lieutenant Colonel Robert, 9

Dort, 48–9, 221

Dow, Lieutenant Archibald, 45, 47–8, 177

Downs, 13, 47, 59, 108, 225

Drake and Long, 65, 80

Dublin, 59

Dundases, the, 24

Dunkirk, 204

Dutch ships, 93, 204. *See also* Netherlands

Earl of Orford transport, return of measurement and inspection of, 114

East Florida, 143, 172, 174; number of troops in, 233. *See also* Florida and West Florida

East India Company, 9, 71, 185, 211; conveyance of troops and stores, 11, 63, 72–6; exports of, 62–3; attempts to obtain ships from, 72; shortage of ships, 73, 74–5

East Indies, 188

Eden, William, 197

Egmont, Lord, 25

Elbe River, 201, 225

Elk, Head of the, 53, 230

Elliot, Ralph, 103

Elphinstone, Captain George Keith, 54

Enterprize transport, 48

Esther & Ann victualler, 50

Extra Commissioners of the Navy, 26, 28, 31

Fanny transport, 58

Fanshawe, Captain Robert, 58

Fathers Desire transport, 50

Favourite transport, compensation paid for loss of, 84

Fawcett, General William, 184, 185

Felicity transport, 14

firewood, problem of obtaining, 126–8

Flora warship, 202

Florida, 168, 173, 174; provisions for, 140

flour, bounty for export removed, 146; warranty of, 152

forage, shortage of at New York, 69–70

foraging, difficulties of, 126–8

Fortitude transport, 109

Foxworthy, T., 59

Free Britain transport, reappraisal of, 119

freight, 86–8, 95, 96, 103–4, 132; rates of, 91, 92, 94, 99, 100, 251–2

Friendship merchant ship, 109

Friendship transport, 183

Fuller, Stephen, 67

Gage, General Thomas, 40, 121, 123

Gambier, Admiral James, 169, 182

Garret, John, 96

George transport, 53

Georgia, 70, 140, 174, 175, 176, 177, 237; number of troops at, 233

Germain, Lord George, 13, 14, 15, 42, 68, 93, 123, 124, 128–9, 138n, 171, 173, 175, 176, 196, 198, 209, 210, 217, 219, 220, 221, 227, 228; use of West India merchant ships to carry troops, 67; opposes

Germain (cont.)
transfer of responsibility for conveyance of army provisions to transport service, 137-8; complains of methods of shipping provisions, 155, 157-8; his directives badly drawn, 198-9; schemes which would have diverted tonnage from reinforcing America, 199; forbids use of *Arwin Galley* and hires *Adamant*, 218

German troops, 221, 225n, 240; conveyance of, 212-14; dates of embarkation, 213, 225; baggage, stores, and equipment of, 213-14; ordered to Europe, 239

Germany, 91, 183, 192, 198, 203, 220; ships hired in, 93

Gibraltar, 40, 50, 63, 91, 140n, 166, 193, 210, 234; troops at, 139; clothing for troops at, 215

Glasgow, 59, 107

Glasgow merchant ship, payment for charter of, 14-15

Good Intent transport, 50

Gordon, Robert, 140n, 145, 155; Treasury's commissary at Cork, 140; disagreements with Harris and dismissal from office, 140-4, 144

Goree, 147, 177

Grand Duke of Russia transport, 48

Grant, General James, 173, 174

Graves, Admiral Thomas, 14

Gravesend, 209

Gravesend, Brooklyn, N.Y., 205

Green Island naval storeship, cargo of, 214

Greenock, 208, 210

Gregory Olive and Company, 65

Gregson, Robert, 22n, 25, 26, 27, 28, 29, 30

Grenada, 199

Grosvenor transport, 48

Guards, 197, 202, 203, 204, 208

Guernsey, 211

gun money, 115

Haldimand, General Frederick, 171

half barrels, 143

Halifax, 66, 149, 168, 169, 178, 179, 180, 202, 224, 234, 238, 239; transports at, 55; provision depot at, 176; army at, 207-8

Hambleton, Robert, 99

Hamburg, 81, 203, 204; agents sent to, 93

Hamilton, Captain Charles, 223

Hamond, Captain Sir Andrew Snape, 155

Hanau troops, 204, 205, 212; embarkation of, 201

Hanoverian troops, 91, 175, 185, 210

Harcourt transport, 48

Harris, Lieutenant Stephen, 39, 47, 48, 59, 144, 155; duties of at Cork, 45-6, 113, 117; disputes with Gordon, 140-2

Hartford transport, 223

Harwich, 212

Hawke transport, compensated for damage sustained through enemy action, 83

Haynes, Lieutenant, Thomas, 40

Henniker and Devaynes, 149

Henslow, John, 27

Hercules victualler, 176

Hesse, Landgrave of, 40, 183

Hessian troops, 196, 197, 205, 208, 212; embarkation of, 202-4; baggage of, 203

Highland troops, 197, 202, 209, 210

Hill, Lieutenant Benjamin, 40

Hill, James, 165

Hinrichs, Captain Johann, 56, 183

Holland, 91; agents sent to, 93. *See also* Netherlands

Hood, Admiral Sir Samuel, 44

Hopewell transport, 220

Horsenail, Samuel, 33, 34

horses, carried on transports, 191

Howe, Admiral Lord, 144, 166, 181, 217

Howe, General Sir William, 40, 41, 51, 53, 123, 124, 126, 128, 191, 192, 198, 199, 202, 206, 207 208, 219, 228, 229, 230
Hudson, Highlands of, 53, 125, 219
Hudson River, 53, 229
Hull, 91
Hunt, Edward, 27–8, 30

Illinois country, 171
impressment, conflict over between Admiralty and Navy Board, 19, 222–3; hampers operations of transport service, 166, 222–3
Impress Service, 20, 59, 223
India, 5, 11, 36, 63, 64, 188n, 211; conveyance of troops and stores to, 72–3, 73–6
Indians, 139; need to provision, 171–2; transportation of presents for, 216
Invalids, 193
Ireland, 5, 44, 192, 193, 194, 195, 196, 208, 209, 210
Iroquois, 171
Isis warship, 196
Isle of Wight, 144

Jackson, George, 6
Jamaica, 3, 4, 41, 58, 67, 165, 173, 177, 190, 234, 237, 238; merchant ships chartered to carry stores to, 64–5
James Dawkins merchant ship, chartered to carry stores to Halifax, 65
James and William transport, ration table of, 188–9
Jane transport, return of having completed refitting, 118
Jason victualler, arrested, 165
Jay, John, 235n
Jenkinson, Charles, 75, 128, 130, 133, 139
Jersey, 211, 231
John (1) merchant ship, 109
John (2) merchant ship, 109–10
John & Bella transport, 44

John & Christopher transport, 48
John & Jane transport, return stating ready to enter into pay, 116; return of appraisal of, 118–19
John's Island, S.C., 54
Johnson, Jam., 114
Jones, John Paul, 34
Jupiter warship, 22
Juliana transport, 48

Kempenfelt, Captain Richard, 31
Keppel, Lord, 41, 100 234
King's stores, responsibility for, 86–7
Kingston, Jamaica, 177
Kinsale, 59, 211
Knowles, Lieutenant John, 40
Knox, William, 13, 14, 15, 137, 176

Lady Hope merchant ship, 107
Lamb, Sergeant, R., 183
La Sybille British prize, 240
Lawrence, George, 59
Leander warship, 97
Le Cras, Captain Edward, 29, 31
Leeward Islands, 220, 224, 236
Leith, 47, 108, 211
Leslie, General Alexander, 169
Lesser Antilles, troops in dispersed, 173; clothing and camp equipage for troops in, 215–16
Leviathan warship, 58
Lexington and Concord, battles of, 90, 121, 172
Liberty merchant ship, 109
light duty, 50
lighter bill, 145
lighters, 141
Lioness storeship, 13
Liverpool, 59, 91, 107, 108, 204, 210
Lloyds Coffee House, advertisements at, 64
Lockie, Patrick, 107
London, 17, 34, 79, 184, 194; ship brokers and merchants of, 80
London duty, 200
Londonderry, 12, 13
Long, Beeston, 67

Long Island, N.Y., 57, 123, 127, 176; firewood from, 127–8

Lord North transport, 85

Loyalists, 131, 139, 172, 207, 232, 237, 238, 239, 240, 241

Loyalist Pennsylvania Militia, 126

Mackenzie, Frederick, 127, 128, 229

Mackenzie, Mr, 145

Mackinac, Mich., 139

Maine, 174, 175, 176

Margery transport, compensation paid for upon being taken into the King's service, 85–6

Marsh, George, 25, 30, 49, 81, 132, 203

Marsh, John, 144n, 145, 149, 150; appointed agent victualler at Cork, 144

Martha's Vineyard, 126

Martin, Governor Josiah, 194

Mary transport, 96

Mathew, General Edward, 168, 237

Mayes, David, 87

measuring, of transports and victuallers, 110–13

Mediterranean, 63, 64, 192; reorganization of garrisons in, 193

Mellish transport, effort required to dispatch to Canada, 32–5; capture of, 217–18

merchant ships, convey troops to West Indies, 66–9

Mercury transport, 48–50

Middlebrook, N.J., 125

Middleton, Sir Charles, 4, 5, 8, 18, 29, 31, 36, 100, 134, 135, 137, 167, 170, 224, 237, 244, 245; thoughts on Admiralty, 7; income of, 21; career and character of, 22–4; thoughts on the Navy Board's methods of conducting business, 31–2; delegates some of his responsibilities, 35; ideas about procurement of shipping, 100–2; thinks there is no plan for the conduct of the war, 221–2; suggests all expeditions leave from western ports, 225; advocates maintaining amphibious reserve in England, 227; plan for evacuation of America, 234–6

Milford Haven, 195

Minorca, 3, 63, 91, 140n, 183, 193; troops at, 139; clothing for troops at, 215

Molly transport, problems encountered unloading coal from, 12–13

Moore's Bridge, battle of, 195

Moran, Matthew, 118

Morristown, N.J., 124, 125

Mosquito Shore, 177

Mulgrave, Lord, 19

Mure, Son, and Atkinson, 80, 132, 135, 169; contract to convey oats to New York, 70–1; contract to ship provisions and manage Treasury victuallers, 129–30; Treasury dissatisfied with, 130; ordered to discharge and then rehire Treasury victuallers, 133

Nancy ordnance transport, 217, 218; capture of, 216

Nantasket Road, Mass., 207

Narragansett Bay, R.I., 127

naval officers, 20n, 59

naval stores, transport of, 214

naval storeships, 214

navy bills, 31; discount on, 68; freight paid in, 87; economics of, 87–8; amount of in circulation, 89

Navy Board, position in administrative machine, 8–12, 18–20; membership of, 17, 20–30; functions of, 17, 20; conduct of business, 30–5; clerical staff, 35–6; coordination and control of shipping, 47–51, 56; short-term chartering of ships and cargo space, 61–71; advertisements, 64–5, 81–2; relations with London brokers and merchants, 80–1;

Navy Board (*cont.*)

sends agents to Out-Ports, 81; payment of compensation for ships lost, 82–6; policy on payment of freight, 86–7; freight rates, 91–2, 94, 95–6, 99, 251–2; to provide shipping to reinforce America, 91; hires ships overseas, 92–3, 99–100; number of ships in service, 93, 94, 95, 105, 249–50; takes over conveyance of army provisions, 95, 135, 136; lowers the number of men and cables required for vessels, 97–8; proposes to buy shipping, 98; unable to charter more ships, 99, 100, 105; outbid for ships by other government departments, 101–2; wants to assume control of all shipping in government service, 101–2; retains in service all ships possible, 102–3; ships under charter to it not earning profit, 103–4; surveying, inspecting, appraisal, and measuring of ships, 106, 108–13, 118–20; tonnage formula, 111, 112; pays gun money, 115; reports of misconduct Treasury victuallers, 130; negotiation about and assumption of responsibility for conveyance of army provisions, 132–5; to have complete control of the administration of the victuallers, 135–6; reforms in the inspection, loading, and dispatch of army provisions, 140–54, 159–60; requests convoys, 154–5, 161; refutes Germain's complaints, 158; cannot rationally employ shipping, 162; requests return of ships to England, 162–4, 175, 230; unable to dispatch provisions owing to shipping shortage, 164–165; suggests setting up central provision depots, 176; attempts to prevent the employment of victuallers in coastwise voyages, 176;

inability to predict amount of tonnage required to transport German troops, 184–5; ordered to procure transports to carry reinforcements to America, 196–7; in confusion, 198–201; shipping of naval and military stores, 214–218; orders issued to without knowledge of outcome of previous campaign, 219–20; complaints to Admiralty, 221–3; proposes a reserve of transports, 226; not informed of intention to withdraw from America, 233

Nelson, Horatio, 22

Nelson, Richard Alexander, 36

Neptune victualler, 176

Netherlands, 92–3, 110. *See also* Holland

New Brunswick, N.J., 124

Newcastle, 200

New England, 122

Newfoundland, 11, 63, 156, 178, 209, 210; trade convoys, 140

New Jersey, 124–5, 127, 205, 229; occupation and evacuation of, 123–4; effects of campaign in, 128

Newport, R.I., 53, 123; firewood problem at, 127–8

newspapers, advertisements in, 64–5, 81–2

New York, shipping at, 52, 55, 167–70; number of horses at and shortage of forage for, 69–71; shortage of firewood at, 126–7; shortage of provisions at, 131–2; convoys to, 140, 156; provisions for, 143, 147, 157; fires at, 167; lack of warehouses at, 167–8; increased consumption of provisions at, 172; troops at, 174, 175, 233, 238; provision depot at, 176; provisions at, 179; campaign in, 205; evacuation of, 238–41

Nonsuch warship, 53

Nore, the, 196, 210, 211, 221, 224

North, Lord, 3, 232

North America, 36, 47, 48, 188, 220; transports in, 55; army in not reinforced, 171; number of troops in, 172; army there dispersed, 173-5; death rate en route to, 191; reinforcements for, 192, 193; dates of departure of convoys for, 224-5. *See also* America

North Carolina, 174; expedition to, 194-5

North River, 230

Northampton transport, 87

Nova Scotia, 63, 70, 122, 169, 173, 176, 178, 180, 209, 210, 238, 239, 240; troops at, 74, 75

oats, contract for conveyance of to New York, 69-71

Ocean transport, 48

Ord and Richardson, 80

Ordnance Board, 9, 10, 23, 52, 88, 101, 181, 186, 194; competes with Navy Board for ships, 78; agreement on freight rates, 91-4; amount of shipping in service, 101; authorized to charter shipping for transport service, 101-2

Out-Ports, 80, 91; agents sent to, 81; arms and munitions shipped from, 115-16

Pallas transport, 40

Palliser, Admiral Sir Hugh, 10, 196, 198

Palmer, William, 25-6, 30

Parrey, Lieutenant Robert, 43-4, 47

Paterson, Governor Walter, 41

Paumier, Peter, 167

Peace & Plenty transport, 48

Pennsylvania, 53, 191, 205, 228

Pensacola, Fla., 174, 178, 216; transports at, 55; difficulties in provisioning, 176-7

Perth Amboy, N.J., 124

Philadelphia, 56, 126, 127, 131, 230, 173

Pitt, William, 5

Plymouth, 12, 13, 31, 50, 65, 107, 117, 192, 199, 201, 204, 211, 225, 226

Polly transport, 49, 103

Pomona victualler, 50

Port Royal warship, 41

Portsmouth, 26, 42, 43, 44, 47, 49, 74, 75, 85, 107, 183, 185, 190, 191, 194, 204, 210, 226; agent for transports at, 41-4

Portsmouth, Va., 169

Preston transport, 210

Prime East India Company ship, 75

Prince Edward Island, 42, 176

Princeton, battle of, 124

Principal Agent for Transports, 39, 175, 213; duties of, 51-2; assumes control of army shipping at New York, 52; report showing deployment of shipping in America, 55; reports against reduction of transport crews, 97

Prohibitory Act, licence required by, 116

Providence, Bahamas, 55, 177

provisions, lack of at Boston, 121-2; failure to obtain in America, 128-129; sent to America, 131-2; Cornwall's plan for managing, 133-4; Navy Board takes responsibility for transport of, 135, 136; loading and stowage of, 141-3; from England and Ireland, 143, 147; transhipment of, 145-6, 147; for America, Canada, West Indies, and West Florida, 147, 157; inspection of, 147, 150-1, 153; late delivery of, 148, 149-50; unfit and in unsound containers, 151-2; warranty of, 151-2; shrinkage of, 152-4; to be shipped in smaller quantities, 159; unable to be shipped because of shipping shortage, 164-5; increased consumption of in Western Hemisphere, 171-2; at New York, 179; issuing of to troops on board transports, 187

Prudence Island, R.I., 127

Quarter Master General's Department, shipping of at New York, 52
Quebec, 33, 46, 63, 69, 122, 140, 173, 178, 179, 180, 183, 190, 192, 195, 197, 202, 205, 206, 234, 237, 238; convoy to, 148; siege and relief of, 195–6, 206; dates of departure of convoys for, 224–5
Queen warship, 29

Rainsford, Colonel Charles, 48–9
Raleigh warship, 156, 160
Randell, Captain James, 39n
Rawdon, Lord, 192
rations, issued to troops on board transports, 10, 186, 188–90
Recovery storeship, 178
refitting, of transports and victuallers, 117–18
Regiments
  Anhalt-Zerbst Battalion, 185
  Edinburgh Regiment, 3
  Kyphausen's Regiment, 203
  Liverpool Regiment, 3, 69
  Mackenzie's Regiment of Highlanders, 221
  Mirbach's Regiment, 203
  Queens Rangers, 126
  Royal Garrison Battalion of Bermuda, 9
  Rall's Regiment, 203
  Seaforth Highlanders, 211
  3rd Regiment, 179, 199
  4th Regiment, 47
  5th Regiment, 47
  6th Regiment, 199
  9th Regiment, 199
  11th Regiment, 192, 199
  13th Regiment, 179
  15th Regiment, 8, 194
  17th Regiment, 126, 193
  19th Regiment, 236, 237
  21st Regiment, 199, 201
  22nd Regiment, 192

  24th Regiment, 199
  25th Regiment, 193
  27th Regiment, 126, 193
  28th Regiment, 193, 195
  29th Regiment, 196
  30th Regiment, 236, 237
  31st Regiment, 236, 237
  31st Regiment, 199, 201
  32nd Regiment, 194, 195
  34th Regiment, 199
  36th Regiment, 194, 195
  37th Regiment, 8, 194, 195
  40th Regiment, 192
  42nd Regiment, 74, 202, 209, 210, 215
  44th Regiment, 192, 220
  45th Regiment, 192
  46th Regiment, 126, 193, 195
  47th Regiment, 201
  48th Regiment, 199
  49th Regiment, 47
  53rd Regiment, 194, 199
  54th Regiment, 194, 195
  56th Regiment, 193
  57th Regiment, 194, 195
  62nd Regiment, 199
  70th Regiment, 209, 210
  71st Regiment, 182, 202, 210, 215
  72nd Regiment, 215
  73rd Regiment, 73–74
  78th Regiment, 17
  79th Regiment, 67
  85th Regiment, 190
  92nd Regiment, 190
  93rd Regiment, 190
  94th Regiment, 190
  98th Regiment, 74
  99th Regiment, 182
  100th Regiment, 74
  101st Regiment, 75
  102nd Regiment, 75
  16th Light Dragoons, 197, 204, 205
  17th Light Dragoons, 193, 215
  23rd Light Dragoons, 75
Resolution merchant ship, 18
Resolution transport, 209, 210

Rhode Island, 69, 124, 172, 174, 219, 225, 228; transports at, 55; provisions at, 140
Richmond transport, 109
Richmond warship, 34, 156, 217
Rising States American privateer, 84–5. *See also Annabella*
Ritzebüttel, 193
Robert & Elizabeth victualler, 177
Robinson, John, 13, 81, 128
Rockingham, Marquis of, 232
Rockingham-Shelburne ministry, 101
Roddam, Admiral Robert, 186
Rodney, Admiral Sir George, 40, 41, 165, 166
Roebuck warship, 155
Rogers, George, 26
Rotherhithe, 143, 144, 145, 148; provision depot removed from, 144
Royal Britain transport, 50, 87
Royal Club transport, appraised three times, 119
Russell warship, 29
Russia, 3
Russia Merchant transport, 53–4

St Ann transport, 50
St Augustine, Fla., 174, 210, 232, 234, 236, 237, 238; evacuation of, 239
St Christophers, troops at, 173
St Eustatius, 122, 165
St Helena transport, 216
St Helens, 44
St John's, 42
St Kitts, 165
St Lawrence River, 140, 196, 224
St Lucia, 165, 173, 228, 234, 238; lack of warehouses at, 167–8; victuallers at, 167–8; central provision depot at, 175–6
St Vincent, 199
Saints, battle of, 233, 235
Sally transport, 96
Salem, N.J., 126

Sandwich, Lord, 2, 7, 8, 22, 24, 31, 40, 123, 137, 196, 197, 198, 217
Sandy Hook, N.J., 166, 176, 178, 205, 230
Saratoga, N.Y., 94
Savannah, Ga., 174, 177, 232, 234, 239; difficulties of unloading victuallers at, 167; evacuation of, 236–7
Savannah River, 167
Saville victualler, 45
Schoolbred, Mr, 69
Schuyler, General Philip, 229–30
Scotch–Dutch troops, 196
Scotland, 208, 209, 210, 211
Seddon, Samuel, 85
Sheerness Dockyard, 27, 28
Shelburne, Lord, 8, 22n, 23, 101, 170, 233, 235, 237
shipping, shortage of, 161, 164–5, 206, 238, 240; importance of, 243–8
Shortland, Lieutenant John, 50, 51
Shuldham, Admiral Molyneux, 51, 227
Six Nations, 171
South Carolina, 53, 54, 175, 176, 177, 179, 191; number of troops at, 174, 233
South Carolina British prize, 240
southern passage, 177
Southouse, Mr, 33
space charter, 65–6
Spanish River, Cape Breton, 127, 169
Speedwell merchant ship, chartered to carry stores to Newfoundland, 65
Spithead, 13, 14, 33, 34, 42, 43, 44, 49, 50, 66, 69, 145, 185, 201, 203, 204, 205, 209, 210, 211, 212, 213, 214, 224, 225, 227, 231, 234, 235
Springfield transport, 216
Stade, 185, 193, 212
Staten Island, N.Y., 204, 208, 241
Stephens, Philip, 6, 7, 12, 14, 15, 160

Stony Point, battle of, 160

storeships, proposal to employ warships as, 217

Suckling, Captain Maurice, 8, 21–2, 92, 134, 245

Suffolk, Lord, 49, 184, 185, 196, 221; directives from badly drawn up, 198–9

surveying of vessels, 108–10

Sutherland, Lieutenant Andrew, 52, 57

Teer, Lieutenant George, 47

Temple, Earl, 28n

Temple, Sir Richard, 28, 30

Terrible warship, 85

Thames River, 27, 79, 83, 98, 143–5, 200, 203, 210, 212, 214, 222, 226, 231

Thompson transport, 50

time charters, short-term, 66

Tonken, Lieutenant Thomas, 39, 48, 49, 53, 55, 56, 162, 166, 178–9

tonnage formulas, 110–13

trade in wartime, effects on shipping market, 78–80

transports, freight withheld, 37; mulct of, 37–8; protested against, 38; under the command of the navy commander-in-chief, 51; transports in America, 55, 56, 206–7, 230, 236; musters of crews of, 56; released from carrying troops to West Indies, 69; sent to India, 74; cost of, 89; number in service, 93, 94, 95, 230–1, 249–50; inspecting and surveying of, 108–110; height between decks, 110; measuring and tonnage of, 110–113; fitting, storing, manning, and arming of, 114–16; entering into pay, 116–17; repair and refitting of, 117–18; appraisals and reappraisals of, 118–20; Ordnance Board's, 181; types of cargo, 181; living conditions on, 181–91; number of troops embarked per ton, 183–5; rations issued to troops on board of, 187–90; sickness and death rates on board of, 190–1; horses carried, 191; difficulty of obtaining, 198; shortage of, 202–3, 204, 206–7, 231, 232; carrying seamen, naval stores, and prisoners, 208–9; in British ports, 209; to be employed to carry military stores, 117; importance of in America, 227–30; strategic importance of maintaining a reserve of, 226–7; turns army into amphibious force, 228; detained overseas, 230; not sufficient number of to evacuate America, 232–41; importance of, 241–2

transport service, subordinate officials of, 37–60; most ships obtained from British merchant marine, 77; advantages of chartering ships to, 79–80; ships from Holland and Germany, 80; payment of compensation by, 82–6; ships of mainly employed in amphibious operations, 94; number of ships in service, 94, 95, 100, 105, 249–50; demands upon increase, 95; operating costs of ships increase, 95; in competition for seamen and naval stores, 95; changing pattern of operations, 96–7; ships in not earning a profit, 103–4; ships of being worn-out by continuous employment, 105; conditions for entering the service the same for every vessel, 106; takes responsibility for conveyance of army provisions, 136; resources of nearly exhausted, 163; largest troop movement carried out by, 192–205; harassment of by Customs Service, 199–200; conveyance of German troops and equipment, 212–14; conveyance of army clothing,

transport service (*cont.*)
    camp equipage, military stores, and Indian presents, 214–16; safety of stores in transit, 216–18; difficulty of punctually dispatching ships from Europe, 218–27; ships employed as hospital ships, prison ships, flags of truce, and guard ships, 228; importance of, 243–8. *See also* freight, transports

Treasury, 9, 12, 13, 14, 15, 18, 24, 138, 140, 143, 187, 188; communicates directly with Navy Board, 11–12; transport service of, 23, 94, 130–2, 135, 136; oats for America, 70–1; competes with Navy Board for ships, 78; freight rates of, 88, 91–2, 94, 132; has responsibility for transport of army provisions, 121, 122, 129; does not want to manage shipping and wishes to transfer responsibility to Admiralty or Navy Board, 129, 131–2, 134–5; contracts for the conveyance of provisions to America, 130; rejects Cornwall's plan, 134; transfers responsibility for conveyance of army provisions to Navy Board, 136; dismisses Gordon, 144; reduces customs procedures for provisions, 145–6; warns provision contractors, 148; requests convoys, 155, 158, 179; setting up of central provision depots, 176

Trenton, N.J., 125; battle of, 124
Trumbull, Jonathan, 229
Tybee Island, Ga., 167

Unanimity transport, 183
Union transport, return of measuring and inspection of, 114
Unity merchant ship, 109

Valiant transport, 50
Valley Forge, Pa., 125

Venus transport, 48
Vernon transport, 50, 216
victuallers, cost of, 89; in Treasury service, 130–2, 135, 136; to sail under convoy, 135, 139; delayed at Cork, 155–6, 157; to be sent with trade convoys, 156–7; more required, 161; not to be used as transports or detained overseas, 162–70; failure to return from overseas, 163–4; shortage of, 163–5, 170–1, 179–80; impressment of seamen off, 166; employed for other purposes, 167–9; at New York and St Lucia, 167–8; diverted on coastwise voyages, 169; employed in provisioning small garrisons, 177; routes to America, 177–8; dispersal of, 178; difficulty of assembling in convoys for return to Britain, 178–9; number in service, 249–50

Victualling Board, 9, 10, 23, 25, 33, 51, 88, 134, 149, 186, 187, 188, 190; shipping of at New York, 51–2; competes with Navy Board for ships, 78; agreement with on freight rates, 91–2; proposes to charter ships on the same terms as the transport service, 102

Virginia, 173, 175, 179, 191; troops at, 174

Walbeoff, Captain Thomas, 41
Waldeck Troops, 196, 204, 205, 212
Wallis, Captain Samuel, 29–30, 35
Walter, Lieutenant Robert, 162
Washington, General George, 216; attacks Trenton, 124; strategy of, 125–6; failure to destroy army of, 205; thoughts on British amphibious capabilities, 229–30
Waterford, 46
Watson, Brook, 180
Weser River, 203, 221
West Florida, 174, 175, 235; provisions for, 143, 147; increased

consumption of provisions in, 171–2; number of troops in, 172

West India Committee, 62, 67

West India merchants, 67, 211; their ships to carry troops, 66–9

West Indies, 36, 41, 44, 64, 66, 122, 129, 168, 207, 220, 234, 235; trade of, 62; troops conveyed to on merchant ships, 66–9; provisions for, 140, 143, 147, 148, 240; troops in, 139; trade convoys to, 156; increased consumption of provisions in, 171; death rate among troops en route to, 191; dates of departure of convoys to, 223–4; army to be deployed in, 232–3

Weymouth, Lord, 210

Whitby, 91, 114

Whitby transport, 48

White, Paul, 45

Whitehaven, 91, 108, 204

Wier, Daniel, 128, 152–3, 157, 188

Wilkinson, John, 80, 85

Wilkinson & Deacon, 65

William transport, 58

William & Elizabeth transport, 216

Williams, Sir John, 27–8, 30

Windward Islands, 168, 170, 173

Winkworth, Lieutenant Grosvenor, 47

Woolwich Dockyard, 20, 21, 25, 26, 29, 214

Wrotham, William de, 18

Yorktown, Va., 84, 174, 175, 234, 238

Young, Captain Walter, 40, 167, 170, 222; duties of at Deptford, 42–3

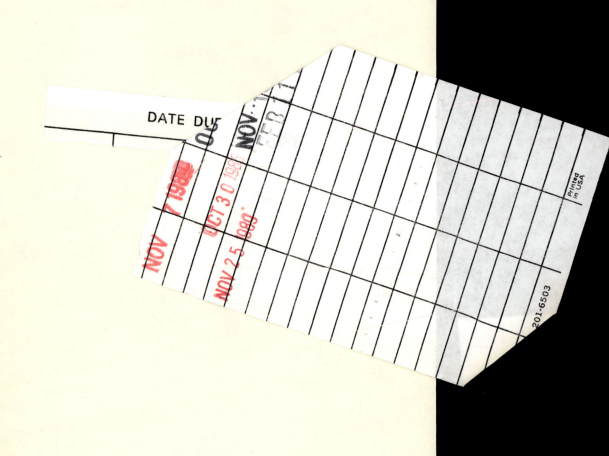